SON OF WOMAN

THE STORY OF D. H. LAWRENCE

BY JOHN MIDDLETON MURRY

NEW YORK

JONATHAN CAPE & HARRISON SMITH

D. H. LAWRENCE 1929

from a Self Portrait

ACKNOWLEDGMENT

NEARLY all the works of D. H. Lawrence are published in England by Mr. Martin Secker, whom I thank for his permission to quote as copiously as was necessary from them. I understand that by the time this book appears, " The Escaped Cock," which is now unobtainable, will have been published by Mr. Secker; and that the *Reflections on the Death of a Porcupine,* which contains the essay "The Crown," will be published shortly after. One considerable work of D. H. Lawrence remains to be printed, a study of the Book of Revelation. This I have read in manuscript. It adds nothing of significance to the total body of his work, though it contains passages of great beauty and deep interest. *The Virgin and the Gipsy,* to which I make no reference, has been over-praised and is comparatively unimportant.

I have to thank the Administrators of the Estate for their permission to print various passages from Lawrence's letters to myself.

For the sake of convenience, I have abbreviated into *Memoirs of Magnus* the full title of this book, which is, " Memoirs of the Foreign Legion, by M. M. with an Introduction by D. H. Lawrence."

To the Reader

THE story told in this book is hard to tell, and perhaps not easy to understand. To the telling of it is necessary language which appears to be the language of judgment and condemnation. I implore those who read it never to forget that Lawrence belongs to the order of men who cannot be judged, but only loved. If, at the end of the story, they feel that this great and frail and lovely man, this man of sorrows, this lonely hero, has been judged by one who was once his friend; then not Lawrence has been judged, but the friend.

This is the story of one of the greatest lovers the world has known: of a hero of love, of a man whose capacity for love was so great that he was afraid of it. We little lovers do not know and cannot dream what it is to be afraid of love as he was. Love grows slowly in us little men, if it grows at all. But in him it was a devouring flame while yet a boy: a love that consumed his soul, and threatened his very life. It was not love of his mother only, but love of all men and all women and all things created: a devouring flame of universal love.

This fierce and devouring flame of love would burn him up; it did burn him up. He was half burned away by it before the great fear took hold of him: a fear as mighty as the love which caused it. So he strove to kill his love; he fled away from it, he hid his face from it, he sought oblivion from it: in woman. The more avidly he sought oblivion from this consuming flame of love, the less he could find it, the less capable he became of finding it. And slowly and inevitably, the love turned into hate. Hate, first and last, of himself who had feared his love and sought to kill it; hate, next, of woman to whom he had fled for refuge from the fire that consumed him, and from whom he could not take the oblivion for which he hungered; hate, finally, of a world of men which had caused him to suffer as scarcely any man has suffered before.

Only he can judge Lawrence, who has loved as he loved. There is no such man living: of that I am convinced. I believe that once there was such a man, who loved as Lawrence loved and did not fear as Lawrence feared, or, if he did, he conquered his fear. He alone could judge Lawrence; and it was he who spoke the word " Judge not, that ye be not judged."

CONTENTS

ILLUSTRATIONS

PART I

SON AND LOVER

SOMEWHERE about the age of thirty-five, men of spiritual genius come to maturity, if they are fortunate enough to live so long. It is the middle of the road of life — *nel mezzo di cammin di nostra vita* — which seldom for the great ones reaches beyond the three score years and ten of the Bible, and often lamentably falls far short of them.

At the age of thirty-five D. H. Lawrence wrote one of his greatest books — *Fantasia of the Unconscious*. It marks the zenith of his mortal course, as will be apparent in this history. In it, he declares a faith, and takes a position, which afterwards he slowly relinquishes. His courage, or rather his simple strength, is not great enough to maintain him in the precarious harmony he has won out of his own conflicting elements. In this halcyon moment, he looks back calmly upon his own life and sees clearly what he is: how compounded, how conditioned, how compelled. And, in essence, *Fantasia of the Unconscious* is the effort, born of this clear self-knowledge, so to change the world of men that in future no child shall be compounded, and conditioned, and compelled as he was.

The relation of marriage between a man and woman, he says in *Fantasia*, is the necessary basis of the new order of society which he desires. In order that this relation should be creative, and not destructive, it is necessary that the man should, at the age of maturity, assume a sacred responsibility for the next purposive step into the future. If this creative responsibility is not undertaken by the man, then the love-craving of the woman will become frenzied and lay waste the family.

The unhappy woman [he goes on] beats about for her insatiable satisfaction, seeking whom she may devour. And usually, she turns to her child. Here she provokes what she wants. Here, in her own son who belongs to her, she seems to find the last perfect response for which she is craving. He is a medium to her, she provokes from him her own answer. So she throws herself into a last great love for her son, a final and fatal devotion, that which would have been the richness and strength of her husband and is poison to her boy. . . .

" *On revient toujours à son premier amour.*" It sounds like a cynicism to-day. As if we really meant: " *On ne revient jamais à son premier amour.*" But as a matter of fact, a man never leaves his first love, once the love is established. He may leave his first attempt at love. Once a man establishes a full dynamic communication at the deeper and the higher centres, with a woman, this can never be broken. . . . Very often not even death can break it.

The establishment of the upper love and cognition circuit inevitably provokes the lower sex-sensual centres into action, even though there be no correspondence on the sensual plane between the two individuals concerned. Then see what happens. If you want to see the real desirable wife-spirit, look at a mother with her boy of eighteen. How she serves him, how she stimulates him, how her true female self is his, is wife-submissive to him as never, never it could be to a husband. This is the quiescent, flowering love of a mature woman. It is the very flower of a woman's love . . . which a husband should put in his cap as he goes forward into the future in his supreme activity. For the husband, it is a great pledge, and a blossom. For the son also it seems wonderful. The woman now feels for the first time as a true wife might feel. And her feeling is towards her son. . . .

And then what? The son gets on swimmingly for a time, till he is faced with the actual fact of sex necessity. He gleefully inherits his adolescence and the world at large, without an obstacle in his way, mother-supported, mother-loved. Everything comes to him in glamour, he feels he sees wondrous much, understands a whole heaven, mother-stimulated. Think of the power which a mature woman thus infuses into her boy. He flares up like a flame in oxygen. No wonder they say geniuses mostly have great mothers. They mostly have sad fates.

And then? — and then, with this glamorous youth? What is he actually to do with his sensual, sexual self? Bury it? Or make an effort with a stranger. For he is taught, even by his mother, that his manhood must not forego sex. Yet he is linked up in ideal love already, the best he will ever know. . . . You will not easily get a man to believe that his carnal love for the woman he has made his wife is as high a love as that he felt for his mother. . . ."

That is Lawrence's history of his own life. It is the history of *Sons and Lovers* told again, eight years later, with the added insight and detachment that comes of maturity. If we are to understand the motions of this greatly gifted, greatly tortured man, we must grasp that fundamental history. Everything derives from it.

Even there he does not tell us everything. There is a secret which even he cannot reveal, and which he will strive to deny, to blot out of his consciousness, until the last. But it will emerge. It was Lawrence's destiny to be able to hide nothing of himself. Everything, down to the innermost secret, must be declared.

In this book we shall reveal nothing which Lawrence himself did not reveal. There is nothing else to be revealed. There is, and can be, but one true life of Lawrence; and it is contained in his works. But in order to read the life therein contained, we must be endowed with imaginative sympathy, and have learned the truth of Keats' word that " a man's life of any worth is a continual allegory, and very few eyes can see the mystery of his life — a life like the scriptures, figurative — which shallow people can no more make out than they can the Hebrew Bible." It is the same truth which Lawrence himself proclaimed in his own more bitter way in the preface to *Studies in Classical American Literature*. " The curious thing about art-speech is that it prevaricates so terribly, I mean it tells such lies. I suppose because we always, all the time tell ourselves lies. . . . Truly art is a sort of subterfuge. But thank God for it, we can see through the subterfuge if we choose. . . . The proper function of the critic is to save the tale from the artist who created it."

To save the truth of Lawrence from " the shallow people who take everything literally "; to save it equally from the veil of self-deception in which Lawrence himself was compelled to hide it, is the purpose of this book. What Lawrence was, not what he pretended to be, is of importance to mankind.

ᧁ

" The first part of *Sons and Lovers*," Lawrence wrote in an account of himself not many months before he died, " is all autobiography." The direct assurance was hardly necessary. We have only to compare *The White Peacock*, which preceded it, with *Sons and Lovers* to be instantly aware of a new element of immediate veracity. *The White Peacock* is a story, *Sons and Lovers* is the life of a man. Moreover, it is easy to see that the experience which is so richly recorded in *Sons and Lovers* had supplied the solid foundation for the imaginative structure of *The White Peacock*.

Strelley Farm of the imaginative story is palpably Willey Farm of the history; Emily is Miriam; George is Edgar;

Cyril is Paul Morel; even the minor character of Alice is the same as Beatrice in *Sons and Lovers*. When these obvious identifications have been made, it is easy to understand why the tiresome and unconvincing Lettie is tiresome and unconvincing and her lover Leslie a nullity. She had no original in life. Lawrence had no such sister; and the sister no such lover.

The White Peacock, then, may fairly be regarded as an imaginative commentary on *Sons and Lovers*, in any effort to reconstruct the fundamental life of Lawrence's youth. His youth ended — he said so himself — with " the great crash," the death of his mother in the winter of 1910. *Sons and Lovers* is the record of that youth. It is a magnificent book: for those who do not care to follow Lawrence in the passionate exploration of life which subsequently engrossed him, it will probably remain his greatest book. If Lawrence is to be judged as the " pure artist," then it is true that he never surpassed, and barely equalled, this rich and moving record of a life. But Lawrence is not to be judged as a " pure artist "; if ever a writer had " an axe to grind " it was he. Set in the perspective — the only relevant perspective — of his own revealed intentions, *Sons and Lovers* appears as the gesture of man who makes the heroic effort to liberate himself from the matrix of his own past. With it he tries to put his youth firmly behind him, and to stand stripped to run his own race. He is the brilliant, jewel-brown horse-chestnut, of his favourite image, newly issued from the burr. He breaks forth from the husk of his youth, from the husk which had been one flesh with him till this emergence, and takes the past into consciousness and cognizance. That knowing is as much a severance, as an acknowledgment. Lawrence therefore tried to make it extraordinarily complete.

Sons and Lovers has a double riches: as the intimate life-history of the youth of a genius, and as a significant act.

The significance of the act of writing the book will only be fully apparent when we have considered the life-history which it records.

∽

Lawrence was born on September 11, 1885, the fourth child of a collier father and a bourgeoise mother. The father was almost the pure animal, in the good and bad senses of the phrase: warm, quick, careless, irresponsible, living in the moment and a liar. The mother was responsible, and " heroic." In *Sons and Lovers* Lawrence makes a great effort to hold the balance fairly between them. Not being God, he found the task impossible. He would have liked to excuse the father, to make the mother bear some part of the blame for the father's slow disintegration.

The pity was, she was too much his opposite. She could not be content with the little he might be; she would have him the much that he ought to be. So, in seeking to make him nobler than he could be, she destroyed him. She injured and hurt and scarred herself, but she lost none of her worth.

But not to have " destroyed " him in this recondite sense would have meant to be destroyed herself, and not only herself, but her children also. To seek, as she did, " to make him undertake his own responsibilities, to make him fulfil his obligations " was not an encroachment, but a sheer necessity. Had she been less his opposite, she might indeed have suffered less, but the family would have collapsed upon itself. In the last issue, the father was responsible. Lawrence declared it again in the *Fantasia*.

So the mother withdrew from the father. There was no help for it. The essential estrangement had happened before Lawrence was born. She had not desired his coming, as she had desired the coming at least of the first of the two

SON AND LOVER 9

brothers before him. A lovely and tender passage of the book describes the sudden birth of her devouring love for the frail little boy, with blue eyes like her own.

In her arms lay the delicate baby. Its deep blue eyes, always looking up at her unblinking, seemed to draw her innermost thoughts out of her. She no longer loved her husband; she had not wanted this child to come, and there it lay in her arms and pulled at her heart. She felt as if the navel string that had connected its frail little body with hers had not been broken. A wave of hot love went over her to the infant. She held it close to her face and breast. With all her force, with all her soul she would make up to it for having brought it into the world unloved. She would love it all the more now it was here; carry it in her love. Its clear, knowing eyes gave her pain and fear. Did it know all about her? When it lay under her heart, had it been listening then? Was there a reproach in the look? She felt the marrow melt in her bones, with fear and pain.

This, if it is wholly imagination — which it is probably not, for there must have been little of her inward history which Lawrence's mother did not eventually confide in him — is an imagination we can trust as truth. The sudden resolve of her heart was fulfilled, and lavishly. She " made it up " in love a hundredfold to the child. He became, as was inevitable in such a case, abnormally sensitive. He expanded preternaturally in this warm atmosphere of love. His capacity for experience was unusually great, so likewise was his shrinking from it. A hungry desire for contact of the same intimate kind as that which he and his mother lavished upon each other was counterpoised by an anguished fear of it. At fourteen, " he was a rather small and rather finely-made boy, with dark brown hair and light blue eyes. His face was becoming . . . rough-featured, almost rugged . . . and it was extraordinarily mobile."

Usually he looked as if he saw things, was full of life, and warm; then his smile, like his mother's, came suddenly and was very lovable; and then, when there was any clog in his soul's quick running, his face went stupid and ugly. He was the sort of boy that becomes a clown and a lout as soon as he is not understood, or feels himself held cheap; and, again, is adorable at the first touch of warmth. He suffered very much from the first contact with anything. When he was seven, the starting school had been a nightmare and a torture to him. But afterwards he liked it.

Those who knew Lawrence well as a man will recognise immediately the truth of this picture of him as a boy. That *is* the boy who became the man they knew.

He grew with his soul sensitized utterly to the determination and the suffering of his mother in the long, unending struggle with her husband. Fortunately for him, it was not a silent and suppressed struggle such as so often, in a like situation, undermines the inmost being of an uncomprehending child. The antagonism was manifest and violent; more terrifying, but less subtly disintegrating. There were outbursts of drunkenness and downright brutality on the father's part, and they were fearful; but they belonged to a child's world. They were plain and elemental. The father does not come home from the pit: his dinner waits, the potatoes go dry. A hundred to one he has stayed drinking at the public house; but there is the agonising chance that something bad may have happened in the pit. If he comes home with too much beer in him, it will be bad; if he is brought home on a stretcher, or jolted off over the cobbles in the ambulance to the hospital, it will be worse. Or perhaps, if the injury is not too bad, it may be better. For there is the club money, and the ten shillings a week that the men of his stall put aside, which together makes more than the twenty-five shillings he has been giving lately. And, if it is beer, the worst won't happen, for he is in his heart afraid of mother.

But then, once or twice, he has done evil things — cut her head open by flinging a drawer at her. There is still the fear. The children listen, with indrawn breath and thumping hearts, to the angry voices contending, one hot, one cold in anger, mingled inextricably and for ever with the shrieking of the ash-tree in the wind.

There is a poem, " Discord in Childhood," about that ash-tree and those voices; it is one of Lawrence's earliest poems, but in the form in which we have it, it has probably suffered from the later rewriting which he inflicted upon many of them — sometimes to their manifest advantage, but sometimes to their distortion. He superimposed the moral judgments of a later Lawrence upon the immediate feelings of an earlier one. The truer memory of the ash-tree is in the prose of *Sons and Lovers*.

In front of the house was a huge old ash-tree. The west wind, sweeping from Derbyshire, caught the houses with full force, and the tree shrieked again. Morel liked it.

" It's music," he said. " It sends me to sleep."

But Paul and Arthur and Annie hated it. To Paul it became almost a demoniacal noise. The winter of their first year in the new house their father was very bad. The children played in the street, on the brim of the wide, dark valley, until eight o'clock. Then they went to bed. Their mother sat sewing below. Having such a great space in front of the house gave the children a feeling of night, of vastness, and of terror. This terror came in from the shrieking of the tree and the anguish of the home discord. Often Paul would wake up, after he had been asleep a long time, aware of thuds downstairs. Instantly he was wide awake. Then he heard the booming shouts of his father, come home nearly drunk, then the sharp replies of his mother, then the bang, bang of his father's fist on the table, and the nasty snarling shout as the man's voice got higher. And then the whole was drowned in a piercing medley of shrieks and cries from the great, wind-swept ash-tree. The children lay silent in suspense, waiting for a lull in the wind to hear what their father was doing. He might hit their mother again. There was a feeling of horror, a kind of bristling in the darkness, and a sense of blood. They lay with their hearts in the grip of an intense anguish. The wind came through the tree fiercer and fiercer. All the cords of the great harp hummed, whistled, and shrieked. And then came the horror of the sudden silence, silence everywhere, outside and downstairs. What was it? Was it a silence of blood? What had he done?

The children lay and breathed the darkness. And then, at last, they heard their father throw down his boots and tramp upstairs in his stockinged feet. Still they listened. Then at last, if the wind allowed, they heard the water of the tap drumming into the kettle, which their mother was filling for morning, and they could go to sleep in peace.

A fearful childhood, judged from one point of view, but from another how rich in the elemental drama that a child could understand and a man never forget! The issue how simple, manifest as the stars! The call upon the children the deepest their souls could sustain. They cleaved like little champions to their mother; they despised their father. And he, who knew that they were right to despise him, who knew that " he had denied the God in him," rotted in his own isolation.

That his father " had denied the God in him " was Lawrence's verdict also in the *Fantasia;* but then it was a still more advised pronouncement. Morel refused to take " the next creative step into the future." It was not an inordinate demand; for Morel the creative step consisted simply in taking responsibility for his children, in being in act, not merely in name, a father, in becoming a man whom his wife must respect and could not despise. He made not even a faint attempt; he slunk away. Inevitably, the mother's starved spirit sought satisfaction through her sons; and two of them, the eldest and the youngest, responded wholly to

BIRTHPLACE OF D. H. LAWRENCE

her call. When the eldest died, evidently on the threshold of a brilliantly successful career, the youngest son became her " man." As his great namesake had said, " Whatever I do, I do it unto the Lord," so Paul Morel could have said, " Whatever I do, I do it unto my mother." She was to live the life of which she had been cheated, through him; he would bring her the spiritual fulfilment she longed for. He had no ambition for himself, but all for her.

Sons and Lovers is the story of Paul Morel's desperate attempts to break away from the tie that was strangling him. All unconsciously, his mother had roused in him the stirrings of sexual desire; she had, by the sheer intensity of her diverted affection made him a man before his time. He felt for his mother what he should have felt for the girl of his choice. Let us be clear, as Lawrence himself tried to be clear in the *Fantasia*. Lawrence was not, so far as we can tell, sexually precocious; he was spiritually precocious. We are told that Paul Morel remained virgin till twenty-three. But his spiritual love for his mother was fully developed long before. What could be more poignant, or in implication more fearful, than the story he tells of the illness which fell upon him at sixteen? (He had told the same story before, in *The Trespasser;* it was a crucial happening in his boyhood.)

Paul was very ill. His mother lay in bed at nights with him; they could not afford a nurse. He grew worse, and the crisis approached. One night he tossed into consciousness in the ghastly, sickly feeling of dissolution, when all the cells in the body seem in intense irritability to be breaking down, and consciousness makes a last flare of struggle, like madness.

" I s'll die, mother! " he cried, heaving for breath on the pillow.

She lifted him up, crying in a small voice:

" Oh, my son — my son! "

That brought him to. He realized her. His whole will rose up and arrested him. He put his head on her breast, and took ease of her for love.

It is terribly poignant, and terribly wrong. Almost better that a boy should die than have such an effort forced upon him by such means. He is called upon to feel in full consciousness for his mother all that a full-grown man might feel for the wife of his bosom.

∽

In this same year, when Lawrence was sixteen, he met the girl Miriam, whose destiny was to be linked with his own for the next ten years, until his mother's death. He also met the farm and the family of which Miriam was the daughter. It became a second home to him. Beautifully situated in a valley about three miles away from the miner's cottage in Eastwood, the small decaying farm, with its pastures nibbled by rabbits to the quick, gave him the full freedom of that natural life which was always washing to the edge of the mining village. There he found the richness of life without which he wilted. He became as one of the family, and the Leivers' kitchen more dear to him than his own.

He loved the family so much; he loved the farm so much; it was the dearest place on earth to him. His home was not so lovable. It was his mother. But then he would have been just as happy with his mother anywhere. Whereas Willey Farm he loved passionately. He loved the little pokey kitchen, where men's boots tramped, and the dog slept with one eye open for fear of being trodden on; where the lamp hung over the table at night, and everything was so silent. He loved Miriam's long low parlour, with its atmosphere of romance, its flowers, its books, its high rosewood piano. He loved the gardens and the buildings that stood with scarlet roofs on the naked edges of the fields, crept towards the wood as if for cosiness, the wild country scooping down a valley and up the uncultured hills of the other side. Only to be there was an exhilaration and a joy to him. He loved Mrs. Leivers, with her unworldliness and her quaint cynicism; he loved Mrs. Leivers, so warm and young and lovable; he loved Edgar, who lit up when he came, and the boys and the children and Bill — even the sow Circe and the Indian game-cock called Tippoo. All this besides Miriam. He could not give it up.

The White Peacock is the poem of that love. In that book Strelley Mill is more than the background; it is almost the substance of the story.

Miriam was about the same age as himself, perhaps a year younger, when Lawrence met her. She encouraged, stimulated, and appreciated his gifts; she saw in him the wonderful being that he was, and she had fallen in love with him long before he with her. She was free to fall in love; he was not. So that when we say that Lawrence fell in love with Miriam, we mean that had he been free, and not bound, and ever more deliberately and tightly bound, he might have fallen in love with her, as she undoubtedly did with him. He fell in love with her only so far as he was capable of falling in love.

The history is painful. In *Sons and Lovers,* Lawrence tells it as though Miriam failed him; and he tried, even at the end of his life in *Lady Chatterley's Lover,* to tell the story thus.

I held forth with rapture to her, positively with rapture. I simply went up in smoke. And she adored me. The serpent in the grass was sex. She somehow didn't have any, at least not where it's supposed to be. I got thinner and crazier. Then I said we'd got to be lovers. I talked her into it. So she let me. I was excited, and she never wanted it. She adored me, she loved me to talk to her and kiss her; in that way she had a passion for me. But the other she just didn't want. And there are lots of women like her. And it was just the other that I *did* want. So there we split. I was cruel and left her.

Lawrence at all times needed desperately to convince himself in this matter of Miriam, and to the end he did not succeed. He does not tell the truth in *Sons and Lovers*, still less in *Lady Chatterley:* he comes closest to the truth in the *Fantasia*. Actually, while his mother still lived, he was incapable of giving to another woman the love without which sexual possession must be a kind of violence done: done not to the woman only, but also and equally to the man: above all to a man like Lawrence. All his life long Lawrence laboured to convince himself, and other people, that sexual desire carried with it its own validity: that the spiritual and the sexual were distinct. In fact, he never could believe it. What he did believe was something quite different, and quite true, namely that, in a man and woman who are whole, as he never was whole, the spiritual and the sexual might be one. This he declared in *Fantasia,* and yet again with his latest breath, in *The Escaped Cock.* He believed in a harmony which it was impossible for him personally to achieve, without a physical resurrection.

So saying, we anticipate: but it is essential to grasp as clearly as we can the subtle human tragedy of the affair with Miriam. It was the tragedy of Lawrence's entry into sexual life, and it haunted him all his days. In *Sons and Lovers* he conceals the truth. He cannot endure really to face it in consciousness. The story told there is subtly inconsistent with itself. At one moment comes a gleam of full recognition, as when he says of his mother: " She bore him, loved him, kept him, and his love turned back into her, so that he could not be free to go forward with his own life, really love another woman." But as he tells the story of the passion itself, he represents that it is not himself, but Miriam who is at fault. She is frigid, she shrinks from sexual passion; and this may have been true in part. But the truth was only partial. When later Lawrence came to a woman who was not frigid, the failure, though long drawn out, was more painful still. In representing that the fault was Miriam's, Lawrence wronged her. But we have to remember that *Sons and Lovers* was written after the death of his mother at a moment when Lawrence believed that he had attained sexual fulfilment. If he had not attained it with Miriam, he had some faint excuse for thinking that the fault was hers. He felt that it was not his own fault, and he had good reason for that. Nevertheless, it was his duty in *Sons and Lovers* to put the blame where it lay — if on a person at all, then upon his mother, who had taken from him that to which she had no right, and had used the full weight of her tremendous influence to prevent her son from giving to a woman the love which she so jealously guarded for herself. The fight was between his mother and Miriam, and it was an utterly unequal battle, between a strong and jealous woman and a diffident and unawakened girl.

In the story, Miriam is sacrificed, because Lawrence cannot tell the truth. Probably he could not tell it even to himself. The physical relation with Miriam was impossible. "You will not easily get a man to believe," he wrote in *Fantasia*, "that his carnal love for the woman he has made his wife is as high a love as that he felt for his mother." If Lawrence could write that when he had found his wife, and when his mother had been dead ten years, what did he feel while his mother was still alive, and he was engaged in talking Miriam into being his lover? He might talk and talk, but how could he convince her of what he did not himself believe — namely, that it was good that she should yield herself to him. He was a divided man. His love and his passion were separated. And because his passion was separated from his love, his passion was not true passion; it had but half the man behind, and to his own thinking, the worse half. This was the poisoned sting. He was, in his own eyes, degrading her, and degrading himself by his demand upon her.

What there was between Miriam and himself was an intense spiritual communion, and mutual stimulation of the mind. Whether it would ever, or could ever, have ripened into love on his side, who can say? Whatever it might have been was cankered in the bud. But I do not believe it ever could have ripened; Lawrence's subsequent history makes that plain to me. Happiness in love was not in Lawrence's destiny.

The appeal he made to Miriam was to her charity. He needed the comfort of her body, and she yielded herself to the sacrifice.

She looked at him and was sorry for him; his eyes were dark with torture. She was sorry for him; it was worse for him to have this deflected love than for herself, who could never be properly mated. He was restless, for ever urging forward and trying to find a way out. He might do as he liked, and have what he liked of her.

Paul did not want her, but, as Mellors says in *Lady Chatterley's Lover,* " he wanted *it.*" Miriam did not want him, but she wanted to give him *it*, because he wanted it. The indulgence of their " passion " was disastrous, because it was not passion at all. On both sides it was deliberate, and not passionate. Miriam's charity was passionate, but she had no sexual desire for Paul; Paul's need for the release and rest of sexual communion was passionate, but not his desire for Miriam. Each was a divided and tortured being. Miriam strove to subdue her body to her spirit, Paul strove to subdue his spirit to his body. They hurt themselves, and they hurt each other. Consider Lawrence's own words in *Sons and Lovers:*

A good many of the nicest men he knew were like himself, bound in by their own virginity, which they could not break out of. They were so sensitive to their women that they would go without them for ever rather than do them a hurt, an injustice. Being the sons of mothers whose husbands had blundered rather brutally through their feminine sanctities, they were themselves too diffident and shy. They could easier deny themselves than incur any reproach from a woman; for a woman was like their mother, and they were full of the sense of their mother.

Yet Paul did the hurt, the injustice, to Miriam, and still more to himself in the process. And the hurt he does her and himself is more delicate than he can acknowledge here. He does not and cannot feel towards her what by his own standards he must feel in order to justify his demand of her. He sacrifices her, or allows her to sacrifice herself, and in so doing, he violates himself. And the consequence is disaster; for their " passion " brings not the release from the torment of inward division which he seeks, but an exasperation of the torment.

From the new torment, new release is sought: and the appeal is always to the woman's charity. Clara Dawes is a married woman, where Miriam was virgin. It is easier for her to give, and easier for Paul to take. But the desire is not for the woman, but for release through the woman; and the woman gives not from desire but from pity.

He needed her badly. She had him in her arms, and he was miserable. With her warmth she folded him over, loved him. . . . She could not bear the suffering in his voice. She was afraid in her soul. He might have anything of her — anything; but she did not want to *know*. She felt she could not bear it. She wanted him to be soothed upon her — soothed. She stood clasping him and caressing him, and he was something unknown to her — something almost uncanny. She wanted to soothe him into forgetfulness. . . . She knew how stark and alone he was, and she felt it was great that he came to her; and she took him simply because his need was bigger either than her or him. . . . She did this for him in his need.

At the crucial moment, we cannot distinguish between Clara and Miriam. One is married, one is virgin; but their attitude towards him is the same, the appeal he makes to them the same.

One's instinct shrinks from it all. It is all wrong, humanly wrong. This man, we feel, has no business with sex at all. He is born to be a saint: then let him be one, and become a eunuch for the sake of the Kingdom of Heaven. For him, we prophesy, sex must be one long laceration, one long and tortured striving for the unattainable. This feverish effort to become a man turns fatally upon itself; it makes him more a child than before. He struggles frenziedly to escape being child-man to his mother, and he becomes only child-man again to other women, and the first great bond is not broken. If the woman is virgin like Miriam, he breaks her, by communicating to her the agony of his own division; if the woman is married like Clara, she breaks him, by abasing him in his own eyes.

To love a woman, in the simplest and most universal sense of the word, was impossible to Lawrence while his mother lived. Whether it was possible afterwards, the event will show. It will need almost a miracle, if he is to find his sexual salvation; for the fearful phrase of his own later invention fits him. It should fit him. He made it for himself. He is a man who is " crucified into sex," and he will carry the stigmata all his life.

Is it, we ask in pity and wonder, just a destiny? Is it simply that the sin of the father is visited through the mother upon the child? Was no escape possible? There is no answer to these questions; yet they return again and again to the mind. Surely, we say to ourselves, he could have broken that fearful bond that bound him to his mother. Was there not some ultimate weakness in the man that held him back? We may say that it was the terror of inflicting pain upon her.

D. H. LAWRENCE 1895 OR 1896

But there is a point at which the rarest and most tender virtue becomes a vice and a weakness; and perhaps to decide where that point lies is not so hard as it seems. When we begin to resent the compulsion of our virtues, they have become vices. Then the necessity of a choice and a decision is upon us: we must either cease to resent, or cease to obey, our virtues. Integrity lies either way. But to continue to obey, and to continue to resent — this means a cleavage which, once past a certain point, can never be healed again. Perhaps the final tragedy of Lawrence — and his life was finally a bitter tragedy — was that he could never make the choice on which his own integrity depended. To the end he resented his virtues, yet in act obeyed them, and in imagination blasphemed them.

Certainly, while his mother lived, until he himself was twenty-six, he resented the compulsion of his fear of paining her more and more deeply, yet he obeyed it. She was determined, consciously or unconsciously, that no woman save herself should have her son's love; and he obeyed her. What genuine and unhesitating passion there was in Lawrence's life before his mother's death went to a man, not a woman.

Miriam's eldest brother, the farmer's eldest son, Edgar Lievers of *Sons and Lovers,* George Saxton of *The White Peacock,* called forth in Lawrence something far more near to what most of us understand by passionate love than either Miriam or Clara. Contact with Miriam made him glow with a kind of spiritual incandescence; they throbbed together in a tense vibration of soul, which Paul strove vainly to convert into a passion of the body. His passion for Clara was from the beginning a physical need. But for the original of George and Edgar he must have felt something for which the best name is the simple one of love. In *Sons and Lovers* this friendship is but lightly touched; in *The White Peacock* the tremor of authenticity is not to be mistaken. Cyril's love for George has more of reality in it than any of the love affairs in the book; it yields in convincingness only to the diffused yet passionate affection for the farm and all its inhabitants which is the real emotional substance of the story. The record of this "friendship at its mystical best" culminates in the chapter, "A Poem of Friendship," and in the description of the two young men bathing together in the lake. They bathed in the morning cool of the hay-harvest, evidently the same hay-harvest which Paul and Edgar worked through together in *Sons and Lovers.*

We stood and looked at each other as we rubbed ourselves dry. . . . He knew how I admired the noble, white fruitfulness of his form. As I watched him, he stood in white relief against the mass of green. He polished his arm, holding it out straight and solid; he rubbed his hair into curls, while I watched the deep muscles of his shoulders, and the bands stand out in his neck as he held it firm. . . .

He saw I had forgotten to continue my rubbing, and laughing he took hold of me and began to rub me briskly, as if I were a child, or rather, a woman he loved and did not fear. I left myself quite limply in his hands, and, to get a better grip of me, he put his arm round me and pressed me against him, and the sweetness of the touch of our naked bodies against each other was superb. It satisfied in some measure the vague, indecipherable yearning of my soul, and it was the same with him. When he had rubbed me all warm, he let me go, and we looked at each other with eyes of still laughter, and our love was perfect for a moment, more perfect than any love I have known since, either for man or woman.

&

The White Peacock alone among Lawrence's novels, belongs wholly to the period before the crucial event of his mother's death. It was written and re-written during the six years before, and his mother held an advance copy of the printed book in her hands before she died. The writing of it, therefore, covered the years when Lawrence's compulsion by his love for his mother, and his vain efforts to liberate himself from that compulsion reached their extreme intensity. *The White Peacock* is a strange document.

The strangest thing about it is its title. We are given a clue to its meaning. The phrase, " a white peacock," occurs in an episode which is quite irrelevant to the deliberate structure of the novel. This seeming excrescence is the story of Annable, the gamekeeper. " The white peacock " is the name coined by Cyril, who is Lawrence himself, for Annable's first wife. Neither Annable's first wife, nor Annable himself, has anything to do with the main events of the story; they have no real contact with, nor influence upon, its characters. If the story of Annable had been completely omitted, the novel would have gained in cohesion and unity. Yet Lawrence, by taking his title for the whole book from that episode, indicated that the episode was to him more significant, in its own kind, than the main narrative itself.

The indication is confirmed by the striking fact that, towards the end of his life, in *Lady Chatterley's Lover,* Lawrence reverted to the figure of Annable. Mellors, the lonely gamekeeper of Lawrence's last novel, is blood-brother to Annable, the lonely gamekeeper of his first. No two imaginary characters in the whole of Lawrence's fiction are more clearly related than these. Essentially, they are the same figure; and the figure is one of great symbolic significance.

In *Lady Chatterley's Lover,* Mellors is more or less identified with Lawrence himself. His past is Lawrence's past, so far as his early relations with women are concerned. Mellors' first entry into sexual life is through Miriam. The

vital difference between Mellors and Lawrence is that Mellors has no mother; there are other vital differences, which
need not concern us now, for they will be apparent hereafter. Mellors tells of his sexual humiliation by Miriam and
Helen.

Annable is the same man as Mellors: their identity is unmistakable; and the story of his own life which Annable tells
is a story of sexual humiliation. It is moreover a story which
ends when Annable is twenty-six. "I thought I'd grown
a solid middle-aged man," he says, confessing his history,
"and here I feel sore as I did at twenty-six, and talk as
I used to." Lawrence was twenty-six, or thereabouts, when
he wrote those words for Annable; Mellors was obviously
twenty-six or thereabouts, when "he wanted a woman who
wanted him, and wanted *it*," for he is manifestly Lawrence
himself — with a concealed but vital difference — at this
very moment in his life. It follows that Annable in *The
White Peacock* is the figure through which, by an obvious
device, Lawrence declares himself.

Thus there are two Lawrences in *The White Peacock*,
Cyril the spiritual and feminine, the son of his mother, and
Annable, the physical and masculine. Cyril is the real Lawrence, Annable the man whom he dreamed that he might be.
This figure of a man haunted Lawrence's imagination all
his life; but at the time of writing *The White Peacock*
he did not dare to attempt to identify himself directly with
Annable, as he identified himself with Mellors in *Lady
Chatterley*. Cyril is himself; Cyril experiences with Emily,
who is Miriam, a certain degree of humiliation. Thus Cyril
says:

A woman is so ready to disclaim the body of a man's love; she
yields him her own soft beauty with so much gentle patience and
regret; she clings to his neck, to his head and cheeks, fondling
them for the soul's meaning that is there, and shrinking from his

passionate limbs and his body. It was with some perplexity, some anger and bitterness, that I watched Emily moved almost to ecstasy by the baby's small innocuous person.

But the tone is gentle. The spiritual man is in control, as in Cyril he is always in control. It is through Annable that Lawrence utters his seething and bitter hatred of woman.

Annable is a strange figure. He is the embodiment of Lawrence's idea of " the pure male." At his first appearance, the two women, Emily and Lettie shrinkingly " kept aloof from the man they instinctively hated." He stands at the quarry-edge " in the rim of light, darkly; a fine, powerful form, menacing us. He did not move, but like some malicious Pan looked down on us." He talks, grinning, of his litter of children — " natural as weasels — that's what I said they should be — bred up like a bunch o' young foxes, to run as they would. . . . They can be like birds, or weasels, or vipers, or squirrels, so long as they ain't human rot, that's what I say."

Cyril (who is Lawrence) thinks him " a fine fellow," Emily (who is Miriam) that " he has no soul." Immediately after the keeper is gone, they encounter the pandemonium of his household: the frenzied mother frantically beating one of the children, then sobbing over and kissing him. " Tha's got a funny Dad, tha' has, not like another man, no, my duckie. 'E's got no 'art ter care for nobody, 'e 'asna, ma pigeon — no, lives like a stranger to his own flesh and blood." It turns out that " 'e never laid a finger on 'em — nor me neither "; but " he's more than a stranger to me this day than 'e wor th' day I first set eyes on 'im." One of the children has a doll; it is " a hideous carven caricature of a woman," made by her father. And he has given her rouge to put on its face.

Cyril cultivates his acquaintance; he is deeply attracted

by Annable, and Annable is attracted by him. He treated Cyril " as an affectionate father treats a delicate son." One evening they met in a deserted churchyard. A peacock is perched on an old stone angel, and it screams. The keeper curses it. " The proud fool! — look at it! Perched on an angel, too, as if it were a pedestal for vanity. That's the soul of a woman — or it's the devil." He throws a sod at the bird, but before it flies away, it fouls its perch. " Just look! " he says, " the miserable brute has dirtied that angel. A woman to the end, I tell you, all vanity and screech and defilement."

Then the keeper tells his story. His father was a big cattle dealer, who had sent his son to Cambridge, and had gone bankrupt while he was there. So Annable had been persuaded to take orders. He became curate to a wealthy and aristocratic rector, who treated him generously. Then the rector's cousin, the Lady Chrystable, set eyes upon him, and determined to marry him.

" We got married. She gave me a living she had in her patronage, and we went to live at her Hall. She wouldn't let me out of her sight. Lord! we were an infatuated couple — and she would choose to view me in an aesthetic light. I was Greek statues for her, bless you. Croton, Hercules, I don't know what. She had her own way too much — I let her do as she liked with me. Then gradually she got tired — it took her three years to be really glutted with me. I had a physique then — for that matter I have now."

He held out his arm to me, and bade me try his muscle. I was startled. The hard flesh almost filled his sleeve.

" Ah," he continued, " you don't know what it is to have the pride of a body like mine. But she wouldn't have children — no she wouldn't — said she daren't. That was the root of the difference at first. But she cooled down, and if you don't know the pride of my body you'd never know my humiliation. I tried to remonstrate — and she looked simply astounded at my cheek. I never got over that amazement."

A year later, Annable completely disappeared. The Lady Chrystable married again. Now, at the moment he is speaking to Cyril, the news has come of her death. " I feel, somehow," he says, " as if I were at an end too. I thought I'd grown a solid, middleaged man, and here I feel sore as I did at twenty-six, and I talk as I used to."

" So she's dead — your poor peacock! " I murmured.

He got up, looking always at the sky, and stretched himself again. He was an impressive figure massed in darkness against the moonlight, with his arms outspread.

" I suppose," he said, " it wasn't all her fault."

" A white peacock, we will say," I suggested.

A few days later, the end comes. The keeper is killed by a fall of stone in the quarry.

In that story Lawrence's hatred of women for his own humiliation by woman attains an intensity of expression which is not equalled again in his work until *Lady Chatterley*. Then it is expressed by the same figure. In his first, and in his last novel, Lawrence is saying the same thing, in the same way, brooding over the same experience. He is unchanged. Eighteen years of experience have passed over him in between; and all that is added essentially is a more bitter hatred of yet another woman — the woman with whom he has spent those eighteen years. Let anyone read the story of Bertha Coutts in *Lady Chatterley* as it follows in Mellors' narrative after the story of Miriam and Helen; when he understands its meaning and its implication, when he recognises the woman to whom it refers, he will be aghast at the intensity of loathing for woman in the sexual relation which Lawrence felt and uttered at the end of his life.

Annable at the beginning, Mellors at the end. The prophetic significance of Annable is frightening, when we realise it fully. We see, with pity and terror, how Lawrence was caught in the toils of a fearful destiny. At twenty-six, something in himself *knows* what is to happen. He cannot escape, though he hides himself in the uttermost parts of the earth; and he will not escape.

The prophetic insight concerning his own destiny which Lawrence reveals in the figure of Annable is astonishing. The chief change which distinguishes Mellors from Annable, is that Mellors is more bitter, more unjust in his hatred. Annable does at least admit that the disaster of his humiliation is not wholly the woman's fault, even though as he tells his story it seems to be wholly hers. Mellors, on the other hand, though he speaks openly of Miriam and Helen, denies that the fault was his at all. True, he says in regard to Miriam that " he was cruel and left her "; but in what his cruelty consisted does not appear: as far as his own story goes he might have said that " he was wise, and left her." As for Helen, " she was a demon," simply. But that is nothing to the truly horrible picture of Bertha Coutts, whom Lawrence at twenty-six had not yet encountered. His loathing of women only grew with the years.

The most striking things in this strange story of Annable are two. The first is that when the Lady Crystabel dies, Annable dies also. It is not a coincidence. Lawrence takes care to underline that the connection is essential. When the news of Crystabel's death comes to him, Annable says: " I feel, somehow as if I were at an end too." And he is. In a day or two he is dead. Realistically judged, it is all wildly improbable; but the realistic judgment is totally irrelevant. The story is manifestly symbolic. What does this simultaneous death of Crystabel and Annable mean? What did Lawrence at twenty-six mean by it? Doubtless, he hardly knew. Probably it meant to him, knowingly, that he knew he was somehow bound to Miriam. Though his devil repudiated her none the less the bond was past all loosing. We shall find that it was. Even though he repudiates her still in *Lady Chatterley's Lover,* he has a later word to say. And transcending this particular reference, the symbolism of their deaths means that though Lawrence longs to repudiate the spiritual, though he dreams of obliterating it in the animal, he knows that it exists, it cannot be denied, and at the last it will claim him. We shall find that it did.

The second striking thing in the story of Annable is the grinding misery of the man when he repudiated Crystabel, and rejected the spiritual. Once more Lawrence insists upon it. Annable has gone his own chosen way, he has reverted to the complete animal, he has begotten a brood of little animal children on a woman with whom he has no spiritual bond at all.

He was a man of one idea: — that all civilisation was the painted fungus of rottenness. He hated any sign of culture. I won his respect one afternoon when he found me trespassing in the woods, because I was watching some maggots at work in a dead rabbit. That led us to discussion of life. He was a thorough materialist — he scorned religion and all mysticism. He spent his days sleeping, making intricate traps for weasels and men, putting together a gun, or doing some amateur forestry, cutting down timber, splitting it into logs for use in the hall, and planting young trees. When he thought, he reflected on the decay of mankind — the decline of the human race into folly and weakness and rottenness. " Be a good animal, true to your animal instinct," was his motto. With all this, he was fundamentally very wretched — and he made me also wretched. It was this power to communicate his unhappiness which made me somewhat dear to him, I think.

No mistake is possible. Annable's creed is the same as Mellors' creed; it is the creed which Lawrence eventually came to proclaim openly. And the grinding misery which Annable felt is the same grinding misery which those who have eyes to see and ears to hear cannot fail to discover everywhere in the work of Lawrence's final period. What Annable has done is what Lawrence was for ever trying to do, to deny the spiritual and return to the animal. No wonder Annable's wretchedness made Cyril wretched; it was Lawrence's prophetic vision of Lawrence's own doom.

უ

In the story of Annable is the key of Lawrence's life and work. In this seemingly irrelevant episode of his first book he lays down the pattern of his own destiny, as it will be accomplished. When we have grasped this, we are safeguarded from the possibility of being deceived. *The White Peacock* was published in 1911, long before the Great War. Lawrence will make us believe, and believe himself, that it was the war which changed him. If there had been no war, Lawrence's destiny would have been essentially the same. By the time he was twenty-six his fate was decided: the irreparable had happened.

We shall be on our guard, therefore, even against Lawrence's own assertion that the death of his mother was " the great crash — the end of his youth." No doubt it seemed so to Lawrence, even to the end of his life, when he made the assertion; but many things about himself appeared to him other than they truly were. The " great crash " was the disaster of his entry into sexual life: only it was not a crash, but a long drawn out torture of self-humiliation.

The death of his mother seemed more important to him. In so far as it was the death of the woman of his life whom Lawrence most deeply loved, it was important. It set him free to find a woman of his own; but to set free is not to make whole. The freedom he gained by his mother's death was wholly external; his soul was in bondage still. Not directly to her, as he seems to say in the *Fantasia* but to that irreparable inward division into which she had compelled him. The plasm of the total organism — the physico-spiritual unity which is man — had suffered vital injury. The mere loosing of a bond by death would not restore it. Long before his mother's death Lawrence had become a conscious, responsible, adult man; what her love had compelled him to do, *he* had done. He had resented the bond that bound him, but he had not been able to break it; he, as a man, had acquiesced in the distortion thrust upon him. He was a victim, but in his own eyes he was guilty too. He had consented to the cleavage within him, he had, by his own act, driven it home. The physical death of his mother could not make him whole again.

Because this was so, the death of his mother was less important than it seemed to him. It changed the outward circumstance rather than the inward pattern of Lawrence's life. That is not to say that it was not an intense experience; on the contrary, it was too intense, humanely excessive. He suffered that agony of extreme and intolerable isolation which comes to other men only at the death of the beloved mistress, or beloved wife. The bond which united him to the universe was suddenly snapped; he was cast out by life, derelict on the naked shore of the great sea wherein before he had moved and had his being. " Whatever spot he stood on, there he stood alone. From his breast, from his mouth, sprang the endless space, and it was there behind him, everywhere. The people hurrying along the streets offered no obstruction to the void in which he found himself." So extreme and perfect a realisation of one's separateness, when the whole universe becomes one vast otherness, might well have been crucial with another man; it might have been the prelude to a rebirth into wholeness. But the occasion would need to have been different.

In the country all was dead still. Little stars shone high up; little stars spread far away in the flood-waters, a firmament below. Everywhere the vastness and terror of the immense night which is roused and stirred for a brief while by the day, but which returns, and will remain at last eternal, holding everything in its silence and its living gloom. There was no Time, only Space. Who could say his mother had lived and did not live? She had been in one place, and was in another; that was all. And his soul could not leave her wherever she was. Now she was gone abroad into the night, and he was with her still. They were together. But yet there was his body, his chest, that leaned against the stile, his hands on the wooden bar. They seemed something. Where was he? — one tiny upright speck of flesh, less than an ear of wheat lost in the field. He could not bear it. On every side the immense dark silence seemed pressing him, so tiny a spark, into extinction, and yet, almost nothing, he could not be extinct. Night, in which everything was lost, went reaching out, beyond stars and sun. Stars and sun, a few bright grains, went spinning round for terror, and holding each other in embrace, there in a darkness that out-passed them all and left them tiny and daunted. So much, and himself, infinitesimal, at the core a nothingness, and yet not nothing.

" Mother! " he whimpered — " Mother! "

She was the only thing that held him up, himself, amid all this. And she was gone, intermingled herself. He wanted her to touch him, have him alongside with her.

But no, he would not give in. Turning sharply, he walked towards the city's gold phosphorescence. His fists were shut, his mouth set fast. He would not take that direction, to the darkness, to follow her. He walked towards the faintly humming, glowing town, quickly.

That is the end of *Sons and Lovers;* and it is beautiful, yet not perhaps so beautiful as the perfect poem which commemorates his mother's death — " The Virgin Mother." She was virgin, because, as Mrs. Morel once whispered to

Paul, " I've never really had a husband "; she was virgin, more subtly, because all the torrents of spring, of the first true love of a man — her son, had been poured out upon her. To be his beloved woman, as his mother was to Lawrence, she must needs be virgin in his imagination. He is her, as she is his, first love. " The Virgin Mother " is one of Lawrence's simplest, and assuredly one of his loveliest poems — universal in its appeal, and final in its felicity.

> My little love, my darling,
> You were a doorway to me;
> You let me out of the confines
> Into this strange countrie
> Where people are crowded like thistles,
> Yet are shapely and comely to see.
>
> My little love, my dearest,
> Twice have you issued me,
> Once from your womb, sweet mother,
> Once from your soul, to be
> Free of all hearts, my darling,
> Of each heart's entrance free.
>
> And so, my love, my mother,
> I shall always be true to you.
> Twice I am born, my dearest:
> To life, and to death, in you;
> And this is the life hereafter
> Wherein I am true.
>
> I kiss you good-bye, my darling,
> Our ways are different now;
> You are a seed in the night-time,
> I am a man, to plough
> The difficult glebe of the future
> For seed to endow.

> I kiss you good-bye, my dearest,
> It is finished between us here.
> Oh, if I were as calm as you are,
> Sweet and still on your bier!
> Oh God, if I had not to leave you
> Alone, my dear!
>
> Is the last word now uttered?
> Is the farewell said?
> Spare me the strength to leave you
> Now you are dead.
> I must go, but my soul lies helpless
> Beside your bed.

It is poignant, and it is lovely. It has a calm of adoration which falls like a still cool air in the fever of the love-poems which surround it in the volume of *Amores*. Yet in that context it is rather terrible. It contains an accent which, though in itself lovely and heart-rending, we are almost ashamed to hear at this moment. For we shall never hear it again save once, and then at the prompting of the same memory of his virgin mother. The exquisite human tenderness which cries to her:

> My little love, my darling. . . .

this was to be reserved for women dead or inaccessible: for a dead mother, for the "spirits summoned west," in the lovely poem which, though written a full twelve years afterwards, is yet the perfect counterpart of "The Virgin Mother." With the woman near and living it is always the heat of struggle, the anguish of humiliation, or the desperate quiet of inviolable otherness. Precisely this tenderness, the virginal tenderness of love that survives the fever and lies open-eyed to the coolness and beauty of the morning, could never visit Lawrence in the presence of the woman to whom he was man. Only in utter separation could it come to him. He could feel it for creatures divided from him by that gulf of " the other dimension " across which the little dog Coasmin was mocked by the parrot. The gulf of death, the gulf of time, the gulf of the other dimension; but gulf there must be. Then, " as 'twere across a vast," this quintessential love could be acknowledged. Then, it made no demands, and involved no consequences.

Yet this tenderness of detachment in love is for the generality of men neither so dangerous nor so rare. They may not have one atom of power to utter it, but they sometimes feel it. It means much to them; by its presence they recognise the angel who stirs the waters, the God made visible. Was it that Lawrence felt it so much more seldom than they? It is scarcely credible; nay, it is certainly incredible. Towards the dumb creation he felt it infinitely more often and more distinctly than we. Could he, then, have felt it less towards his fellow men and women? The idea to those who knew him intimately will seem fantastic.

Then, why was it suppressed and concealed? Or was it merely forgotten? And the answer is, I believe, that it was suppressed and concealed, but not, in the last resort, deliberately. In his life it was radiant; it is by this thing, chief among many others, that his friends remember him. Yet there is this strange discrepancy between the work they read and the man they knew. The cause lies deep down; and we have tried to reveal it. Of this one thing, of his own wonderful tenderness, of his own most godlike quality, Lawrence was afraid; as though he said to himself, this is my weakness which must not be exposed.

It is, indeed, this convulsive struggle against his own tenderness which marks Lawrence from the beginning. He struggles against the tenderness he feels for his mother. It is strangling him, cankering his life, that he cannot inflict upon her the pain that he ought to inflict — the pain of cleavage. He turns to Miriam, and because he cannot inflict pain on his mother, he tortures Miriam. He cannot help it; he " gets thinner and crazier," as Mellors says. But not with passionate desire for the woman, but with the passionate longing for respite and release from a consciousness tortured by the suffering he is inflicting. Lawrence was not a physically passionate man; he was not more passionate than the common run of men, but less passionate — almost a sexual weakling. Whether this was the cause or the effect of the excessive and misplaced love between him and his mother, who shall say? Sex, for him, is the escape from the torture of tenderness, the chance of oblivion; never an equal relation.

To overcome his own tenderness — this is the strange problem of Lawrence's life, as it presented itself to him. And once we have presented it to ourselves in these terms, the impossibility of any *judgment* upon him is apparent. If we say, as we shall say, that his effort to escape from his own tenderness was mistaken, we do not imply that it was a mistake which it lay within his power to avoid. If we say, as we shall say, that he ought to have accepted his own deepest nature, we shall say it in the full realisation that this act of acceptance would have been one of incredible, and perhaps of superhuman difficulty. Lawrence's tenderness was not a thing that happens often in human history; it is rare, rarer far than even sensitive men and women imagine. We cannot tell what suffering it entails for the handful of wonderful human beings who have possessed it. If we ourselves have any spark of real human tenderness, then we know that tenderness involves the capacity for a kind of suffering which can drive men mad. We suffer, like Miranda, with those that we see suffer; and we cannot bear it. The anguish is intolerable; the human organism cannot sustain it. What shall we do?

Only those to whom this problem has been a real one, those who have known what it is to be on the brink of insanity or death through the torture of sympathy, can understand Lawrence; and, because they understand, they know they cannot judge him. If their suffering has been past bearing, what was his? And let us never forget, he had known the extremity of this suffering when he was young. Between sixteen and twenty-six, he touched the pinnacle — the extremity of anguish, the extremity of desperation, the extremity of cleavage. I do not believe that there was in him, afterwards, any essential change. There were new experiences, but they came to him in forms now predetermined by the inward structure of his being, which is established and will not change.

The most certain of these forms is that woman is the means of escape from the anguish of his own inward division, and from the sense of isolation that is inseparable from it. This is Lawrence's fundamental " mistake," his ineradicable bias. Woman is the means to oblivion, the sexual connection the only waters of true Lethe. It is a " mistake " for many reasons. It is a " mistake " because Lawrence's tenderness, which is deeper even than his desire to escape from it, rebels at the notion that a living woman should be a means at all; it is a " mistake " because Lawrence will never be able to believe in his inmost soul that he has the right to seek escape from the consequences of his own tenderness, and he will be haunted by the thought that he has failed in the courage of his own isolation; it is a " mistake," because he will always be conscious that his being is not his own, but is dependent upon a woman's charity; it is a " mistake," because for all these reasons his sexual experience will be inordinately mental, an agony of self-consciousness; it is a

" mistake," because his surpassing tenderness, his amazing delicacy of spiritual response, which is the cause of his seeking escape, has been purchased at the cost of his own physical virility; the healthy animal has been sacrificed to make a man of genius. For all these reasons, sex is for Lawrence a *pis-aller*, a means of escape that will give him neither refuge nor rest, a perpetual thorn in the spirit, a reminder of his own insufficiency and weakness and lack of courage; it will tell him always that he is not greater, but less, than his fellow men. The frail, delicate animal that he is will come to loom as a thing of contempt before his eyes, quite blotting out the magnificence and beauty of the spiritual being that he was. By choosing the way of sex, he will come to lose that core of living belief in himself as a single and integral human being which could make him, what in his soul he desires to be, and knows he ought to be, a leader of men. He will gradually disintegrate his own integrity, and become the anti-type of the man who is from the beginning, and will be to the end, his veritable hero — Jesus Christ. The anti-type in whom is manifest that " he who will save his life, shall lose it."

But there is this to say. In the order to which Lawrence belongs, nothing is lost. He is a symbolic man, one of the world's great exemplars of what a man may be; one of the chief of those rare spirits who bring men to a consciousness of their own strange destinies. Through Lawrence we learn to know ourselves, in a way which men have never known themselves before. If he was tortured, as he surely was, it was for us that he was tortured. If his tenderness turned into a frenzy of hatred, if at the last he was a thing of fragments dreaming impossible dreams — it was tragedy for him who suffered the destiny, but for us who behold it, it is illumination, " He lived through this experience for us; we owe him homage."

From seventeen to twenty-one Lawrence had been teaching miners' children in a rough and fierce elementary school; the next two years he was at Nottingham University. At the age of twenty-three, he left Nottingham University, and went to teach in an elementary school at Croydon. While there he made his entrance into the literary world. In the spring of 1909 Miriam had copied and sent a few of his poems to Ford Madox Hueffer at *The English Review*. " Discipline," " Dreams Old and Nascent," and " Baby Running Barefoot " were among them; and it is not to be wondered at that Hueffer was impressed, for all are beautiful, and the first, manifestly addressed to Miriam herself, memorable in other ways.

I came to the boys with love, dear, and only they turned on me;
With gentleness came I, with my heart 'twixt my hands like
    a bowl,
Like a loving-cup, like a grail, but they spilt it triumphantly
And tried to break the vessel, and violate my soul.

And perhaps they were right, for the young are busy deep down
    at the roots,
And love would only weaken their under-earth grip, make shallow
Their hold on reality, enfeeble their rising shoots
With too much tincture of me, instead of the dark's deep fallow.

I thought that love would do all things, but now I know I am
    wrong.
There are depths below depths, my darling, where love does not
    belong.
Where the fight that is fight for being is fought throughout the
    long
Young years, and the old must not win, not even if they love and
    are strong.

Alas that, in Lawrence himself, the old must win! But the immediate power of the poems impressed Hueffer. He accepted them, and invited Lawrence to call upon him. Shortly afterwards, Hueffer passed on " the ragged and bulky manuscript" of *The White Peacock* to Heinemann the publisher, and Edward Garnett, who was then Duckworth's reader, wrote appreciatively to Lawrence, and successively arranged for the publication of *The Trespasser, Love Poems,* and *Sons and Lovers.* Garnett became (in Lawrence's own words) " a generous and genuine friend." Thus Hueffer and Garnett launched Lawrence into the literary world.

Evidently, this year 1910 was feverish. To it seems to have belonged the painful culmination of his love for Miriam and the affair with Helen of the " Poems," who is obviously the Helena of *The Trespasser.* Says Mellors in *Lady Chatterley's Lover:*

I was cruel, and left her [Miriam]. Then I took on with another girl, a teacher, who had made a scandal by carrying on with a married man and driving him nearly out of his mind. She was a soft, white-skinned soft sort of a woman, older than me, and played the fiddle. And she was a demon. She loved everything about love, except the sex. Clinging, caressing, creeping into you in every way: but if you forced her to the sex itself, she just ground her teeth and sent out hate. I forced her to it, and she could simply numb one with hate because of it. So I was balked again.

The account is not to be trusted, any more than the account of Bertha Coutts which follows: the whole narrative is coloured by the extremity of Lawrence's loathing for sex and woman which runs floodgate in his last novel. None the less, it obviously is an account of the happening which underlies the story of *The Trespasser.* Siegfried, in that disappointing book, is obviously a composite character; he is partly the married man of Mellors' narrative, and partly Lawrence himself. (For example, the crucial experience of

Lawrence's illness at sixteen is given to him.) *The Trespasser* compared to *The White Peacock*, is a poor book:
the feverish, confused and death-haunted book of a soul-
sick man, written out of a turmoil of unresolved experience.
One would guess that it was hurriedly written. It has neither
the romantic glamour, nor the symbolic profundity of its
predecessor. The substantial difference is that there are
evident traces of sexual experience and sexual disappointment in it; so that one would be tempted to guess that the
Annable episode was added to *The White Peacock* at this
time. But the supposition is unnecessary; Lawrence was a
man capable of anticipating experience.

The episode with Helen seems to have been brief, and —
if we may accept the time order of the poems — to have followed hard upon " the test on Miriam." Soon afterwards
came the death of his mother; followed " a weary and bitter
year," a second serious attack of pneumonia, and, apparently, a last abortive attempt to renew the relation with
Miriam. Then *Sons and Lovers* must have been begun. With
a renewed vitality, Lawrence made the attempt to bring the
past wholly into consciousness. As a writer, he took a giant
stride forward. And at this moment he met the woman who
was to be his wife, who enters now into the very substance of
his work, and remains in it to the end. This was in May 1912.

It is the end of the first period of Lawrence's life and
work, and the beginning of the second. Of these clearly
marked periods there were four. The first ends with his
mother's death; the second begins with his meeting with his
wife and ends with the end of the war; the third begins,
roughly, with his leaving England in 1919 and ends with his
abortive return to England at the end of 1923; the fourth
and last period ends with his death, on March 3rd, 1930.

PART II

I

THE SEXUAL FAILURE

IN *Sons and Lovers* Lawrence had made the effort to liberate himself from his own past. His mother was dead; he was free to make the attempt to bring the past into consciousness and utterance. He was also free to find the woman of his choice, and cleave to her. The weary and bitter year was over. Lawrence had let his grief for his mother have its way with him. The corn of wheat had fallen into the ground and died, and a new life seemed to spring forth again. The " Hymn to Priapus " tells of the resurrection.

> My love lies underground
> With her face upturned to mine,
> And her mouth inclined in the last long kiss
> That ended her life with mine.
>
> She fares in the stark immortal
> Fields of death;
> I in these goodly, frozen
> Fields beneath.
>
> Something in me remembers
> And will not forget.
> The stream of my life in the darkness
> Deathward set!

And something in me has forgotten,
Has ceased to care.
Desire comes up, and contentment
Is debonair.

I, who am worn and careful,
How much do I care?
How is it I grin then, and chuckle
Over despair?

Grief, grief, I suppose, and sufficient
Grief makes us free
To be faithful and faithless together
As we have to be.

A little while after this poem was written, Lawrence met his wife. I imagine that the amazing poem " Snapdragon " tells of their thrilling meeting, in the late spring of 1912:

Again I saw a brown bird hover
Over the flowers at my feet;
I felt a brown bird hover
Over my heart, and sweet
Its shadow lay on my heart.
I thought I saw on the clover
A brown bee pulling apart
The closed flesh of the clover
And burrowing in its heart.

She moved her hand, and again
I felt the brown bird cover
My heart; and then
The bird came down on my heart,
As on a nest the rover
Cuckoo comes, and shoves over
The brim each careful part

Of love, takes possession, and settles her down
With her wings and her feathers to drown
The nest in a heat of love.

So the new and sudden passion took violent possession of him. The brief prose argument of *Look! We Have Come Through!* tells the story that was to ensue.

After much struggling and loss in love and in the world of man, the protagonist throws in his lot with a woman who is already married. Together they go into another country, she perforce leaving her children behind. The conflict of love and hate goes on between the man and the woman, and between these two and the world around them, till it reaches some sort of conclusion.

Every process in life at any point has reached " some sort of conclusion." Lawrence knew what he was doing when he chose the vague and non-committal phrase. There was to be more struggle than conclusion in this history of himself and his woman.

Both the record of the poems themselves, and the sudden change which comes over the beautiful and evidently auto-biographical story of the " honeymoon " of Will Brangwen and Anna Lensky in " The Rainbow," concur in showing that the golden time was quickly over and the struggle quickly begun. Neither is free; each feels chained to the past. In " First Morning," the man says:

> I could not be free,
> not free myself from the past, those others —
> and our love was a confusion,
> there was a horror,
> you recoiled away from me.

What is it that she recoils from? It is hard to say; she herself finds it hard to say. In " In the Dark," she cries:

" I am afraid of you, I am afraid, afraid!
　There is something in you destroys me — ! "

　　　" Ah, you are horrible;
　You stand before me like ghosts, like a darkness upright."

And the man answers:

" In the darkness we all are gone, we are gone with the trees
　And the restless river; — we are lost and gone with all these."

The woman answers:

" But I am myself, I have nothing to do with these. . . ."
" But let me be myself, not a river or tree."

What lies behind the words we shall gather hereafter. It
is connected on the one hand with the man's desire for total
eclipse,

Not sleep, which is grey with dreams,
nor death, which quivers with birth,
but heavy, sealing darkness, silence, all immovable. . . .

and with his appeal to the " Gods of the living Darkness,
powers of Night " to overcome her recoil from him. One
feels that the desire of the man is to find in the sexual relation a kind of death, an utter lapse from daylight consciousness, a mutual immolation; and from this the woman recoils in horror. But underneath we sense some deep physical
incompatibility of the kind which Mellors describes so painfully in *Lady Chatterley's Lover*.

At the spiritual level the cause of his hatred of her is that
the woman's soul turns back to her children.

Yet how I have learned to know that look in your eyes
Of horrid sorrow!
How I know that glitter of salt, — dry, sterile, sharp, corrosive salt!
Not tears, but white sharp brine
Making hideous your eyes.

I have seen it, felt it in my mouth, my throat, my chest, my belly,
Burning of powerful salt, burning, eating through my defenceless
    nakedness.
I have been thrust into white, sharp crystals,
Writhing, twisting, superpenetrated. . . .

Lot's Wife! — Not Wife, but Mother.
I have learned to curse your motherhood,
You pillar of salt accursed.
I have cursed motherhood because of you,
Accursed, base motherhood!

But if the woman were carrying Lawrence's child in her
womb, all this would be over. " Rose of all the World " tells
us that in her heart the woman believes that the birth of a
child is the appointed end of sex-fulfilment, and the ecstasy
only the blossom on its way to become ripe seed. The man
seeks to convince her that it is not so, but in vain. If she
were fulfilled, according to her own desire, there would be
no turning back, or if there were, it would be only a momentary turning back, of which the man need not be afraid. But
he is afraid; and the fear turns into hatred.

The agony of fear, the agony of hatred — these are the
most memorable and recurrent moods of this sequence of
naked poems. The thought that she should leave him drives
him to a frenzy of anguish.

        A cripple!
        Oh God, to be mutilated!
        To be a cripple!

        And if I never see her again?

I think if they told me so
I could convulse the heavens with my horror.
I think I could alter the frame of things in my agony.
I think I could break the System with my heart.
I think, in my convulsion, the skies would break.

Need so naked as that must inevitably pass into hate. No
man can be so dependent upon a woman, without hating her
for the humiliation of which she is the cause. And some of
these poems are terribly painful to read — in particular, the
one which bears the very name " Humiliation."

I have been so innerly proud, and so long alone,
Do not leave me, or I shall break.
Do not leave me. . . .

God, that I have no choice!
That my own fulfilment is up against me
Timelessly!
The burden of self-accomplishment!
The charge of fulfilment!
And God, that she is *necessary!*
Necessary, and I have no choice!

Do not leave me.

Humiliation, indeed. She gives him fulfilment; he does not
give it her, or this agonised fear of her leaving him would
not exist.

When the relation of sex is equal, there is on both sides
simple security in the essential. Here is none. It is self-
deception for the man to claim fulfilment — " I am myself
at last; now I achieve my very self " — when the woman
sees him as "limping and following rather at my side, moaning for me to love him." Fulfilment in sex cannot be so one-
sided; if it is, it is something less than fulfilment. In " The

Song of a Man who is not Loved," he is utterly overwhelmed by the thought of his own isolation without her. " The space of the world is immense, before me and around me." It is the same feeling which swept over Paul Morel at the death of his mother; and it has not been conquered. All that has happened is that he has found a refuge from it in the woman. And that, deep down, he feels is cowardice, as though he had shirked a destiny, or betrayed a God.

Fulfilment — the word returns again and again, until we begin to shrink from its grim, unconscious irony. What is this fulfilment? What is it that is fulfilled? The sexual man? There is no such thing as the sexual man. He is an abstraction, as remote from human reality as the economic man. Seek to fulfil the physical man alone, and you starve the spiritual man; you get the kind of " fulfilment " which turns spiritual love into hatred. Lawrence is " fulfilled "; and yet,

> This love so full
> Of hate has hurt us so,
> We lie side by side
> Moored — but no,
>
> Let me get up
> And wash quite clean
> Of this hate. . . .
>
> It is all no good
> I am chilled to the bone
>
> Now the hate is gone;
> There is nothing left;
> I am pure like bone,
> Of all feeling bereft.

By the very feeling of this all-consuming hatred, the man is humiliated, as by an impurity into which he is plunged.

He is caught in a destiny of degradation, engulfed in a flood
of vileness rising from his own depths. From humiliation he
reacts into frenzied self-assertion. He strikes out wildly, like
a blinded man. " This misery of your dissatisfaction and
misprision stupefies me," he cries.

> Here I am — get up and come to me!
> Not as a visitor either, nor a sweet
> And winsome child of innocence; nor
> As an insolent mistress telling my pulse's beat.
> Come to me like a woman coming home
> To the man who is her husband, all the rest
> Subordinate to this, that he and she
> Are joined together for ever, as is best.
>
> Behind me on the lake I hear the steamer drumming
> From Austria. There lies the world, and here
> Am I. Which way are you coming?

Big brave words, but we have not forgotten the anguished
horror of " Do not leave me! " We can hardly be convinced
by this sudden masculinity. The man who cried " God, that
she is necessary! " may ask for submission from his wife, but
he cannot compel it. Against the memory of that reluctant
confession, the manly voice cannot prevail.

> Put ashes on your head, put sackcloth on
>   And learn to serve.
> You have fed me with your sweetness, now I am sick
>   As I deserve. . .
>
> And serve now, woman, serve, as a woman should,
>   Implicitly.
> Since I must serve and struggle with the imminent
>   Mystery.

D. H. LAWRENCE SEPTEMBER 11, 1906

Serve then, I tell you, add your strength to mine,
Take on this doom.
What are you by yourself, do you think, and what
The mere fruit of your womb?

What is *he* by himself? she might answer; and, alas for
him, the question would be more devastating. He has already
answered it in good set terms in " Humiliation ":

What should I do if you were gone again
So soon?
What should I look for?
Where should I go?
What should I be, I myself,
" I "?
What would it mean, this
" I "?

No doubt, it would have meant a very great deal. But
then it would have been a different " I." What is certain by
now about the actually existing " I " of Lawrence is that it
does not intend to make the experiment of finding out what
it might become in isolation. The situation, in this regard, is
simple. When it comes to imposing terms, it is the necessary person who can impose them; for the other to claim to
do so is a mere gesture, a salving of pride, a saving of face,
the reverse of an obverse of humiliation.

There are moments of simple happiness, when it seems
that the fight is over; and we may be sure the simple happiness was much greater and much more frequent than appears from the poems themselves, where it seems to come
and go " as the lightning in the collied night." But when,

in such a moment of peace, Lawrence assures us that it is
final,

> We have died, we have slain and been slain,
> We are not our old selves any more.
> I feel new and eager
>   To start again

we cannot help being dubious. Wherein, we ask, have the essentials of the relation been changed? In the very next poem
the acknowledgment of dependence is absolute once more.

> How quaveringly I depend on you, to keep me alive,
> Like a flame on a wick. . . .

> Suppose you didn't want me! I should sink down
> Like a light that has no sustenance
> And sinks low. . . .

> Nourish me, and endue me, I am only of you,
> I am your issue.

It is almost a sacrilege to pry into this poem, " Wedlock,"
so naked and quivering with tremulous hope. But the hope
was to be blasted; and the need is upon us to understand
why it was to be blasted. And the cause is that the dependence of the man upon the woman is excessive; it is an
extremity of dependence against which he must rebel. He
can surrender himself to it for the moment, but he will hate
himself and her for the humiliation of his own surrender.
Therefore the tender and tremulous hope arouses within us
only the pain of foreboding.

> There will be something come forth from us.
> Children, acts, utterance.
> Perhaps only happiness.

Perhaps only happiness will come forth from us.
Old sorrow, and new happiness.
Only that one newness.

But that is all I want.
And I am sure of that.
We are sure of that.

When a man is sure that all he wants is happiness, then most grievously he deceives himself. All men desire happiness, but they need something far different, compared to which happiness is trivial, and in the lack of which happiness turns to bitterness in the mouth. There are many names for that which men need — " the one thing needful " — but the simplest is " wholeness." When a man is whole, then there is something in himself which looks no more for happiness, and smiles at the child in himself who still dreams of it. Lawrence at this moment is a child full of childish things.

So I hope I shall spend eternity
With my face down buried between her breasts;
And my still heart full of security,
And my still hands full of her breasts.

That is the place and posture of the child in arms; an eternity of infancy. Yet if the woman takes him for an instant at his word, he is all angry resentment. She dares to admire his body, to chide him with the physical shyness that makes him hide it even from her.

" Why shouldn't your legs, and your good strong thighs
be rough and hairy? — I'm glad they are like that.
You are shy, you silly, you silly shy thing. . . .
And I love you so! Straight and clean and all of a piece is the
     body of a man,
Such an instrument, a spade, like a spear, or an oar,
Such a joy to me — "

Difficult, one would have thought, to take offence at that. If Lawrence had so chanted the praise of his woman's body, he would have been thunderstruck to find that she resented it. But he resented it.

So she said, and I wondered,
feeling trammeled and hurt.
It did not make me free.

Now I say to her: "No tool, no instrument, no God!
Don't touch me, and appreciate me.
It is an infamy.
You would think twice before you touched a weasel on a fence
as it lifts its straight white throat.
Your hand would not be so flig and easy.
Nor the adder we saw asleep with her head on her shoulder
curled up in the sunshine like a princess;
when she lifted her head in delicate, startled wonder
you did not stretch forward to caress her though she looked
    rarely beautiful
and a miracle as she glided away with such dignity.
And the young bull in the field, with his wrinkled, sad, face,
you are afraid if he rises to his feet,
though he is all wistful and pathetic, like a monolith, arrested,
    static.

Is there nothing in me to make you hesitate?
I tell you there is all these.
And why should you overlook them in me?

It is a beautiful poem; but as a document it is evidence of a hyper-sensitive masculinity. A man might well feel embarrassed by a woman's open admiration of his naked body; but surely if the admiration were warm and sincere the cause of his unease would not be that she treated as tame and domesticated an animal who knew himself for wild and dangerous.

But we remember Lady Crystabel's " aesthetic raptures " over Annable's body, and how " he was Greek statues to her." The wild and untamed masculinity which is here affronted, precisely as it was affronted in Annable, is here as there something which Lawrence desires to possess, and does not possess. He is a child to the woman, and resents the humiliation. In his dream he is a wild, untamed, dominant male. Yet he wants to be child: that is happiness and oblivion. And he wants to forget that he has been a child; above all he wants the woman to forget it. She must forget it instantly their naked flesh is parted. It must be blotted out of her memory. She must see him then as a wild and dangerous creature who has pounced upon her. And, of course, she cannot thus forget, she cannot see him thus. She cannot thus deliberately deceive herself. " Submit! Serve! " he cries. And since he cannot compel her either to submit or serve, it seems to her the petulance and vanity of a child, ashamed of his own dependence.

There is nothing to be done about it; there never will be anything to be done about it. The only thing that could be done is that Lawrence should cease to depend upon the Woman, should cease to find in her the soul refuge from the isolation which threatens him and is an intolerable horror to his mind. And this he cannot do. The discord is really ultimate and lies within himself. The Woman must be his mother; and, being made his mother, she cannot do otherwise than regard him as her child. It is not in her power to do otherwise. Neither is it in his power to cease to rebel against this fundamental humiliation of the man in him. Unless Lawrence can find within himself the strength to be veritably alone, to withdraw finally from this sexual relation, he is doomed to spend his life distraught between humiliation and extravagant masculine assertion.

It is vain to imagine that with a different woman he might

have found peace and unity. The choice — and he will acknowledge it plainly in *The Rainbow* — is not between the Woman and another; but between the Woman and no woman. What he needs from woman this woman will give, abundantly, generously; his life will be rooted in her, and her alone. That is what he needs, and against the compulsion of that need he will always rebel. Many other women will imagine themselves his perfect wife; he will try at the least to imagine the perfect wife for himself: in vain. He cannot conceive her. She is inconceivable.

II

THE RAINBOW

IN *The Rainbow* is a still more intimate record of the experience confessed in *Look! We Have Come Through!* The correspondence is exact and unmistakable. The story of Anna Lensky and Will Brangwen is, in essentials, the story of the poems; but the story is told more richly, and more fearfully. I know nothing more beautiful or more powerful in all Lawrence's writing than the opening of the long chapter ominously entitled "Anna Victrix." It describes their "honeymoon"; the rebirth of the shy and shamefaced man in a long world-forgetful ecstasy of passion with a carefree, beautiful, passionate, unashamedly physical woman.

She didn't care. *She* didn't care in the least. Then why should he? Should he be behind her in recklessness and independence? She was superb in her indifference. He wanted to be like her.

Lawrence's favourite image comes to him to describe his new felicity. " Suddenly, like a chestnut falling out of a burr, he was shed naked and glistening on to a soft, fecund earth, leaving behind him the hard rind of worldly knowledge and experience." He is surrendered to the woman utterly: he gives himself up into her keeping.

She got up at ten o'clock, and quite blithely went to bed again at three, or at half-past four, stripping him naked in the daylight, and all so gladly and perfectly, oblivious quite of his qualms. He let her do as she liked with him, and shone with strange pleasure. She was to dispose of him as she would. He was translated with gladness to be in her hands. And down went his qualms, his maxims, his rules, his smaller beliefs, she scattered them like an expert skittle-player. He was very much astonished and delighted to see them scatter.

We are, we have learned to be, afraid in Lawrence of that yielding of himself to the woman's leading. It is delightful, it is ecstasy; but it is also, to him, humiliation. We look for the reaction. It comes with sickening speed. " Shame at his own dependence upon her drove him to anger. . . . Driven by fear of her departure into a state of helplessness, almost of imbecility, he wandered about the house." And she is irritated beyond bearing by his helplessness, his clinging.

There followed two black and ghastly days, when she was set in anguish against him, and he felt as if he were in a black, violent underworld, and his wrists quivered murderously. And she resisted him. He seemed a dark, almost evil thing, pursuing her, hanging on to her, burdening her.

The struggle becomes nightmarish, and ends in a frenzied sexual consummation. It is the story of the poem " In the Dark," re-enacted in large. " He was not interested in the *thought* of himself or of her: oh, and how that irritated her. . . . The verity was his connection with Anna and his connection with the Church, his real being lay in his dark emotional experience of the Infinite, the Absolute." And as in the poem, Anna reacts in horror. " But I am myself, I have nothing to do with these."

What did she want herself? She answered herself that she wanted to be happy, to be natural, like the sunlight and the busy daytime. And, at the bottom of her soul, she felt he wanted her to be dark, unnatural. Sometimes, when he seemed like the darkness covering and smothering her, she revolted almost in horror, and struck at him. She struck at him, and made him bleed, and he became wicked. Because she dreaded him and held him in horror, he became wicked, he wanted to destroy. And then the fight between them was cruel.

She began to tremble. He wanted to impose himself on her. And he began to shudder. She wanted to desert him, to leave him a prey to the open, with the unclean dogs of the darkness setting on to devour him. He must beat her, and make her stay with him. Whereas she fought to keep herself free of him.

As in the poems, he does foolish, frantic things. " Frantic is sensual fear," he asserts his rights as master and as male.

" Fool! " she answered. " Fool! I've known my own father, who could put a dozen of you in his pipe and push them down with his finger-end. Don't I know what a fool you are! "

He knew himself what a fool he was, and was flayed by the knowledge. Yet he went on trying to steer the ship of their dual life. He asserted his position as captain of the ship. And captain and ship bored her. . . . She jeered at him as master of the house, master of their dual life. And he was black with shame and rage. He knew, with shame, how her father had been a man without arrogating any authority.

Then the story of *The Rainbow* departs from the naked facts of Lawrence's experience. Anna Brangwen is with child; she is fulfilled. But, since that is an imaginary fulfilment, the struggle goes on, ever more fearful, and always the same.

Then she turned fiercely on him, and fought him. . . . What horrible hold did he want to have over her body? Why did he want to drag her down, and kill her spirit? Why did he want to deny her spirit? Why did he deny her spirituality, hold her for a body only? . . .

Some vast hideous darkness he seemed to represent to her.

" What do you do to me? " she cried. " What beastly thing do you do to me? . . . There is something horrible in you, something dark and beastly in your will. What do you want of me? What do you want to do to me? . . ."

He hated her for what she said. Did he not give her everything, was she not everything to him? And the shame was a bitter fire in him, that she was everything to him, that he had nothing but her. And then that she should taunt him with it, that he could not escape! The fire went black in his veins. For try as he might, he could not escape. She was everything to him, she was his life and his derivation. He depended on her. If she were taken away, he would collapse as a house from which the central pillar is removed.

And she hated him, because he depended on her so utterly. He was horrible to her. . . . It was horrible that he should cleave to her, so close, so close, like a leopard that had leapt on her, and fastened.

He went on from day to day in a blackness of rage and shame and frustration. How he tortured himself, to be able to get away from her. But he could not. She was as the rock on which he stood, with deep, heaving water all round, and he was unable to swim. He *must* take his stand on her, he must depend on her.

What had he in life, save her? Nothing. The rest was a great heaving flood. The terror of the night of heaving, overwhelming flood, which was his vision of life without her, was too much for him. He clung to her fiercely, and abjectly. . . .

He wanted to leave her, he wanted to be able to leave her. For his soul's sake, for his manhood's sake, he must be able to leave her.

But for what? . . . The only tangible, secure thing was the woman. He could leave her only for another woman. And where was the other woman, and who was the other woman? Besides, he would be in just the same state. Another woman would be woman, the case would be the same.

" He could leave her only for another woman. . . . Another woman would be woman, the case would be the same."

There is the adamantine fact, the grim and fatal destiny. He is ruthless in his self-knowledge. The naked confession goes on.

The only other way to leave her was to die. The only straight way to leave her was to die. His dark raging soul knew that. But he had no desire for death. . . .

A woman, he must have a woman. And having a woman, he must be free of her. It would be the same position. For he could not be free of her.

For how can a man stand, unless he have something sure under his feet? . . . And upon what could he stand, save upon a woman? Was he then like the old man of the seas, impotent to move save upon the back of another life? Was he impotent, or a cripple, or a defective, or a fragment?

It was black, mad, shameful torture, the frenzy of fear, the frenzy of desire, and the horrible, grasping back-wash of shame.

The quotation is long; but it cannot be avoided. It takes us, with pitiless intimacy, closer to the core of Lawrence's strange and fearful experience than anything he has yet written.

In the story, Will Brangwen escapes from the horror which, it seems, he cannot escape. Anna, at last, finds the oppressive darkness of his physical contact unbearable. She makes him sleep alone. He is so wretched, that she takes him back; and again it is too much for her. She sends him away again. "He went and lay down alone. And at length, after a grey and livid and ghastly period, he relaxed, something gave way in him."

So he reached a sort of rebirth. It consists in the fact that "he could sleep with her, and let her be." But it is claimed as a veritable rebirth.

He could be alone now. He had just learned what it was to be able to be alone. It was right and peaceful. She had given him

a new deeper freedom. The world might be a welter of uncertainty,
but he was himself now. He had come into his new existence. He
was born for a second time, born at last unto himself, out of the
vast body of humanity. Now at last he had a separate identity,
he existed alone, even if he were not quite alone. Before he had
only existed in so far as he had relations with another being.
Now he had an absolute self — as well as a relative one.

But we cannot be deceived. This is the experience of the
child who no longer sleeps in his mother's bed, but in a room
alone. " To have learned to be alone," for a man, is an in-
comparably sterner experience; that death, for which "he
had no desire." An absolute self is hardly to be had at a
lesser price; and even in the story, the dawn is a false dawn.
Will Brangwen cannot believe in himself, apart from Anna.
In the end, he is as he was. " In the long run he learned to
submit to Anna. She forced him to the spirit of her laws,
while leaving him the letter of his own." The dark, destructive rage comes on him as before. " Their fights were horrible, murderous. And then the passion between them came
just as black and awful." But a certain human wisdom arose
between them. She left him alone in his rage, and he struggled to submit to her, " for at last he learned that he would
be in hell until he came back to her."

But she has destroyed his belief in himself, and his belief absolutely. She has undermined his own separate creative purpose. He has lost faith in his own ideal, his own
vital illusions. In their symbolic visit to Lincoln Cathedral,
Anna deliberately shatters her husband's passionate ecstasy
in the pure upsurge of the building by insisting upon the
gargoyles. The mason, she said, had carved the portrait of
his detested wife. " You hate to think he put his wife in your
cathedral, don't you? " And, of course Will Brangwen did
hate to think it. The symbol of pure spirituality was degraded. " Yet somewhere in himself he responded more

deeply to the sly little face that knew better, than he had done before to the perfect surge of his cathedral." The meaning of all this symbolism is patent. Through the woman, through sex, the spiritual ideal is destroyed; and it is good that it should be destroyed. For the spiritual ideal is partial and false. It is based on the negation of sex, of the mighty principle of life itself. But Will Brangwen, in whom the old spirituality has been thus, and rightly destroyed, cannot move forward to create and embody a new harmony. He lapses into the woman, lapses and rebels, and at last is content to lapse altogether.

At this point Lawrence's own destiny is distinct from that of his creation. Will Brangwen, so to speak, is a Lawrence who has given up the effort — the effort to make the spirit and the flesh dwell together into harmony. But Lawrence, who conceived and contained him, has not given up the effort. The effort is to find the rainbow — the bright arch that spans in beauty the conflicting elements. Both Will and Anna come to have a sense of the goal; but it is not they, but their child, Ursula, who will reach it. " The child she might hold up, she might toss the child forward into the furnace, the child might walk there, amid the burning coals and the incandescent roar of heat, as the three witnesses walked with the angel in the fire."

So the story passes to the next generation. Ursula grows, and her sister Gudrun. Their final history is chronicled in *Women in Love.* In the remainder of *The Rainbow,* Gudrun is nothing, simply a small girl. Ursula becomes the chief figure, with her lover, Anton Skrebensky. Once more the sexual struggle between them is a nightmare, a worse nightmare than the sexual struggle between Anna and Will.

Anton is also a spiritual man, but of a lower (or later) order of spirituality than Will Brangwen. Will is an artist, with a direct creative purpose; Anton an engineer in the army, with a consciousness of his mission as the servant of the nation. Again, he is like Lawrence: not, indeed, so like him as Will Brangwen, who apart from his paternity and his final submission was Lawrence himself; but like enough. Ursula and he together met a man and woman who live on a canal boat.

He was envying the lean father of three children for his impudent directness and worship of the woman in Ursula, a worship of body and soul together, the man's body and soul wistful and worshipping the body and spirit of the girl. . . .

Why could not he himself desire a woman so? Why did he never want a woman, not with the whole of him; never loved, never worshipped, only just physically wanted her. But he would want her with his body, let his soul do as it would.

The struggle begins, in these now familiar conditions. Ursula, unlike her mother, and unlike her essentially in only this, resists from the first. Not with any ordinary resistance, but with the instinctive will to entice and destroy her man. The scene in the moonlight, after the dance, becomes a phantasmagoria. Anton "was afraid of the great moon-conflagration of the corn-stacks rising above him. His heart grew smaller, and began to fuse like a bead. He knew he would die."

She was afraid of what she was. Looking at him, at his shadowy, unreal, wavering presence a sudden lust seized her, to lay hold of him and tear him and make him into nothing. . . . She tempted him.

And temerously, his hands went over her, over the salt, compact brilliance of her body. If he could but have her, how he would enjoy her! If he could but net her brilliant, cold, salt-burning body in the soft iron of his own hands, net her, capture her, hold her down, how madly he would enjoy her! . . . Obstinately, all his flesh burning and corroding, as if he were invaded by some consuming, scathing poison, still he persisted, thinking at last he might overcome her. Even, in his frenzy, he sought her mouth with his mouth, though it was like putting his face into some awful death. . . .

She took him in the kiss, hard her kiss seized upon him, hard and fierce and burning corrosive as the moonlight. She seemed to be destroying him. He was reeling, summoning all his strength to keep his kiss upon her, to keep himself in the kiss.

But hard and fierce she had fastened upon him, cold as the moon and burning as a fierce salt. Till gradually his warm, soft iron yielded, yielded, and she was there fierce, corrosive, seething with his destruction, seething like some cruel, corrosive salt around the last substance of his being, destroying him in the kiss. And her soul crystallised with triumph, and his soul was dissolved with agony and annihilation. So she held him there, the victim, consumed, annihilated. She had triumphed: he was not any more.

The experience, as one might expect, is fatal. Though Ursula is horrified at what she has done or at what has been done through her, and is kind to him thereafter, Anton's "core is gone," it has been irreparably destroyed. "His triumphant, flaming, overweening heart of the intrinsic male would never beat again. . . . She had broken him." Rather strangely, he seems to forget about it, when he has gone off to fight in the Boer war. But we are given to understand that the killing of the intrinsic male in him, and his unhesitating acceptance of service to the state, are complementary. One nullity is corollary to the other.

∽

With Anton's return, six years later, the struggle becomes more intense and ghastly, for now the need for physical union is upon them both. The record is difficult to follow, because it is beyond the range of ordinary experience, and also because it seems to be in itself inconsequent, without the convincing inevitability of the story of Anna and Will. At first, Anton and Ursula seem to be happy as lovers, in spite of her destruction of his " intrinsic male core " six years before. But, Lawrence insists, they are happy like two wild animals, outlaws and enemies of the light of social day. Ursula goes about " in a dark richness, her eyes dilated and shining like the eyes of a wild animal, a curious half-smile which seemed to be gibing at the civic pretence of all the human life about her "; while Anton " watched as a lion or a tiger may lie with narrowed eyes watching the people pass before its cage, the kaleidoscopic unreality of people." Both live " in the sensual sub-consciousness all the time." So for a few weeks they live together in London. Suddenly, Ursula has a desire to leave England. She insists on staying at Rouen.

For the first time, in Rouen, he had a cold feeling of death; not afraid of any other man, but of her. She did not want him. The old streets, the cathedral, the age and monumental peace of the town took her away from him. She turned to it as if to something she had forgotten. This was now the reality; this great stone cathedral slumbering there in its mass, which knew no transience nor heard any denial. It was majestic in its stability, its splendid absoluteness.

To judge by the symbolic significance of the cathedral in the history of Will and Anna, Lawrence must have meant by this that Ursula at this crucial moment has a recoil from the sensual sub-consciousness to spirituality. From this time onward both have a premonition of " the death towards which they are wandering."

Ursula returns home. And, when she leaves him, a cold

horror takes possession of Anton. " He went mad. He had
lived with her in a close, living, pulsing world, where everything pulsed with rich being. Now he found himself struggling amid an ashen-dry, cold world of rigidity, dead walls
and mechanical traffic, and creeping, spectre-like people."
She is his one salvation from " the horror of not-being which
possesses him." To marry her, " to be sure of her " — that is
all. He writes to her desperately, she answers easily: his
agony means nothing to her, really. But she believes she
loves him. They are together again for a few days.

She owned his body and enjoyed it with all the delight and
carelessness of a possessor. But he had become gradually afraid
of her body. He wanted her, he wanted her endlessly. But there
had come a tension into his desire, a constraint which prevented
his enjoying the delicious approach and the lovable close of the
endless embrace. He was afraid. His will was always tense, fixed.

Suddenly she declares open war upon his " idealism," his
democratic humanitarianism. " I'm against you, and all your
old, dead things," she cries in fury. He " felt cut off at the
knees, a figure made worthless." She does not esteem him.
He tries to make her esteem him by flirting with other women.
Then, the secret is out.

In passionate anger she upbraided him because, not being man
enough to satisfy one woman, he hung round others.
" Don't I satisfy you? " he asked of her, again going white to
the throat.
" No," she said. " You've never satisfied me since the first
week in London. You never satisfy me now. What does it mean
to me, your having me — "
She lifted her shoulders and turned aside her face in a motion
of cold, indifferent worthlessness. He felt he would kill her.
When she had aroused him to a pitch of madness, when she saw
his eyes all dark and mad with suffering, then a great suffering

overcame her soul, a great, inconquerable suffering. And she loved him. For oh, she wanted to love him. Stronger than life or death was her craving to be able to love him.

And at such moments, when he was mad with her destroying him, when all his complacency was destroyed, all his everyday self was broken, and only the stripped, rudimentary, primal man remained, demented with torture, her passion to love him became love, she took him again, they came together in an overwhelming passion, in which he knew he satisfied her.

But it all contained a developing germ of death. After each contact, her anguished desire for him or for that which she had never had from him was stronger, her love was more hopeless. After each contact his mad dependence on her was deepened, his hope of standing strong and taking her in his own strength was weakened. He felt himself a mere attribute of her.

Gradually, Anton breaks down. Ursula says she does not want to marry him, and he collapses upon himself. Yet although she is afraid of the fearful compulsion of his utter dependence upon her, tacitly she seems to have given in to marrying him. They go away together to a house by the sea as an engaged couple. The physical contact goes on, but she is indifferent. One night, once more in the presence of a great burning moon, beneath which once more Anton " felt himself fusing down into nothingness, like a bead that rapidly disappears in an incandescent flame," they reach their terrible consummation.

Then there in the great flare of light, she clinched hold of him, hard, as if suddenly she had the strength of destruction, she fastened her arms round him and tightened him in her grip, whilst her mouth sought his in a hard, rending, ever-increasing kiss, till his body was powerless in her grip, his heart melted in fear from the fierce, beaked, harpy's kiss. The water washed again over their feet, but she took no notice. She seemed unaware, she seemed to be pressing in her beaked mouth till she had the heart of him.

Then, at last, she drew away and looked at him — looked at him. He knew what she wanted. He took her by the hand and led her across the foreshore back to the sand-hills. She went silently. He felt as if the ordeal of proof was upon him, for life or death. He led her to a dark hollow.

" No, here," she said, going out to the slope full under the moonshine. She lay motionless, with wide-open eyes looking at the moon. He came direct to her, without preliminaries. She held him pinned down at the chest, awful. The fight, the struggle for consummation was terrible. It lasted till it was agony to his soul, till he succumbed, till he gave way as if dead, and lay with his face buried, partly in her hair, partly in the sand, motionless, as if he would be motionless now for ever, hidden away in the dark, buried, only buried, he only wanted to be buried in the goodly darkness, only that, and no more.

This is the end. Anton has failed at the proof. Ursula lies in a cold agony of un-satisfaction, and he creeps away a broken man.

To discover all that underlies this fearful encounter, we should have to go to *Lady Chatterley's Lover*, to Mellors' account of his sexual experience with Bertha Coutts. That is, in the present state of affairs, unquotable. But in that page and a half the curious will find not only the naked physical foundation — " the blind beakishness " — of this experience of Ursula and Anton, but also Lawrence's final account of the sexual experience from which both the sexual experience of Will and Anna, and of Anton and Ursula is derived. *The Rainbow* is, radically, the history of Lawrence's final sexual failure.

It is much beside that; but that it is. And unless we grasp the fact, the inward meaning of *The Rainbow* and its sequel, *Women in Love,* must be concealed from us. One shrinks from the necessity of thus laying bare the physical secrets of a dead man; but in the case of Lawrence we have no choice. To the last he conceived it as his mission to teach us the way to sexual regeneration, and he claimed to give the world the ultimate truth about sex. If we take him seriously, we must take his message seriously. Continually, in his work we are confronted with sexual experience of a peculiar kind; it is quite impossible to ignore it. The work of a great man, as Lawrence was, is always an organic whole. If we shrink from following the vital thread of experience from which it all derives, then we shrink from him altogether. It is all or nothing, with such a man as Lawrence; and, since it must not be nothing, it must be all.

The Rainbow is the story of Lawrence's sexual failure. The two men, who have succumbed to the woman, are one man — himself. The rainbow, in the symbolic sense of a harmony between spirit and flesh, is as far away as ever at the end of the book. It shines over the first generation, where man is really man, and does not need to arrogate authority over woman; it begins to be remote in the second, where the woman begins to establish the mastery; in the third, where woman is not only " victrix " but " triumphans," it fades into the dim future. Ursula, the woman, becomes the protagonist; the man is secondary, an attribute of the woman. Nevertheless, Ursula is an unconvincing character in *The Rainbow*. She is a composite figure, made of the hated sexual woman, and of some of Lawrence's own manly experiences. Thus she is made to carry much of his experience as a schoolmaster, and of his own disappointment with the university; and more important, she is made to undergo a sort of physical-mystical experience, an annihilation of the personality. When in the last chapter the horses stampede upon her, she dies, and rises again in a new world: she becomes the mouthpiece of Lawrence's own visions.

The chief vision of which she is the vehicle is the vision of the darkness with which the conscious, personal, deliberate, social life of mankind is surrounded.

This inner circle of light in which she lived and moved . . . suddenly seemed like the area under an arc-lamp, wherein the moths and the children played in the security of blinding light, not even knowing there was any darkness, because they stayed in the light. . . .
Nevertheless the darkness wheeled round about, with grey shadow-shapes of wild beasts, and also with dark shadow-shapes of the angels, whom the light fenced out, as it fenced out the more familiar beasts of darkness. And some, having for a moment seen the darkness, saw it bristling with the tufts of the hyæna and the wolf; and some, having given up their vanity of the light, having died in their own conceit, saw the gleam in the eyes of the wolf and hyæna, that it was the flash of the sword of angels, flashing at the door to come in, that the angels in the darkness were lordly and terrible and not to be denied, like the flash of fangs.

It is not easy to be sure what Lawrence means by this. Is the surrounding darkness the darkness of " the sensual subconsciousness " which Ursula and Anton inhabited like wild animals? Or is it that darkness whose " unclean dogs " Will Brangwen feared would devour him if Anna left him? Or are both these darknesses the same darkness? Is this darkness beneficent, or is it horrible? — creative, or destroying?
It would be hard to say. For this conception of the surrounding " darkness," which will return in many forms in Lawrence's work, is an intensely personal conception. It derives, once more, from his peculiar experience. It is the darkness of pure animality as conceived and experienced by an intensely spiritual man. It is, therefore, essentially a horrible darkness of sin and evil, the enemy and destroyer of the light. To explore it, to surrender to it, is for Lawrence

a self-violation, a perversity. Of this deliberate and willed surrender to the horror of darkness, the woman really knows nothing; because the woman is not spiritual. To her, what darkness she knows is warm and natural. Her darkness is not the same as his, because she is not divided. In the religious phrase, she has no sense of sin.

Therefore, to represent her in Ursula as realising the horror and majesty of the darkness is false. Neither the conception nor the experience belongs to her at all. All that she knows of this darkness comes to her from and through the man. She represents that darkness to him; indeed she *is* that darkness to him: but she is completely unconscious of it. That the man should regard her as the creature and embodiment of *his* darkness horrifies her. She repudiates it utterly. She does not belong to his darkness at all. She recoils instinctively away. The truth of the whole strange situation is in the momentous poem " In the Dark," where she cries:

> *" I am afraid of you, I am afraid, afraid!*
> *There is something in you destroys me — ! "*

And it is so. His darkness is necessarily death to her. For she is the real animal, unconscious of evil; but he is a spiritual man, willing himself into animality, into a deadly darkness, which if once she really entered, her innocent integrity would be shattered, and she would be destroyed.

This profound conflict is terrible indeed. The man is trying to compel the woman out of her own innocent darkness into the utterly different darkness of depravity. Neither he nor she knows quite what is happening; but he knows far better than she. She is simply conscious of a horror from which she shrinks. And in creating the character of Ursula in *The Rainbow*, Lawrence has begun an effort of imaginative duplicity which will be decisive. For, in creating

Ursula, he makes the woman a denizen of his darkness, not of her own; and he makes her in the final pages consciously submit herself and do homage to the darkness in which she would die. Ursula Brangwen of *The Rainbow,* is, in fact, a completely incredible character. She is the woman who accepts the man's vision of herself; accepts it, believes in it, and obeys it. She therefore, becomes a monster, a chimaera.

Only in *Women in Love* does Ursula Brangwen really come alive; and then she is manifestly her mother, Anna Brangwen, continued from the point at which her imaginary child-bearing began. She becomes the Woman who is constant in Lawrence's books — the Woman whom Lawrence can never really understand, the innocent sensual woman, whom he can only watch and wonder at, love and hate, and cleave to until the end.

III

SPIRIT AND FLESH

LAWRENCE had always the need to universalize his own experience. Two great efforts at universalization correspond with the phase of personal experience uttered in the story of Ursula and Anton. At about the time that he finished *The Rainbow,* he rewrote his beautiful travel-sketches, *Twilight in Italy,* and wrote an essay called *The Crown,* which was to remain one of his most important essays. He spoiled his travel-sketches by rewriting them, for the rewriting consisted chiefly in the interpolation of passages belonging to a later phase of experience.

But these added and discordant passages of *Twilight in Italy* are a precious commentary upon *The Rainbow.* For instance, the following:

The Italian is attractive, supple, and beautiful, because he worships the Godhead in the flesh. We envy him, we feel pale and insignificant beside him. Yet at the same time we feel superior to him, as if he were a child and we adult.

Wherein are we superior? Only because we went beyond the phallus in the search of the Godhead, the creative origin. . . . We have exalted Man far above the man who is in each one of us. Our aim is a perfect humanity, a perfect and equable human consciousness, selfless. And we obtain it in the subjection, reduction, analysis, and destruction of the self. So on we go, active in science and mechanics, and social reform.

But we have exhausted ourselves in the process. We have found great treasures, and we are now impotent to use them. So we have said: " What good are these treasures, they are vulgar nothings." We have said: " Let us go back from this adventuring, let us enjoy our own flesh, like the Italian." But our habit of life, our very constitution prevents our being quite like the Italian. The phallus will never serve us as a Godhead, because we do not believe in it: no Northern race does. Therefore, either we set ourselves to serve our children, calling them " the future," or else we turn perverse and destructive, and give ourselves joy in the destruction of the flesh.

Granted we understand that the reference of the last phrase " the destruction of the flesh " is sexual, the passage forms a perfect " argument " for the whole of the last two sections of *The Rainbow*. Anna and Will set themselves to serve their children, calling them " the future "; Ursula and Anton turn to perverse and destructive sensuality. And, a few pages earlier in *Twilight in Italy*, there is a further commentary on this process of " destruction of the flesh " in conscious sensuality.

The mind, that is the Light; the senses, they are the Darkness. Aphrodite, the queen of the senses, she, born of the sea-foam, is the luminousness of the gleaming senses, the phosphorescence of the sea, the senses become a conscious aim to themselves; she is the gleaming darkness, she is the luminous night, she is goddess of destruction, her white cold fire consumes and does not create. . . . Ecstatic sensual delight, the intense, white-cold ecstasy of darkness and moonlight, the raucous, catlike, destructive enjoyment, the senses conscious and crying out in their consciousness in the pangs of the enjoyment. . . . The flesh, the senses are now self-conscious. Their aim is in supreme sensation. They seek the maximum of sensation. They seek the reduction of the flesh, the flesh reacting upon itself, to a crisis, an ecstasy, a phosphorescent transfiguration in ecstasy. . . . This is one way of transfiguration into the eternal flame, the transfiguration through ecstasy in the flesh.

There we have the reason why the mutual annihilation of Anton and Ursula takes place in the full moonlight and at the edge of the phosphorescent sea. It is all symbolism. Full moonlight for the extreme of consciousness in the sensual darkness; the sea for its salt corrosiveness, and because Aphrodite is sea-born.

∽

But we cannot forget that all this generalisation is born of a peculiar sexual experience; it is, in fact, as generalisation, unconvincing, but of intense interest as the projection and elaboration of Lawrence's sexual experience. Moreover, we absolutely need the personal clue to interpret the more sustained effort at generalisation which is contained in the essay, *The Crown*. A passage in *Twilight in Italy* leads us thither.

It is past the time to cease seeking one infinite (that is the spiritual striving for a perfect selfless humanity), ignoring, striving to eliminate the other. The Infinite is twofold, the Father and the Son, the Dark and the Light, the Senses and the Mind, the Soul and the Spirit (*sic*), the self and the not-self, the Eagle and the Dove, the Tiger and the Lamb. The consummation of man is twofold in the Self and in Selflessness. By great retrogression back to the source of darkness in me, the Self, deep in the senses, I arrive at the Original, Creative Infinite. By projection forth from myself, by the elimination of my absolute sensual self, I arrive at the Ultimate Infinite, Oneness in the Spirit. They are two Infinites, twofold approach to God. And man must know both.

But he must never confuse them. They are eternally separate. The lion shall never lie down with the lamb. The lion eternally shall devour the lamb, the lamb eternally shall be devoured. Man knows the great consummation in the flesh, the sexual ecstasy, and that is eternal. Also the spiritual ecstasy of unanimity, that is eternal. But the two are separate and never to be confused. To neutralize the one with the other is unthinkable, an abomination.

Now this, if it were possible, would deceive the very elect; for it is divided only by a hair's breadth from the enunciation of a great truth. Instead, it is a great falsehood. To explain why it is a great falsehood may be hard, because the great truth which it stimulates, and from which it must be distinguished, is known to few. We must follow the simplest clue to unravel the deception. We begin by an absolute assertion.

Sexuality is right; sensuality is wrong. This assertion is absolutely true, for the simple reason that sensuality *is* sexuality which is conscious of guilt. It is the consciousness of guilt that makes sensuality of sexuality. Take the unconsciousness of guilt away from sensuality, and it becomes sexuality once more — completely innocent.

The problem which tormented Lawrence, and it may be the great problem of our day, was how to regain innocence in sex. The tragedy of his life, from this point of view, was that he could not regain it. The natural way of regaining innocence is through love. This may be rare, to-day; perhaps it has always been rare. It is very hard for a man and a woman to love each other, very hard for them to know when they love each other. It is a thing which we have to learn, in order that our children may learn it from us.

Lawrence was incapable of loving a woman. It was not his fault, he was so conditioned. Since he could not wholly love a woman, sexual innocence was for ever unknown to him, save as a dream of a thing that might be. Sexuality was to him always sin, because he was always conscious of sin.

Hence his final cry, in *Pansies:* " Sex is a state of grace, and you'll have to wait." It is true. Sex *is* a state of grace; but there is a natural way of attaining that state of grace, which Lawrence, by destiny, had forfeited. He had sought sexuality, having no entire love and knowing that he had no entire love, to the woman. Therefore, he had sinned; for sin *is,* where there is a sense of sin.

Sexuality, therefore, was always sensuality to Lawrence. It was always evil, always something to which he was tempted, and into which he fell. He was a fallen angel, because he believed he was, and the darkness of sex into which he had fallen was an evil darkness. Good and Evil were, therefore, his two realities; and they were the Spirit and the Flesh. The two eternities between which man is poised were, for him, the Good, which is selfless spirituality, and the Evil, which is self-assertion in sensuality. His eternal principles were Good and Evil. By making Good and Evil eternal principles he perpetuated in himself a cleavage which is fatal to human integrity. He embarked irrevocably on a course which led him to complete disintegration.

The doctrine which is the true doctrine, of which Lawrence's doctrine is a fearful parody, is this. The two eternities between which man is poised are both beyond good and evil, both utterly innocent, both having no opposite. The true unconscious, or true flesh, into which sexuality is the great gateway, is beyond good and evil because it is prior to good and evil. The true spirit is beyond good and evil, because it is consciousness become innocent; it is the final completion of consciousness. Flesh is innocent and unconscious; Spirit is innocent and conscious. Once the innocence of true Flesh is lost, there is no way of regaining it except by gaining the innocence of Spirit. True Spirit is not only not the enemy of true Flesh; it is the only condition by which true Flesh can be restored, once it has been corrupted. When true Spirit is born in a man (and it cannot be born in him except through a death) then he becomes nothing but true Flesh and true Spirit. He is a complete and entire unity which no power in earth or heaven or hell can disrupt: he passes, once and for ever, out from the dominion of Good and Evil. They are annihilated in him, and for him. He lives, in every moment of every day, in a " state of grace."

Lawrence's doctrine is a doctrine of complete disruption and denial of the unity of man. Lawrence's two Infinites are the ecstatic satisfactions of the " higher " and " lower " desires of man. And these desires are for ever in conflict. The " spiritual " man hates the " sensual " man, in the same person. This was, indeed, painfully true of Lawrence. The cleavage was agonising in him. But to fulfil the " spiritual " man, and to fulfil the " sensual " man, where such a fearful division exists, is impossible. The " spiritual " man can be fulfilled only by the annihilation of the " sensual " man; and the " sensual " man only by the annihilation of the " spiritual " man. To fulfil both is to fulfil neither, but only to maim both, and finally to kill them.

For at bottom these two Infinities of Lawrence's are simply Love and Hatred: the " spirit " seeking the ecstasy of universal love, the " flesh " seeking the sensual ecstasy in which " having drunk all blood and devoured all flesh, I am become again the eternal Fire, I am infinite." In other words, the only Love is " spiritual " Love; Love in and through the flesh is inconceivable and impossible, in fleshly " love " there is only hatred and mutual destruction. This is only too true, as we have seen, in Lawrence's experience of carnal love, but when put forward as a general and final truth of human experience it is, to me, a fatal falsehood. In such a matter one can only declare one's faith, or one's experience. I have no doubt that physical " love " can become a thing of horror and hatred, but I have still less doubt that physical love can be a thing of beatitude and innocence and bliss, a true and perfect consummation of two human beings into unity. Therefore, to me, the assertion that the spirit and the flesh are eternally opposed is a fatal lie. If it were true, then there would be no hope for humanity at all. For if it were true, then mankind must choose: either the way of Spirit, and a total asceticism, and an eventual self-annihilation: or the way of the Flesh, and a total repudiation of the Spirit, and a relapse into the pure animality of hatred and lust, from which Man has so painfully won his way.

✍

Lawrence, indeed, says there is a third way: to recognise the eternal opposition between the Spirit and the Flesh, and to seek both ecstasies — to hunt with the lion and lie down with the lamb. In the language of *Twilight in Italy,*

The two Infinites, negative and positive, are always related, but they are never identical. They are always opposite, but there exists a relation between them. This is the Holy Ghost of the Christian Trinity. And it is this, the relation which is established between the two Infinites, the two natures of God, which we have transgressed, forgotten, sinned against. The Father is the Father, and the Son is the Son. I may know the Son and deny the Father, or know the Father and deny the Son. But that which I may never deny, and which I have denied, is the Holy Ghost which relates the dual Infinites into One Whole, which relates and keeps distinct the dual natures of God. To say that the two are one, this is the inadmissible lie. The two are related, by the intervention of the third, into a Oneness.

The Holy Ghost was to become, henceforward, a favourite term of Lawrence's. What is the Holy Ghost, then, according to Lawrence? The Holy Ghost is that which unites the eternal opposites of the Spirit which is love, and the Flesh which is hatred. But can they be united? It depends what we mean by unity. If a man feels in himself, as Lawrence feels, the extreme desire of the Spirit towards love, and the extreme desire of the Flesh towards hatred, and if he still lives, feeling these conflicting desires in their extremity, then it is true that he himself is, in a sense, the unity of those conflicting and destructive desires. He embodies them in a single body. His body obeys now the one desire, now the other, and the body remains one. And this is a kind of unity. Every living man on this earth is necessarily such a unity, while he lives. And this unity, of mere bodily existence, is the only unity that can exist between the desire of the Spirit towards love, and the desire of the Flesh towards hatred. So that the Holy Ghost of Lawrence, no matter how he may strive to conceal it, consists simply in his bodily unity. Whatever he does — his total "behaviour" in the largest sense — his deeds, words, no matter how contradictory or hostile, everything that is him and his: this is his Holy Ghost. And the total "behaviour" of any other man, be he Christ or cretin, is his Holy Ghost. Lawrence will try to conceal this from himself and from others; not least by this very device of calling this animal and inevitable unity, which all men have by the fact of their living at all, by the tremendous and awful name of the Holy Ghost.

Here we glimpse the nature of the inordinate difficulty of understanding Lawrence's words and works at this moment. He desires — what man of his composition could not desire it? — a true and not a specious unity. He is racked and tortured by the knowledge of his own inward division. And for him the rainbow is a symbol of the true unity he de-

sires. But the unity is impossible: spirit and flesh have been
torn asunder in him, and cannot be united. His effort is to
reconcile the unity which he desires, with the division which
he knows; and sometimes he writes out of his desire for
unity, and sometimes out of his knowledge of division. So
that he may, as we have said, deceive the very elect, if that
were possible. *The Crown,* written at this moment, is the
most difficult, the most fascinating, and the most deceptive of all Lawrence's essays. " The Lion and the Unicorn
were fighting for the Crown." The Lion — in *Twilight in
Italy* it is the Tiger — is the symbol of carnality, the Unicorn of spirituality, and the Crown for which they fight,
which they hold up between their rampant and hostile bodies,
is the symbol of their unity in division. The Crown means the
same as the Rainbow, or the Holy Ghost. Consider this beautiful passage:

I know I am compounded of two waves, I, who am temporal and
mortal. When I am timeless and absolute, all duality has vanished.
But whilst I am temporal and mortal, I am framed in the struggle
and embrace of the two opposite waves of darkness and of light.

There is the wave of light in me which seeks the darkness,
which has for its goal the Source and the Beginning, for its God
the Almighty Creator to Whom is all power and glory. Thither
the light of the seed of man struggles and aspires, into the infinite darkness, the womb of all creation.

What way is it that leads me on to the Source, to the Beginning?
It is the way of the blood, the way of power. Down the road of
the darkness, further and further into the darkness, I come to the
Almighty God Who was in the beginning, is now, and ever shall
be. I come to the Source of Power. I am received back into the
utter darkness of the Creator, I am once again with Him.

This is a consummation, a becoming eternal. This is an arrival
into eternity. But eternity is only relative.

I can become one with God, consummated into eternity, by

D. H. LAWRENCE

NEW MEXICO

taking the road down the senses into the utter darkness of power, till I am one with the darkness of initial power, beyond knowledge of my opposite.

It is thus, seeking consummation in the utter darkness, that I come to the woman in desire. She is the doorway, she is the gate to the dark eternity of power. . . .

Gradually my veins relax their gates, gradually the rocking blood goes forward, quivers on the edge of oblivion, then yields itself up, passes into the borderland of oblivion. Oh, and then I would die, I would quickly die, to have all power, all life at once, to come instantly to pure eternal oblivion, consummation, the source of life. But patience is fierce at the bottom of me; fierce, indomitable, abiding patience. So my blood goes forth in shock after shock of delirious passing-away, in shock after shock entering into consummation, till my soul is slipping its moorings, my mind, my will fuses down, I melt out and am gone into the eternal darkness, the primal creative darkness reigns, and I am not, and at last *I am*. . . .

Till, new-created, I am thrown forth again on the shore of creation, warm and lustrous, goodly, new-born from the darkness out of which all time has issued.

And then new-born on the knees of darkness, new-issued from the womb of creation, I open my eyes to the light and know the goal, the end, the light which stands over the end of the journey, the everlasting day, the oneness of the spirit.

The new journey, the new life has begun, the travelling to the opposite eternity, to the infinite light of the Spirit, the consummation in the Spirit.

My source and issue is in two eternities, I am founded in the two infinities. But absolute is the rainbow that goes between; the iris of my very being.

That passage, taken in and for itself alone, seems to contain fundamental truth. One or two of the phrases are faintly disturbing: chiefly among them the insistence on " power " as the element of darkness. (In fact, the word " power " was added, in every case, ten years later.) But what, we ask again, is this rainbow that goes between?

Towards the end of the essay he seems to tell us. He elaborates the statement made in *Twilight in Italy*.

God is not the one infinite, nor the other, our immortality is not in the original eternity, neither in the ultimate eternity. God is the utter relation between the two eternities, He is in the flowing together (i.e. unanimity and love in the spirit) and the flowing apart (i.e. separateness and hatred in the flesh.)

This utter relation is timeless, absolute and perfect. It is in the Beginning and the End, just the same. Whether it be revealed or not, it is the same. It is the Unrevealed God: what Jesus called the Holy Ghost.

My immortality is not from the beginning, in my endless ancestry. Nor is it on ahead in life everlasting. My life comes to me from the great Creator, the Beginner. And my spirit runs towards the Comforter, the Goal far ahead. But I, what am I between?

These two halves I always am. But I am never *myself* until they are consummated into a spark of oneness, the gleam of the Holy Ghost. And in this spark is my immortality, my non-mortal being, that which is not swept away down either direction of time.

The rainbow is thus the self, the true self. But how is the self to be achieved out of the hostile and destructive elements of spirit and flesh, love and hatred? Lawrence tells us.

I am not immortal till I have achieved immortality. And immortality is not a question of time, of everlasting life. It is a question of consummate being. Most men die and perish away, unconsummated, unachieved. It is not easy to achieve immortality. It is supremely difficult. It means undaunted suffering and undaunted enjoyment both. And when a man has reached his ultimate of enjoyment and his ultimate of suffering, *both*, then he knows the two eternities, then he is made absolute, like the iris,

created out of the two. Then he is immortal. It is not a question
of time. It is a question of being. It is not a question of submission, submitting to the divine grace; it is a question of submitting
to the divine grace, in suffering and self-obliteration, and it is a
question of conquering by divine grace, as the tiger leaps on the
trembling deer, in utter satisfaction of the Self, in complete fulfilment of desire. The fulfilment is dual. And having known the
dual fulfilment, then within the fulfilled soul is established the
Divine relation, the Holy Spirit dwells there, the soul has achieved
immortality, it has attained to absolute being.

It is clear enough. We have to seek the ecstasy of the
spirituality and the ecstasy of sensuality; the consummation of love, and the consummation of hatred. The spirit
loves and suffers, the flesh hates and exults; when the love
and suffering of the spirit and the hatred and exultance of
the flesh have reached each their separate extremity, the
true self is born.

The doctrine is false and deathly; it must, if followed,
inevitably lead through a slow disintegration to a death. For
it rests on a total repudiation of all true growth. No progress
towards a more perfect unity is possible in man, the only
movement is towards a more utter division; when the division
has reached a point beyond which it cannot go while the body
it inhabits still remains alive, at that point is the true self
of man.

That is the doctrine implicit in *The Crown;* and Lawrence was to follow it to the bitter end. As his doctrine derived from his experience, so his experience will conform to
his doctrine. The duality and division will become more
intense, more irremediable; it will invade and dominate all
his conscious thought and his unconscious creation. Already in *Twilight in Italy* and in *The Crown* we see the
process beginning. *The Crown* ends with the question
" Why do we not create a new revelation of God? " But the

only revelation of God is man. To create a new revelation
of God means to become a new man. There is no other way.
As Lawrence puts it, " there is nothing for a man to do but
to behold God, and to become God." But how? According
to Lawrence's doctrine, man is God already, if he will only
obey his impulse to love and suffer, *and* his impulse to hate
and exult. By so doing, his ego is annihilated; it is cloven
in sunder. But what then?

IV

WOMEN IN LOVE

THE autobiographical sequence of *Look! We Have Come Through!* ends strangely with a handful of poems which appear to record an annihilation of the ego. The annihilation of the ego is an essential phase in the mystical experience; it is the preliminary to a rebirth. And these final poems seem to assert a rebirth. We must examine them carefully.

The first is entitled " New Heaven and Earth." Lawrence records his shy entry into a new world. He was so weary of the world, he says; everything was tainted with himself.

> I was a lover, I kissed the woman I loved
> and God of horror, I was kissing also myself.

In the end it was an unforgettable, maniacal horror. But at last came death, sufficiency of death. Apparently this " sufficiency of death " came partly through an imaginative enduring of the horrors of the war. Lawrence died, because he in imagination endured the deaths of many men. He, with them, was " dead and trodden to nought in the sour black earth of the tomb; dead and trodden to nought, trodden to nought."

Then came a resurrection, " risen, not born again, but risen, body the same as before." And the manner of the resurrection was this:

I, in the sour black tomb, trodden to absolute death,
I put out my hand in the night, one night, and my hand
touched that which was verily not me,
verily, it was not me.
Where I had been was a sudden blaze,
a sudden flaring blaze.
So I put my hand out further, a little further
and I felt that which was not I,
it verily was not I,
it was the unknown.

Ha! I was a blaze leaping up!
I was a tiger bursting into sunlight.
I was greedy, I was mad for the unknown.

And the unknown that he touched was " the flank of his wife," at whose side " he had lain for more than a thousand nights."

and all that previous while, she was I, she was I

But now she is other, and she who is other has " strange-mounded breasts and strange sheer slopes, and white levels."
The next poem, " Elysium," which seems to be intimately connected with this, tells of his finding

a place of loneliness
Lonelier than Lyonesse,
Lovelier than Paradise.

Again, it is through the woman that he finds it. But whereas she was passive in the former poem, she is active in this. There, he put out his hand in the night and discovered her as other; here it is she who releases him.

Invisible the hands of Eve
Upon me travelling to reeve
Me from the matrix, to relieve

Me from the rest! Ah, terribly
Between the body of life and me
Her hands slid in and set me free.

Ah, with a fearful, strange detection
She found the source of my subjection
To the All, and severed the connection.

I do not pretend to understand that; nor can I positively say
that this deliverance of the man by the woman " from the
womb of the All, the monstrous womb of time " is the same
as that separation of himself from a universe which was
wholly himself of which the former poem speaks. But they
appear to be intimately connected.

The next poem, " Manifesto," is much more explicit; it
belongs to a year later, to 1916. It begins: " A woman has
given me strength and affluence." She has freed him from
his direst hunger,

> more frightening, more profound
> than stomach or throat or even the mind;
> redder than death, more clamorous.

the hunger for the woman. She fed that hunger in him at
last.

She stood before me like riches that were mine.
Even then, in the dark, I was tortured, ravening, unfree,
Ashamed, and shameful, and vicious.
A man is so terrified of strong hunger;
and this terror is the root of all cruelty.
She loved me, and stood before me, looking to me.
How could I look, when I was mad? I looked sideways, furtively,
being mad with voracious desire.

But he lost at last " the fierceness that fears it will starve."
He knew he would never go hungry, and he was fulfilled.

Yet hunger remains, the ultimate hunger — " the ache for being." And the satisfaction of this hunger depends on being known by her even as he knows her. This knowledge which he has of her, but which she has not of him is that

> ultimately, she is all beyond me,
> She is all not-me, ultimately.
> It is that that one comes to.
> A curious agony, and a relief, when I touch that which is not me
>   in any sense,
> it wounds me to death with my own not-being; definite, inviolable
>   limitation,
> and something beyond, quite beyond, if you understand what that
>   means.

But she does not know him thus. She touches him as if he were herself, her own.

> I want her to touch me at last, ah, on the root and quick of my
>   darkness
> and perish on me, as I have perished on her. . . .
> When she has put her hand on my secret, darkest sources, the
>   darkest outgoings,
> when it has struck home to her, like a death, " this is *him!* "
> she has no part in it, no part whatever,
> it is the terrible *other,*
> when she knows the fearful *other flesh,* ah, darkness unfathomable
>   and fearful, contiguous and concrete,
> when she is slain against me, and lies in a heap like one outside
>   the house,
> when she passes away as I have passed away,
> being pressed up against the *other,*
> then I shall be glad, I shall not be confused with her,
> I shall be cleared, distinct, single as if burnished in silver,
> having no adherence, no adhesion anywhere,
> one clear, burnished, isolated being, unique,

and she also, pure, isolated, complete,
two of us, unutterably distinguished, and in unutterable conjunction.

Once more I do not claim to understand this wholly. But,
even though one may not understand the experience which
is recorded, one may reach certain conclusions.

The man hungers " for being "; yet his achievement of
" being " depends upon the woman. She must know him in
the same way as he knows her; and this knowledge is a
carnal and a sensual knowledge, physical touch of the naked
other flesh, physical touch of " his secret, darkest sources,"
accompanied by a realisation of his otherness. He came to
this knowledge of her a year before; she does not, or cannot
come to this knowledge of him. The knowledge is mysterious.
But why, we ask, should his achievement of " being " depend upon how the woman knows him? Surely it must be a
very precarious sort of " being " that thus depends upon
the woman's ratification. If he knows himself as isolated
and unique, with a true and certain knowledge, what does
it matter to him whether the woman recognises him as isolated and unique? Certainty is certainty. But, if his certainty
is uncertain, then its ratification by the woman will bring
him comfort, though not certainty. Still more, if he desires
to have " no adhesion anywhere," surely it is a queer way
to sever himself by asking the woman to recognise that he
is severed. " Tell me," he says in effect, " that I do not
adhere to you "; and the appeal is a confession that he does
adhere to her, that he cannot separate himself. " Be terrified
of me," he says in effect; and the summons is a confession
that she is not likely to be terrified of him.

There is, we suspect, a great and grievous weakness here.
We simply cannot believe in any achievement of " being "
which thus depends upon another's recognition of it. " Being " is achieved alone, and if it is achieved it is self-sufficient,
and calls for no allowance. But no such self-sufficiency is
here. This condition is rather one of excessive dependence,
assuming a last disguise. " I am myself, isolated, independent, and alone," says the man to the woman, "but tell me
that I am, otherwise I cannot believe it." Neither can we.
It is the old situation, in a new form. We remember the
agonised self-questioning of Will Brangwen:

Why could he not leave her? He could not, he could not. A
woman, he must have a woman. And having a woman he must be
free of her. It would be the same position. For he could not be free
of her.

That is the psychological position, unchanged. The physical situation is more mysterious. The dependence upon the
woman is physical: the ravening hunger is satisfied. But
he seems to be now demanding a new kind of physical contact, or rather a physical contact in which the woman shall
feel a new emotion, of fear and terror, in contact with him.
And again we recall the poem " She said as well to me,"
which immediately precedes " New Heaven and Earth."

" Don't touch me and appreciate me
It is an infamy.
You would think twice before you touched a weasel on a fence
as it lifts its straight white throat.
Your hand would not be so flig and easy. . . .
Is there nothing in me to make you hesitate? "

He is asking that she shall feel, in physical contact, the
same terror that he feels for her. Somehow, she must be
made to respect and fear him, sexually; until she does, he

will be "confused with her." When she does, ah, then, it
will be heaven. After that it will only remain that all men
and women go through the same process of coming to final
sexual terror of each other; then,

> Every man himself, and therefore, a surpassing singleness of
> mankind.
> The blazing tiger will spring upon the deer, undimmed,
> the hen will nestle over her chickens,
> we shall love, we shall hate,
> but it will be like music, sheer utterance,
> issuing straight out of the unknown.

Since the habits of the actual tiger would not be affected by
this consummation among men and women, the tiger is
symbolic. It is the sexual tiger, in Lawrence, who will be
undimmed, because the woman will know that it is a tiger,
instead of mistaking it for a milder animal.

✍

    This endeavour to enforce upon the woman a sexual or
sensual homage to the man is the chief clue to Lawrence's
next novel, *Women in Love*. In that novel Ursula Brangwen becomes, quite recognisably, *the* Woman; and Lawrence himself also appears, quite recognisably, as Rupert
Birkin. The culmination of their relation is described in
the chapter " Excurse." To anyone who reads the novel in
isolation, and without the necessary clue, it is an obscure and
difficult chapter; but it strikes even the unadvised reader
as invented and untrue. He scents in it a fundamental falsity,
as of a forced conclusion. Perhaps Lawrence himself half-
acknowledged this by giving the chapter its curious title,
" Excurse."
    What is certain is that it can be readily understood only

by reference to the poem " Manifesto " which we have been examining. The poem was written in 1916, so was the novel; and there are good reasons for supposing that the poem was written almost at the same moment as this particular chapter of the novel. The situation is the same. Birkin is dissatisfied with Ursula; he demands of her a kind of physical contact which she will not give.

He wanted her to come to him. But he was angry at the bottom of his soul, and indifferent. He knew she had a passion for him, really. But it was not finally interesting. There were depths of passion when one became impersonal and indifferent, unemotional. Whereas Ursula was still at the emotional personal level — always so abominably personal. He had taken her as he had never been taken himself. He had taken her at the roots of her darkness and shame — like a demon, laughing over the fountain of mystic corruption which was one of the sources of her being, laughing, shrugging, accepting, accepting finally. As for her, when would she so much go beyond herself as to accept him at the quick of death?

I do not know what " the fountain of mystic corruption " in Ursula really means, though it is certain that there was no such thing in her; but it is obvious that Birkin's demand of Ursula is the same demand as Lawrence makes upon the woman in the poem. The difference in mood — the poem is passionate, the prose cynical — is due to the fact that the prose is a little later, and Lawrence has become cynical, through the woman's resistance. With pitiless fidelity Lawrence, immediately afterwards, gives utterance to Ursula's repulsion. She bursts upon Birkin in fury:

" You love the sham spirituality, it's your food. And why? Because of the dirt underneath. Do you think I don't know the foulness of your sex life — and hers? — I do. And it's the foulness you want, you liar. Then have it, have it. You're such a liar. . . .

"*You!*" she cried. "You! You truth-lover! You purity-monger! It *stinks*, your truth and your purity. It stinks of the offal you feed on, you scavenger dog, you eater of corpses. You are foul, *foul* — and you must know it. Your purity, your candour, your goodness — yes, thank you, we've had some. What you are is a foul, deathly thing, obscene, that's what you are, obscene and perverse. You, and love! You may well say, you don't want love. No, you want *yourself*, and dirt, and death — that's what you want. You are so *perverse*, so death-eating."

It was, within the limits of the story, quite impossible for Ursula to know anything about "the foulness of the sex-life" of Birkin and Hermione Roddice. Their liaison is over before Ursula ever meets Birkin; and he tells Ursula nothing about it. We must say, if we keep to the rules of the game, that Ursula's knowledge was due to a flash of imaginative intuition. But, with Lawrence, it is impossible to keep to the rules of the game; with him, there is no "game." He did not conceal himself, and we cannot conceal him. Rupert Birkin is Lawrence, and what Lawrence knew about Birkin, he knew about himself. Birkin, indeed, makes no attempt to deny the truth of Ursula's knowledge. On the contrary,

He knew she was in the main right. He knew he was perverse, so spiritual on the one hand, and in some strange way, degraded on the other. But was she herself any better? Was anybody any better?

Wherein did this depravity, of which Lawrence was conscious, consist? It consisted in this demand that the woman "should take him as he had taken her," with a sense "of the contiguous, concrete, terrifying *other flesh*." It is a demand for sexual contact, without the oblivion of passion, without the ecstasy of union — cold, conscious, calculating sensuality. And the woman, instinctively, repels it; probably, she is completely incapable of it. Probably, the vast majority of ordinary men and women are completely incapable of it; probably, it is only practicable in a man of physical and spiritual constitution resembling that of Lawrence.

~

The point, and the falsity of " Excurse," is that it represents Ursula as giving way to Birkin's demand. In Lawrence's quasi-mystical language, " she had thought there was no source deeper than the phallic source;" now, at his demand, she discovers it. " She had had lovers, she had known passion. But this was neither love, nor passion." That was true enough. But what is completely false is that Ursula, or her original, acknowledged its supremacy. The evidence of this is Lawrence's work. This ultra-phallic consummation, in which Birkin and Ursula are represented as finding complete fulfilment, disappears almost completely from Lawrence's subsequent books. If it really had been the consummation which he represented it to be, this disappearance would be inconceivable. The true fulfilment between man and woman is not discovered simply in order to be forgotten: for it is, for Lawrence, and for many men, the Holy Grail itself. One does not throw the Holy Grail into the kitchen-midden. That alone is evidence enough that this consummation was not what Lawrence represented it to be. But it is not the only evidence.

This consummation is not actual at all. It is a wish-fulfilment. Let us examine it. One would need, to be wholly precise, to quote nearly the whole chapter. A few passages must suffice.

She had a full mystic knowledge of his suave loins of darkness, dark-clad and suave, and in this knowledge there was some of the inevitability and the beauty of fate, fate which one asks for, which one accepts in full.

He sat still like an Egyptian Pharaoh. . . . He felt as if he were seated in immemorial potency, like the great carven statues of real Egypt, as real and as fulfilled with subtle strength, as these are, with a vague inscrutable smile on the lips. He knew what it was to have the strange and magical current of force in his back and loins, and down his legs, force so perfect that it stayed him immobile, and left his face subtly, mindlessly smiling. He knew what it was to be awake and potent in that other basic mind, the deepest physical mind. And from this source he had a pure and magic control, magical, mystical, a force in darkness, like electricity.

This is the re-assertion of his masculinity, of which he is always dreaming. In this realm of mindless sensuality, he is like Pharaoh, and " immemorially potent." And, still more important, the woman recognises it. She bows down to him; she becomes purely feminine, receptive, and submissive before him.

She was next to him, and hung in a pure rest, as a star is hung, balanced unthinkably. Still there remained a dark lambency of anticipation. She would touch him. With perfect fine finger-tips of reality she would touch the reality in him, the suave, pure, untranslatable reality of his loins of darkness. To touch, mindlessly in darkness to come in pure touching upon the living reality of him, his suave perfect loins and thighs of darkness, this was her sustaining anticipation.

And he too waited in the magical steadfastness of suspense, for her to take this knowledge of him as he had taken it of her. He knew her darkly, with the fullness of dark knowledge. Now she would know him, and he too would be liberated.

As a matter of fact, Lawrence is so immersed in his personal experience that he forgets his story. Birkin had not taken this knowledge of Ursula in the novel. Lawrence had taken it of the woman in life, and the record is in " Manifesto." There it only remained for him to be known even as he knows, without which he cannot be free. Now, in the novel, where he is master, he gives himself this " liberation." Ursula Brangwen is made to desire what the poet of " Manifesto " desired that his woman should desire.

They threw off their clothes, and he gathered her to him, and found her, found the pure lambent reality of her forever invisible flesh. Quenched, inhuman, his fingers upon her unrevealed nudity were the fingers of silence upon silence, the body of mysterious night upon the body of mysterious night, the night masculine and feminine, never to be seen with the eye, or known with the mind, only known as a palpable revelation of living otherness.

She had her desire of him, she touched, she received the maximum of unspeakable communication in touch, dark, subtle, positively silent, a magnificent gift and give again, a perfect acceptance and yielding, a mystery, the reality of that which never can be known, vital, sensual reality that can never be transmuted into mind-content, but remains outside, living body of darkness and silence and subtlety, the mystic body of reality. She had her desire fulfilled. He had his desire fulfilled. For she was to him what he was to her, the immemorial magnificence of mystic, palpable, real otherness.

So the dream is made to come true. Ursula has " the full mystic knowledge of his suave loins of darkness "; she has discovered that " there were strange fountains of his body, more mysterious and potent than any she had imagined or known, more satisfying, ah, finally, mystically-physically satisfying. She had thought that there was no source deeper than the phallic source." Now, she knew better. The something that remained, that something which prevented Lawrence from satisfying the ultimate hunger of his " ache for being," is achieved. And we see what this " ache for being " really is; it is the ache to establish his own masculinity. It cannot be done in sexual possession, in which he is always the dependent, the victim; but it can be done in this new

mode of sexuality, which consists in touch, in which there
is none of the "abhorred mingling." In the sexuality of
touch, of complete separateness, he may be lord and master
— a very Pharoah.

When we grasp this, we grasp the meaning of the strange
chapter, " Moony," where Birkin throws stone after stone, in
an unintelligible frenzy, at the reflection of the moon in a
pool, while Ursula watches him in agony. It seems quite
meaningless, until we realise that Birkin is destroying Aphrodite, the divinity under whose cold light Ursula annihilated
the core of intrinsic male in Lawrence's last incarnation as
Anton Skrebensky. To annihilate the female insatiably de-
manding physical satisfaction from the man who cannot
give it her — the female who has thus annihilated him —
this is Lawrence's desire. To make her subject again, to
re-establish his own manhood — this is the secret purpose
of *Women in Love*. In imagination, he has his desire. He
creates a sexual mystery beyond the phallic, wherein he is
the lord; and he makes the woman acknowledge the existence of this ultra-phallic realm, and his own lordship in it.
He triumphs over her in imagination, but not in life. Aphrodite can only be appeased within the phallic realm, and
Lawrence is no master there.

To the working out of this personal argument in the
imaginary consummation of Birkin and Ursula, all else is
really subsidiary in the novel. But, once we understand the
true situation, we shall not be surprised at the definite
emergence of a new theme — the hunger for a man. The
hunger for a woman has proved disastrous, in spite of the
assertions of actual, and the reports of imaginary fulfilment; it was inevitable that Lawrence should turn towards

the possibility of a relation with a man. There is the same confusion between spirituality and sensuality. The love between Rupert Birkin and Gerald Crich is, on Birkin's side, half-spiritual, half-sensual. "We are mentally, spiritually intimate," says Birkin to Crich, "therefore we ought to be more or less physically intimate." Accordingly, the two men wrestle naked together, and Birkin swoons away. But the main interest of their relation is the indecision which Birkin reveals. He says to Crich:

"You've got to take down the love-and-marriage ideal from its pedestal. We want something broader. I believe in the *additional* perfect relationship between man and man — additional to marriage."

That, indubitably, was in Lawrence's own mind at this moment; he expressed his thought, even more strongly, in his letters. But, since we know what underlay the "perfect" marriage-relation between Ursula and Birkin, and that its "perfection" consisted precisely in the substitution of "the mystery beyond the phallic" for the phallic mystery, we know that it is not the addition of one perfection to another that he is seeking, but rather to escape to a man from the misery of his own failure with a woman. This has always appeared to Lawrence a way out. In *The White Peacock* his love for a man is more perfect than his love for a woman; and, truly, in actual fact I believe it was a happier and less tortured relation for him. But always it was brief and fugitive. Lawrence was always, and inevitably, disappointed.

"We ought to swear to love each other, you and I," says Rupert to Gerald, "implicitly and perfectly, finally, without any possibility of going back." Again he pleads: "We will swear to stand by each other — be true to each other — intimately — infallibly — given to each other, organically, without possibility of going back." Gerald withdraws from the proffered alliance, puts it gently aside, and the novel purports to show us how, in consequence of this refusal, he is destroyed. He chooses Ursula's sister, Gudrun. This, Birkin says (and Lawrence makes it so), is a disaster. " He was willing to condemn himself in marriage . . . but he would not make any pure relationship with any other soul. Marriage was not the committing of himself into a relationship with Gudrun." This is very obscure, and perhaps Lawrence himself did not know what he meant. But manifestly " the pure relationship " with a woman is what Birkin attains with Ursula. Gerald and Gudrun are to remain under the dominion of Aphrodite the deathly.

The other way was to accept Rupert's offer of alliance, to enter into the bond of pure trust and love with the other man, and then subsequently with the woman. If he pledged himself with the man he would later be able to pledge himself with the woman: not merely in legal marriage, but in absolute, mystic marriage.

Such " absolute, mystic marriage," namely, as Rupert and Ursula achieve: their imaginary ultra-phallic consummation. Since the desire for this consummation, and the hunger for the man also, is the effect of Lawrence's phallic failure, Rupert's demand of Gerald is the last extremity of self-deception. It means nothing, or if it means anything, it means that his man-friend must be the repetition of himself: just such another phallic failure, just such another sex-crucified man.

Lawrence's hunger for a man could never have been satisfied. He came to know, and in part to confess it later, in *Kangaroo*. But at this time he did not know it, he was only vaguely aware of the depth upon depth of self-deception in which he was involved. He was gratifying himself with a dream. Gerald, because he refuses Rupert's offer of alliance, is delivered over to the destructive Aphrodite and to death: he goes the way of the tiger, as described in *Twilight in Italy* — the tiger " whose *essential* fire is white and cold, a white ecstasy." In a sensual ecstasy, Gerald seeks to murder Gudrun, and dies in a final ecstasy of dissolution in the snow, in the light of a painful brilliant-shining moon, " from which there was no escape."

The book comes to a close with a conversation between Rupert and Ursula about the dead man.

" Did you need Gerald? " she asked one evening.

" Yes," he said.

" Aren't I enough for you? " she asked.

" No," he said. " You are enough for me, as far as a woman is concerned. You are all women to me. But I wanted a man friend, as eternal as you and I are eternal."

" Why aren't I enough? " she said. " You are enough for me. I don't want anybody else but you. Why isn't it the same with you? "

" Having you, I can live all my life without anybody else, any other sheer intimacy. But to make it complete, really happy, I wanted eternal union with a man too: another kind of love," he said.

" I don't believe it," she said. " It's an obstinacy, a theory, a perversity."

" Well — " he said.

" You can't have two kinds of love. Why should you? "

" It seems as if I can't," he said. " Yet I wanted it."

" You can't have it, because it's false, impossible," she said.

" I don't believe that," he answered.

Was he or Ursula right? Surely, Ursula. Not that love of a woman and love of a man are incompatible. That is not the question at all. The question is entirely personal: whether Lawrence can find an issue, by way of a relation with a man, from the strange and terrible situation in which he is now caught. Lawrence is bewildered and lost. He feels that he is disintegrating; his inward division is become terrible to himself; his life a nightmare.

THE NIGHTMARE

T
HE NIGHTMARE " is the title of a retrospective and autobiographical chapter of his later novel *Kangaroo,* which covers the three years from the beginning of 1916 to the end of 1918: that is, the period of writing *Women in Love* and two years after. In that record, which is of a veritable nightmare, and sometimes seems definitely to cross the border-line of sanity, there are clear traces of an endeavour by Lawrence to satisfy his hunger for a man. The threads of the narrative are mingled, and the one which is apparently dominant is Lawrence's horror of the war, and the effect of that horror upon him. Lawrence's horror of the war was real and profound, so were its effects upon him. Nevertheless, the war was only the secondary cause of his suffering. Even if there had been no war, some such experience as " The Nightmare " was bound to have befallen him. It lay in his destiny.

Two things existed together in Lawrence: they were, perhaps, in the last analysis, dependent upon each other. One was an extraordinary spiritual sensitiveness, the other a less than normal sexual vitality. So that, instead of being strengthened by his relation with a woman, he was weakened by his own vain struggle to be dominant and lacerated by his sense of guilt; instead of being refreshed and renewed by physical communion, he was only the more en-

feebled and divided by it. His sexual life was an added burden to his spirit, instead of a release from burdening. The
horror of the war doubled the burden of his spirit, and made
more agonised and desperate his attempts to find release in
the woman. Defeat became only the more inevitable; and
the burden increased till it became intolerable. I knew Lawrence well at the beginning of the period of " The Nightmare "; I lived for some three months in close contact with
him in Cornwall. He had made a desperate call to Katherine
Mansfield and me to join him and his wife, and live together
in unity. And we responded, because we loved him and his
wife. He was to us a wonderful and beloved being. And, I
think, he was depending upon us. " There remain only you
and Murry in our lives," he wrote to Katherine, beseeching
her to come. " We look at the others as across a grave. . .
Let us all live together and create a new world."

The attempt was a painful failure. There were moments
of blissful happiness: when were there not moments of
simple bliss for any one who lived with Lawrence? But the
failure was only the more painful. Katherine and I were
bewildered by Lawrence. All the knowledge of him contained in this book was completely hidden from me then;
it was, in the main, concealed from me all through his life.
When he died, something broke in my heart: but all I knew
was that I had loved him, and that, at times at least, he had
loved me. I knew that our relation had been a miserable and
tragic failure, and I felt that the failure had been inevitable,
necessary as fate. And that was all I knew when Lawrence
died. Only since his death have I been driven by some inward compulsion to try to understand him. The attempt
would have been impossible while he yet lived.

Katherine and I were completely ignorant of the nature
of the struggle which was then devouring him like a disease.
We saw, and felt on our pulses, only the incredible mingling

of love and hatred that was in him. He seemed to us like a man possessed, now by an angel, now by a devil. Both were beyond our comprehension; but to the angel we responded, the devil tortured us beyond endurance. It was pain to see him so transformed and transfigured by the paroxysms of murderous hatred, of his wife, of us, of all mankind, that swept over him. They would leave him white, bowed, spent, silent and shuddering. Such a happening was beyond our experience and beyond our understanding. Gradually, we became oppressed and frightened; it seemed as though we could not breathe, and that our only hope was to get away. We packed up our few possessions and went away to the other side of Cornwall.

We did not understand; but we could have done nothing if we had understood. The horror of the war was not the cause of his strange and terrifying condition. We also felt the horror of the war, but Lawrence's horror was a frenzy. It utters itself as such in the " The Nightmare " chapter of *Kangaroo*, written years later.

And now, if circumstances had roped nearly all men into the horror, and it was a case of adding horror to horror, or dying well, on the other hand, the irremediable circumstance of his own separate soul made inevitable Richard Lovat's standing out. If there is outward, circumstantial unreason and fatality, there is inward unreason and inward fate. He would have to dare to follow his inward fate. He must remain alone, outside of everything, everything, conscious of what was going on, conscious of what he was doing and not doing. Conscious he must be, and consciously he must stick to it. To be forced into nothing.

But there was, and Lawrence knew it, no danger of his being forced into anything. He was completely unfit for any kind of military service. The most obtuse doctor had only to put a stethoscope to his chest for a second to know that as a soldier he was unthinkable. Moreover, for his own occupation — he had now, after finishing *Women in Love*, practically given up writing — he was working hard on the farm below his cottage at Zennor; he was, though not with that intention, doing " national service " of the most necessary kind. All that could happen to him in the normal course was a periodic summons for medical examination, of which the conclusion was foregone. But this had become to him an unspeakable horror: the mere recollection of it, six years later when he was writing *Kangaroo*, drove him once more to insane fury.

Not while life was life, should they lay hold of him. Never again. Never would he be touched again. And because they had handled his private parts, and looked into them, their eyes should burst and their hands should wither and their hearts should rot.

That refers to the last medical examination in 1918. The war had ended before Lawrence's resolution could be put to the test.

∾

Lawrence was, at this time, suffering from a kind of persecution-mania. He believed he was a marked man, and that " the authorities " had taken good note of his inward resistance. This was, I believe, pure delusion; but Lawrence had more excuse for the delusion than most people who suffer from persecution mania. He had as good an excuse as Jean-Jacques Rousseau. He knew himself to be an extraordinary man; and to suppose that the vague " authorities " knew it also was only natural to him. Moreover, *The Rainbow* had been suppressed, and no one had uttered a word in its defence. It was put aside, annihilated, as unspeakable. Lawrence had some excuse for believing that the powers that were, were determined to destroy him.

These convictions worked on him in his isolation in Cornwall. His behaviour became deliberately intransigent. Among the ignorant and often malicious Cornish peasantry, the fact that his wife was German was suspicious. The submarine menace was at its height, their cottage looked directly over the Bristol Channel; they had no visible means of subsistence. Another man, even Lawrence himself at another moment, would simply have removed inland. But the devil of perversity had now taken hold of him; he willed to stay and be persecuted by skulking coast-watchers; he wanted to drink the cup to the dregs and make the potion as bitter as he could. So he stuck fast in Cornwall, and sang German songs to the spellbound ears of the coast-watchers crouching beneath his cottage-windows. The longer he stayed, the more suspect he inevitably became. *Why* did he stay there, when any other man would simply have gone somewhere else? The answer was as natural as the question to the local jacks-in-office. He was there for no good.

And, of course, if someone had been there to answer the question correctly, and to say that he stayed there because he wanted to be persecuted, because he wanted to suffer, because he wanted to hate them and mankind for making him suffer, because he wanted to be able to spew England out of his mouth, the answer would have seemed pure nonsense. But it would have been true. Lawrence wanted the darkness and the horror and the sense of malignancy that he felt in Cornwall.

The Cornish night would gradually come down upon the dark shaggy moors, that were like the fur of some beast, and upon the pale-grey granite masses, so ancient and so Druidical, suggesting blood-sacrifice. And as Somers sat there on the sheaves in the underdark, seeing the light swim above the sea, he felt he was over the border, in another world. Over the border, in that

twilight awesome world of the previous Celts. The spirit of the
ancient pre-Christian world, which lingers still in the truly Celtic
places, he could feel it invade him in the savage dusk, making him
savage too, and at the same time strangely sensitive and subtle,
understanding the mystery of blood-sacrifice: to sacrifice one's
victim, and let the blood run to the fire, there beyond the gorse
on the old grey granite: and at the same time to understand most
sensitively the dark flicker of animal life about him, even in a
bat, even in the writhing of a maggot in a dead rabbit. Writhe
then, Life, he seemed to say to the things — and he no longer
saw its sickeningness.

Not to see its sickeningness is one thing; Lawrence wanted
something different. He wanted to exult in its sickeningness,
to let himself lapse into an ecstasy of decay and disintegration. The tendency thus to escape from the burden of the
spiritual consciousness was always in him. Even so far back
as *The White Peacock* it is with Cyril's fascinated watching
of the maggots in a dead rabbit that his friendship with
Annable begins. Lawrence was now deliberately seeking that
decomposition of the spiritual consciousness which circumstance and place offered him. He consciously sought to lapse
from consciousness. " He could feel himself metamorphos-
ing. He no longer wanted to struggle consciously along, a
thought-adventurer. He preferred to drift into a sort of
blood-darkness." Of this deliberate drift out of consciousness, Richard Somers' affair with the young Cornish farmer
was an integral part. It was also deliberately directed against
his wife: against " the love and marriage ideal," as embodied in her. The relation with the young farmer was in
malignant opposition to her: a consciously willed destruction
of his wife's being.

Poor Harriet spent many lonely days in the cottage. Richard
was not interested in her now. He was only interested in John
Thomas and the farm-people, and he was growing more like a

labourer every day. And the farm-people didn't mind how long *she* was left alone, at night too, in that lonely little cottage, and with all the tension of fear upon her. . . . Richard . . . neglected her and hated her. She was driven back on herself like a fury.

It was the deliberate seeking of a death-relation — the farmer and he "would talk of death, and the powers of death " — a deliberate denial of the life-relation. It was the proving, in bitter life-experience, of the truth of Ursula Brangwen's instinct that Birkin's wanting " another kind of love " with a man was an obstinacy, a theory, a perversity. " Somers seemed to come home (from his farmer-friend) like an enemy, with that look on his face, and that pregnant malevolency of Cornwall investing him."

Inevitably, Lawrence felt that he was violating himself. This conscious perversion, this wilful degradation, of his spirit could never have the entire man behind it. He was not, and never could be, " mindless "; the spirit was still there, watching him.

" I declare! " said John Thomas, as Somers appeared in the cornfield, " you look more like one of us every day." And he looked with a bright Cornish eye at Somers' careless, belted figure and old jacket. The speech struck Richard: it sounded half triumphant, half mocking. " He thinks I'm coming down in the world — it is half a rebuke," thought Somers to himself. But he was half pleased: and half he *was* rebuked.

Even in the simple human way his man-friend failed him. Subtly, it is easy to see from the story, Buryan despised Lawrence. He left Lawrence's passionate letters unanswered, made no response to his appeals, treated him as of no account. Lawrence would have us and himself believe that it was because he was afraid of his association with a marked man. But the explanation does not fit with Buryan's deliberate neglect of him in the episode of the journey to the market town. The cause is plain to see: at bottom Buryan despised Lawrence for his own self-degradation.

Of this strange period, Lawrence said that " it changed his life for ever." It may have done; in the sense that it may have confirmed and made inveterate his appetite towards disintegration and death, his mood of loathing and hatred for all mankind. But both were manifest long before, and long before the war. What had happened now was that he had given rein to his devil, and the devil was never afterwards in subjection very long. But whether in fact he had any real power to choose, who shall say? I am no believer in free-will; it seems to me a childish superstition. Humanly speaking, I wish that Lawrence had been an undivided man; but since it seems plain to me that those precious qualities in him which made him wonderful were corollary to that weakness which I would have had him spared, even the human wish seems childish to me.

❧

So with *Women in Love,* the novel of this period. I hold it to be built upon a lie, or on many lies; yet I would not have it otherwise. The haunted, tortured, divided, angel-devil of a man is in it. He is not like the Lawrence whom I loved; but (as I learned to my sorrow) the Lawrence whom I loved was only half the Lawrence whom I knew.

Women in Love is an amazing book; amazing for the subtlety of its falsity, amazing for the intricacy of its self-deception. It is the imperishable monument of one of the strangest moments of Lawrence's strange destiny.

The main argument of the book, which is the distinction between the " love " of Rupert and Ursula on the one hand, and of Gerald and Gudrun on the other, is false. Rupert and Ursula are represented as in the way of salvation, Gerald

and Gudrun as in the way of damnation: and this is superficially plausible for the simple reason that Rupert and
Ursula are in the main real people, while Gerald and Gudrun
are not. But when we consider the principles which these
opposed couples really embody, we discover that the difference between them is that Rupert and Ursula are a whole
stage further on in the process of damnation, for Gerald
and Gudrun simply represent Rupert and Ursula at their
previous stage of sensual self-destruction. Lawrence claims
that Rupert and Ursula escape from it into the ultra-phallic
realm, of utter separateness and mindless sensuality. It was
untrue. What happened was that Lawrence tried to escape
thither, and left Ursula where she was; and some record of
what happened in consequence of this escape is written in
" The Nightmare."

Lawrence, who was a supremely conscious man, was not
unaware of the deception he was trying to work upon himself. There is a point in the story where Birkin wonders
whether he has done wrong to refuse Ursula's proffered
love. " Perhaps," he thinks, " he had been wrong to go to
her with an idea of what he wanted." The idea of what he
wanted is expressed in fifty different ways in the novel;
sometimes very deceptively, but the substance beneath is
always the same. The phallic relation is to be superseded,
by a new sexuality of separateness and touch. Perhaps the
" idea " is most clearly expressed, with much that lay behind
it, in this passage:

On the whole he hated sex, it was such a limitation. . . . He
wanted sex to revert to the level of the other appetites, to be
regarded as a functional process, not as a fulfilment. He believed
in sex-marriage. But beyond this he wanted a further conjunction,
where man had being and woman had being, two pure beings, each
constituting the freedom of the other, balancing each other like
two poles of one force, like two angels, or two demons.

He wanted so much to be free, not under the compulsion of any need for unification, or tortured by unsatisfied desire. . . . The merging, the clutching, the mingling of love was become madly abhorrent to him. But it seemed to him, woman was always so horrible and clutching, she had such a lust for possession, a greed of self-importance in love. She wanted to have, to own, to control, to be dominant. Everything must be referred back to her, to Woman, the Great Mother of everything, out of whom proceeded everything and to whom everything must be rendered up.

It filled him with almost insane fury, this calm assumption of the Magna Mater. . . . He had a horror of the Magna Mater, she was detestable.

Were it not that we have learned to read this language, it might be plausible. Lawrence seems half to have deceived himself by his phrases. For Birkin, when he wonders whether he was wrong to go to Ursula with this idea of what he wanted, asks himself: "Was it really only an idea, or was it the interpretation of a profound yearning? If the latter, how was it he was always talking about sensual fulfilment? The two did not agree very well together." They agreed, in reality, perfectly well together. Sensual domination, not sexual fulfilment, is his desire. A sexual marriage in which he does not have to satisfy the woman, where the sexuality, being transformed into sensuality, may give him the opportunity of reasserting the manhood he had lost — this is precisely Lawrence's dream. It is the dream of a man who would give his soul to be free of the woman, but has not the courage to make himself free of her.

Suddenly he found himself face to face with a situation. It was as simple as this: fatally simple. On the one hand, he knew he did not want a further sensual experience — something deeper, darker than ordinary life could give. [He thinks of an African carving of a negro woman, which is for him the expression of the

" deeper, darker " sensual mystery.] Thousands of years ago, that which was immanent in himself must have taken place in these Africans: the goodness, the holiness, the desire for creation and productive happiness must have lapsed, leaving the single impulse for knowledge in one sort, mindless progressive knowledge through the senses, knowledge arrested and ending in the senses, mystic knowledge in disintegration and dissolution. . . .

Birkin shrinks back in horror from the lapse from goodness that is imminent in himself. No, there is another way, he cries in anguish.

There was the paradisal entry into pure, single being, the individual soul taking precedence over love and desire for union, stronger than any pangs of emotion, a lovely state of free proud singleness, which accepted the obligation of the permanent connection with others, and with the other, submits to the yoke and leash of love, but never forfeits its own proud individual singleness, even while it loves and yields. There was the other way, the remaining way. And he must run to follow it. . . .

He goes off to ask Ursula to marry him. Which eventually she does. And then we find, as we have found, that the consummation between them has nothing whatever to do with these brave words of spiritual achievement, this mutual acknowledgment of the proud single soul; on the contrary, it is an attempt, to which Ursula is represented (falsely, as " The Nightmare " shows) to have been converted, to experience precisely those " sensual subtle realities far beyond the scope of phallic investigation," those mindless but not unconscious ecstasies of dissolution, which Birkin has ostensibly rejected for " the paradisal way " of marriage with Ursula.

I believe that Lawrence changed while *Women in Love* was actually being written: that he really did mean to reject the way of sensuality and dissolution, and that he succumbed to it in spite of himself. And Lawrence at the end of his novel is trying to persuade himself that his defeat is a victory; to deceive himself and his reader into the belief that the mutual acknowledgment of the proud single soul (which is spiritual) and the mutual exploration of " the ultra-phallic otherness " (which is sensual) are the same. Somewhere in his inward soul Lawrence must have known what he was doing; just as Birkin " knew that his spirituality was concomitant of a process of depravity, a sort of pleasure in self-destruction. There really *was* a certain stimulant in self-destruction, for him — especially when it was translated spiritually. But then he knew it — he knew it, and had done." That was an easy thing to say; but a man who, like Lawrence, " is damned and doomed to the old effort at serious living," cannot violate himself with impunity. He has finally broken something, deliberately riven his secret soul in sunder; and no power in earth or heaven can make him whole again.

The fundamental equivocation of *Women in Love* repels me. It is not that I blame Lawrence for yielding to a longing from which in his inward soul he shrank away. Lawrence was Lawrence — a destiny-driven man, if ever there was one. If the realm of mindless sensuality offered or seemed to offer the only way of escape for his tortured spirit, then he was driven to explore it. But I think he is to be condemned for painting his devil as an angel, for the duplicity with which he represents himself as turning away from this mindless sensuality towards a paradisal relation with the woman, yet subtly perverts this very relation (in defiance of all truth, factual or imaginative) into a form of that mindless sensuality from which it was to be an escape. Lawrence, in the essential and vital argument of *Women in Love*, behaves like a cheat. To behave like a cheat in these momentous issues of human destiny is to play the Judas to humanity. The man who betrays himself in such an issue betrays all men.

The failure was momentous. Lawrence, in the essential, was never to recover from it. He would make the heroic effort — a truly heroic effort — to assert himself against the consequences of his own spiritual suicide. But he was, henceforward, veritably a doomed man. He had made the great refusal, and it was irrevocable.

My mind tells me that this was inevitable, my heart tells me that it was not. When I think, childishly, of what Lawrence might have been, and of what he actually became, my heart is wrung with anguish. The slow recantation of all that was most precious to him, the gradual disintegration which an inexorable justice exacted from him, is fearful to contemplate. To mitigate the tragedy of this retribution, let us remember this, which I believe to be true.

Lawrence was denied the basic strength to bear the burden of the human spirit which lay more heavily on him than any other man of his time. The extreme knowledge of the burden to be borne, the secret inability to bear it — these were, I believe, given together. The excessive sensitiveness to the demands of the spirit, prematurely awakened in him, prevented that true physical maturity which would have enabled him either to maintain himself in physical isolation, or to draw upon the woman's vital strength, to take through her the healing virtue of the unknown which is beyond and below life itself. So he was driven consciously to seek not the unconscious, which he could not fully enter, but the mindless, which he believed he could. But even this he could not do, without his woman. She must submit her instinctive knowledge to his strange necessities; she must believe in his unnatural consummations; she must be convinced that humanity was involved in a destiny of mindless dissolution; she must submit to the idea that sex was a functional process not a fulfilment; she must acknowledge that they were not

man and woman, discovering and rediscovering their own
integral being through their perfect union, but polarised
demons inhabiting the mindless realm. She submits, believes,
is convinced; in the book she obeys. In life she resists; and
the victory is hers, as it must be.

But there was still more. Precisely because Lawrence was
denied that utter fulfilment in a woman which would have
given him the strength to bear his spiritual isolation, he
needed a friend, needed friends — men and women who
were his equals in spiritual development. And they did not
exist; or, if they did exist, he did not know them. Here I
speak with some authority, for it was to Katherine Mansfield and to me that he turned with longing in the crucial
winter of 1915–16 after which *Women in Love* was written,
and simply because I was a man, he turned primarily to me.
And I failed Lawrence, not from any lack of love, or of will
to avail him. I was never lacking in love towards Lawrence;
but I lacked understanding, the understanding that is born
of absolute experience, and can come from no other source
whatever.

Yet it is plain to me now that, even if I had understood
Lawrence, I should still have been bound to fail him, and
that it was better to fail him in ignorance, than to be impotent to help him, in knowledge. If I had known his secret,
I would have been his master, not he mine. And he needed
to be the master. The defect of his own manhood which
gnawed at him, demanded this spiritual compensation. If he
had been able to accept the fact of his own dependence,
Lawrence would never have been driven to his dire necessity.
The man who can finally accept himself is a free man. If
Lawrence could have accepted his own intrinsic dependence,
then he would, by that very act, have become independent:
his dependence would have fallen away from him. It sounds
a miracle, perhaps it is a miracle, but this miracle is inevi-

table in the progress of the human spirit. If it is a miracle it is a natural miracle — that eternal rebirth of human soul, without which life, to the sensitive spirit, must become an unendurable agony. This eternal rebirth of the soul Lawrence could not achieve: he fled from the naked isolation of self-knowledge without which it is inconceivable.

Women in Love was written during 1916. It was not published here in England till some six years later, owing to the prejudice against Lawrence because of the condemnation of *The Rainbow.* Its writing marked the end of a period in Lawrence's development. For nearly three years afterwards he wrote nothing. He endured in England till the end of the war. In the late autumn of 1919, he left for Italy. He speaks of this last year in " The Nightmare."

A lovely summer went by, a lovely autumn came. But the meaning had gone out of everything for him. He had lost his meaning. England had lost its meaning for him. The free England had died, this England of the peace was like a corpse. It was the corpse of a country to him.

In October came the passports. He saw Harriet off to Germany — said good-bye at the Great Eastern Station, while she sat in the Harwich-Hook of Holland express. She had a look of almost vindictive triumph, and almost malignant love, as the train drew out. So he went back to his meaninglessness at the cottage.

Then, finding the meaninglessness too much, he gathered his few pounds together and in November left for Italy. Left England, England which he loved so bitterly, bitterly — and now was leaving, alone, and with a feeling of expressionlessness in his soul. It was a cold day. There was snow on the Downs like a shroud. And as he looked back from the boat, when they had left Folkstone behind and only England was there, England looked like a grey, dreary-grey coffin sinking in the sea behind, with her dead grey cliffs and the white, worn out cloth of snow above.

Lawrence never returned to England again. In the flesh he came, once, twice, thrice, for brief weeks: in the spirit, never. He was henceforward a stranger in his own country, and among his own kin.

PART III

THE ESCAPE FROM ENGLAND

THE next, the third period, of Lawrence's life and work is to me the greatest. In the work of this period more nearly than in any other is expressed the man I knew. It is a period, brief and fleeting, of harmony between the conflicting elements within him. The harmony is precarious; one has the sense that it cannot endure: and it is the more wonderful for that. It is a great and truly heroic effort, to conquer his hatred, and to restore the spiritual man — the truly spiritual man — to the supremacy he has lost. The halcyon moment is brief: it trembles to its own perfection in two books — of which *Fantasia of the Unconscious* is the finer, and the more profound. *In Aaron's Rod* — to me the greatest of his novels — we sense the faint beginnings of a new decline. But common to both these books of Lawrence is a wonderful clarity of insight into his own nature. And in the *Fantasia* he touches a strange and significant perfection: he consciously conceives it as his mission to create, or help to create, a world in which men so divided as himself shall be impossible.

Lawrence left England alone in November 1919. His wife went to Germany. When he arrived in Florence, he tells us in the *Memoirs of Magnus,* he had nine pounds in his pocket, twelve pounds at home in the bank, and no prospects in particular. *Women in Love* was still unpublished in England. He was looked at askance by all the publishers and all the editors in England. Since *Women in Love* Lawrence had written practically nothing. He was engrossed in mindlessness.

But, with the end of the war, the creative impulse had begun to thrust forth again. In the winter of 1918–19 he had written one of his finest short stories, *The Fox*, where the argument is human once more. The manner of the capture of March by young Henry the soldier is, we feel, a victory for life not merely in the destinies of those two characters, but in Lawrence himself. The suffocating cloud of death and dissolution is lifted; deliberate disintegration by mindlessness and sensuality is the goal no longer. A profound submission of the woman to the man in unconsciousness is indeed demanded, a surrender of all her wakeful, independent and unsatisfied spirit; and this may be called mindless also. But it has not very much to do with the consummation of *Women in Love*. It is a fulfilment. Something of Lawrence's own personal ache and personal hope finds expression in Henry's thought.

He was waiting, waiting to go West. He was aching almost in torment to leave England, to go West, to take March away. To leave this shore! He believed that as they crossed the seas, as they left this England which he so hated, because in some way it seemed to have stung him with poison, she would go to sleep. She would close her eyes at last and give in to him.

And then he would have her, and he would have his own life at last. He chafed, feeling he hadn't got his own life. He would never have it till she yielded and slept in him. Then he would have all his own life as a young man and a male, and she would have all her own life as a woman and a female. There would be no more of this awful straining. She would not be a man any more, an independent woman with a man's responsibility. Nay, even the responsibility for her own soul she would have to commit to him. He knew it was so, and obstinately held out against her, waiting for the surrender.

But more impressive than the re-emergence of this basic argument is the re-emergence of Lawrence's blitheness of heart. *Women in Love* was deathly in word and spirit. *The Fox* is, in the very texture of the writing, filled with the promise of spring.

✍

Very notably, in the novel which Lawrence began to write soon after he had left England in 1919, is manifest the same argument, the same blitheness, the same returning faith. I believe that Lawrence wrote *The Lost Girl* in the hope that it would have some popular success. In intention, it was his "best-seller." Lawrence kept out of it, accordingly, any character remotely resembling himself or his wife and thus allowed no occasion for the explicit "thought-adventure" which had become, for him, the *raison d'être* of the novel. *The Lost Girl*, like *The Fox*, is pure story, and like *The Fox* it is a beautiful story. It had life, and a delicate flickering humour, and a deep seriousness below; and it had little or no success. Those who were offended with Lawrence when he was serious, were offended with him for not being serious. Of course, Lawrence was as serious as ever, but in a different and most captivating way. He was celebrating his escape from the prison of his own deathly conclusions, declaring anew through the lips of Alvina Houghton his "faith in life." Alvina, in her effort to break free from the impoverished and thin-blooded gentility into which she had been born, becomes a maternity nurse. She goes back to her native town in the midland collieries and finds no patients; then she becomes involved in her father's last desperate commercial adventure as proprietor of a fourth-rate music-hall. There she meets Cicio, an Italian member of a cosmopolitan troupe of " Redskin" Indians — The Natcha-Kee-Tawaras — and eventually becomes his lover. With him she knows a true consummation; she suffers and surrenders. Even when he wants her against her will, still she surrenders.

There comes a moment when fate sweeps us away. Now Alvina felt herself swept — she knew not whither — but into a dusky region where men had dark faces and yellow eyes, where all speech was foreign, and life was not her life. It was as if she had fallen from her own world on to another, darker star, where meanings were all changed. She was alone, and did not mind being alone. It was what she wanted. In all the passion of her lover she had found a loneliness, beautiful, cool, like a shadow she had wrapped round herself and which gave her a sweetness of perfection. It was a moment of stillness and completeness.

Yet afterwards Cicio is a stranger to her, and Alvina feels herself, and is, disregarded. She leaves him, and the Natcha-Kee-Tawaras, and takes up a position as an official maternity nurse far away, in which capacity she attends Effie Tuke, the wife of a composer, and a good specimen of the feminine *intelligentsia*. But Cicio now feels the hunger for her: she *is* his woman. Catching sight of her by chance, he seeks her out, and serenades her with a despairing Neapolitan song — *Ma nun me lasciar*. He stands outside the house singing, as Effie Tuke's pains come on. The scene is beautifully done; Lawrence never more perfectly harmonized his symbolism and his realism. " Oh, the flesh is a *beastly* thing," cries Effie. " To make a man howl outside there like that, because you're here. And to make me howl because I've got a child in me. It's unbearable! " Alvina goes down to Cicio, and brings him up that Mrs. Tuke may see him. The pains come on again, and he departs.

" Nurse! " cried Effie. " It's no use trying to get a grip on life. You're just at the mercy of *Forces*," she shrieked angrily.

" Why not? " said Alvina. " There are good life-forces. Even the will of God is a life-force."

" You don't understand. I want to be *myself*. And I'm *not* myself. I'm just torn to pieces by *Forces*. It's horrible — "

" Well, it's not my fault. I didn't make the universe," said Alvina. " If you have to be torn to pieces by forces, well, you have. Other forces will put you together again."

" I don't want them to. I want to be myself. I don't want to be nailed together like a chair, with a hammer. I want to be myself."

" You won't be nailed together like a chair. You should have faith in life."

" But I hate life. It's nothing but a mass of forces. *I* am intelligent. Life isn't intelligent. Look at it at this moment. Do you call this intelligent? Oh — Oh! It's horrible! Oh — ! " She was wild and sweating with her pains. . . . The moment Mrs. Tuke recovered her breath she began again.

" I hate life, and faith, and such things. Faith is only fear. And life is a mass of unintelligent forces to which intelligent beings are submitted. Prostituted. Oh — oh!! — prostituted — "

" Perhaps life itself is something bigger than intelligence," said Alvina.

" Bigger than intelligence! " shrieked Effie. " *Nothing* is bigger than intelligence. Your man is a hefty brute. His yellow eyes *aren't* intelligent. They're *animal* — "

" No," said Alvina. " Something else. I wish he didn't attract me — "

And Alvina tries finally to escape. But Cicio follows her, and she accepts her destiny. There is a grain of Effie-like resistance left in her, that drives her to escape, but it is dissolved away, and she marries him. " There was no wonderful intimacy of speech, such as she had always imagined and always craved for. No. He loved her, but it was in a dark mesmeric way which did not let her be herself. . . ."

But "somewhere she was content. Somewhere, she was vastly proud of the dark veiled eternal loneliness she felt, under his shadow."

So Alvina submits to the "forces," that are not intelligent. She is the lost girl. And Cicio takes her away with him to his home in the Alban Mountains south of Rome; and there she suffers and endures. She is isolated among a half-savage peasantry, with only her deep and unspoken communion with Cicio to sustain her; and he half-lapses back into the indifference of a hopeless peasant life. The war breaks out. Even if he would, he cannot now return. He will be called up for service, and he awaits the summons with an unmindful indifference which goes near to breaking the life of Alvina who is with child. He cannot respond to her appeal for hope and faith. " You will come back, won't you? " she says and says again.

He sat motionless for a long while: while she undressed and brushed her hair and went to bed. And still he sat there unmoving, like a corpse. It was like having some unnatural, doomed, unbearable presence in the room. She blew out the light that she need not see him. But in the darkness it was worse.

At last he stirred — he rose. He came hesitating across to her.

" I'll come back, Allaye," he said quietly. " Be damned to them all." She heard unspeakable pain in his voice.

" To whom? " she said, sitting up.

He did not answer, but put his arms round her.

" I'll come back, and we'll go to America," he said.

" You'll come back to me," she whispered, in an ecstasy of pain and relief. It was not her affair, where they should go, so long as he really returned to her.

" I'll come back," he said.

᧒

The relation of that beautiful ending to the story told in " The Nightmare " is evident; we need not insist upon it.

In the last three chapters of *The Lost Girl* Lawrence's exquisite tenderness comes to a full and delicate flowering. The description of the bitter winter and the gleams of spring in the mountains is perfectly beautiful, yet not one whit more delicate than the picture of the human struggle which is, as it were, part of the same desperate beauty. Background and events are one. Whether or not it is true, as Alvina said, that men are so much masters of their fates that it depended on Cicio himself whether he should come back safe from the war, the issue with which he struggles with such pain is real. He is struggling not merely for faith, but to break forth finally from the ultimate apathy of peasant generations. His victory over himself is her victory; it is his surrender to her, as she has surrendered to him: and whether Cicio comes back or not, in actual destiny, the hard-won decision of his soul is a victory for the spirit of man, in whom there is no distinction of male or female. The last chapter of *The Lost Girl* is a declaration of faith, made with the subtle simplicity of genius.

Continually, throughout the story, appear indications of this curious and winsome change of temper in Lawrence. For this halcyon moment, at least, Lawrence is infinitely tolerant. He is kind, utterly kind, to his odd and pathetic and comical characters — to James Houghton, to Mr. May the impresario (who is obviously drawn from Maurice Magnus), to Miss Frost, and to Miss Pinnegar; he positively loves the Natcha-Kee-Tawara and their calculating, bourgeoise Kishwégin, who has yet the soul of an artist. And the implicit tolerance is explicitly asserted many times. It is the old fundamental wisdom of acknowledging that "it takes all sorts to make a world." Why condemn Alvina's ineffectual spendthrift father? " He should have been somebody else and not himself. Which is the *reductio ab absurdum* of idealism. The universe should be something else and not what it is: so the nonsense of Idealistic conclusion."

That is the doctrine of love, which has a flickering victory in Lawrence's soul at this moment of escape from the winter of his discontent. Not even the memory of his bitter years in Cornwall can embitter him when he makes the Natcha-Kee-Tawara suffer the attentions of police-spies. When Alvina leaves England with Cicio, she leaves it just as Lawrence had done in mid-winter, a few months before. It is the same picture of the "ash-grey, corpse-grey cliffs, and streaks of snow on the Downs above" that he was to draw again at the end of "The Nightmare."

Her heart died within her. Never had she felt so utterly strange and far-off. Cicio at her side was as nothing, as spell-bound she watched, away off, behind all the sunshine and the sea, the grey, snow-streaked substance of England slowly receding and sinking, submerging. She felt she could not believe it. It was like looking at something else. What? It was like a long ash-grey coffin, winter, slowly submerging in the sea. England?

But again there is no bitterness; so that one wonders whether Lawrence himself really felt quite all that unspeakable bitterness which he was afterwards to impute to himself in "The Nightmare." Was it perhaps all exaggerated in retrospect at the bidding of some deep desire to justify a rejection of England and his fellow-men about which his heart was never, and never could be, completely at ease? What is certain is that at this moment Lawrence buried what hatred he felt. He did not want to feel it now. Perhaps he wanted only to think of an England untouched by the war. But the same desire to remember only things lovely and of good report is manifest in his magnificent chapters on their life in the Alban Mountains. In reality, Lawrence had but just made trial of the Alban mountains in the winter of 1919, and fled away beaten by the vigours of the climate and the people. He tells us so in the *Memoirs of Magnus*. It was too grim; and he fled to Capri. What he could not endure, Alvina Houghton could not have endured.

Nor, even in the story, is she expected to endure it for ever. " I'll come back," says Cicio at the last, " and we'll go to America." And this choice of Cicio's is meant to be significant. With it he conquers his own mindless apathy. There is no return for conscious man back to the mindless world, Lawrence is saying, and recanting his own immediate past; man must go on and on. In the final chapters of *The Lost Girl* he says it plainly enough. First, he makes Alvina feel the nostalgia, the temptation to return. The same spell of the pre-mental world that was upon Lawrence himself in Cornwall is upon Alvina in the Alban Mountains.

How unspeakably lovely it was, no one could ever tell, the grand, pagan twilight of the valleys, savage, cold, with a sense of ancient gods who knew the right for human sacrifice. It stole away the soul of Alvina. She felt transfigured in it, clairvoyant in another mystery of life. A savage hardness came in her heart. The gods who had demanded human sacrifice were right, immutably right. The fierce, savage gods who dipped their lips in blood, these were the true gods. . . . And a wild terrible happiness would take hold of her, beyond despair, but very like despair. No one would ever find her. She had gone beyond the world into the pre-world, she had reopened in the old eternity.

The peasants are kind to her, and she is deceived by their kindness. Cicio, and his old uncle Pancrazio, who has lived in England and " has known the social confidence of England and who, coming back, is deeply injured by the ancient malevolence of the hill-peasantry," undeceive her. The peasants are kind to her, but it is not with a human kindness, of brother to brother or sister to sister. They are kind to her, as savages would be kind to a strange divinity who had visited them; they serve her, because they think she will go away again. They see in her what Pancrazio sees, " a fairness, a luminousness in the northern soul, something free, touched with divinity, such as ' these people here ' lacked entirely." They serve, and revere her, because she is distinct — the promise or symbol of a fuller, freer life. If once she becomes merged into them, if she becomes a denizen instead of a visitant, they will serve her no longer; she will be the victim of their ancient and inhuman malevolence.

So the glamorous pre-mental world unsheathes its fangs. Alvina's temptation to return to it gives place to a revulsion.

The more she wandered, the more the shadow of the bygone pagan world seemed to come over her. Sometimes she felt she would shriek and go mad, so strong was the influence on her, something pre-world and, it seemed to her now, vindictive. She seemed to feel in the air strange Furies, Lemures, things that had haunted her with their tomb-frenzied vindictiveness since she was a child. . . . Black and cruel presences were in the under-air. They were furtive and slinking. They bewitched you with loveliness, and lurked with fangs to hurt you afterwards. There it was: the fangs sheathed in beauty: the beauty first, and then, horribly, inevitably, the fangs.

"You will not stop here," says a young Italian to her. " Nobody young can stop here." And she knows the word is true. The pre-mental world is a sub-human world. Alvina enters the darkness of a church and recoils in horror from the " repulsive fetish-worship." As was the inside of the church, so were the inward souls of the people, dark, degraded and repulsive. Only those were truly human who longed to escape, and were resolved to escape: of whom, by his final choice, Cicio is one.

So *The Lost Girl* marks a decisive moment. It records Lawrence's own revulsion against his former nostalgia. A man must not put off his humanity; the allurement of the pre-mental world is a temptation, a lure to death.

The pre-mental world has failed him: the lapse back from the human consciousness offers no solution. But the problem remains. What is the problem? In universal terms, it is the fundamental human problem of the divided being of man. Be fully conscious, fully sensitive, and the spectacle of the human universe drives you to isolation and despair; seek to become unconscious, insensitive, and a sense of degradation and betrayal takes hold of you. In personal terms, it is the problem of Lawrence's effort to achieve his own unity. He had been seeking refuge from his own division the communion of mindlessness. He had found that it was not possible. He had sought a mindless communion with Buryan, yet he had looked in it for loyalty — no mindless quality — and had been bitterly grieved because he had not found it. The mindless human being is malevolent.

ఌ

Lawrence fled to Capri from the Alban Mountains. The longing for communion remained. Within a week or two he went to the great Benedictine monastery at Monte Cassino. Perhaps the Roman Catholic Church is the answer to the problem. The story of that visit in January 1920 is told in the *Memoirs of Magnus*. I remember that, in the winter of 1923, Lawrence told me that he thought that introduction was the best thing he had ever written. Indeed, as a piece of writing it is magnificent. But I think the importance he attached to it was due less to the mastery of his medium which it showed than to the fact that it contained the record of a crucial experience in Lawrence's life. Magnus was the occasion of Lawrence's being invited to Monte Cassino.

It is evident that Lawrence wanted to go; he was looking

for something, and he felt it might be there. It was not there. Lawrence had meant to stay a week, and he stayed only a day or two. But those two days were days of intense realisation and intense suffering. He describes his first morning at the monastery.

It was a sunny day. I looked down on the farm-cluster and the brown fields and the sere oak woods of the hill-crown, and the rocks and the bushes savagely bordering it round. Beyond the mountains with their snow were blue-glistery with sunshine, and seemed quite near, but across a gulf. All was still and sunny. And the poignant grip of the past, the grandiose, violent past of the Middle Ages, when blood was strong and unquenched and life was flamboyant with splendours and horrible miseries, took hold of me till I could hardly bear it. It was really agony to me to be in the monastery and to see the old farm and the bullocks slowly walking in the fields below, and the black pigs rooting among weeds, and to see a monk sitting on a parapet in the sun, and an old, old man in skin sandals and white bunched, swathed legs come driving an ass slowly to the monastery gate, slowly, with all that lingering nonchalance and wildness of the Middle Ages, and yet to know that I was myself, child of the present. It was so strange from Magnus' window to look down on the plain and see the white road going straight past a mountain that stood like a loaf of sugar, the river meandering in loops, and the railway with glistening lines making a long black swoop across the flat and into the hills. To see trains come steaming, with white smoke flying. To see the station like a little harbour where trucks like shipping stood anchored in rows in the black bay of railway. To see trains stop in the station and tiny people swarming like flies! To see all this from the monastery, where the Middle Ages live on in a sort of agony, like Tithonus, and cannot die, this was almost a violation to my soul, made almost a wound.

The Church, too, like the pre-mental world, is past. It represented a great victory of the human spirit over the pre-mental world; but the victory was won long ago, and it is not the Church which maintains that victory to-day, but the fully conscious individual soul. The Church in its relation to the souls of the pre-mental world was majestic and divine, positive and true. Lawrence feels it, and sees it.

They were the old-world peasants still about the monastery, with the hard, small bony heads and deep-lined faces and utterly blank minds, crying their speech as crows cry, and living their lives as lizards among the rocks, blindly going on with the little job in hand, the present moment, cut off from all past and future, and having no idea and no sustained emotion, only that eternal will-to-live which makes a tortoise wake up once more in spring, and makes a grasshopper whistle in the moonlight nights even of November. Only these peasants don't whistle much. The whistlers go to America. It is the hard, static, unhoping souls that persist in the old life. And still they stand back, as one passes them in the corridors of the great monastery, they press themselves back against the white-washed walls of the still place, and drop their heads, as if some mystery were passing by, some God-mystery, the higher beings, which they must not look closely upon.

But that reverence belongs, like the static unhoping souls who alone now truly feel it, to the past. Other men, cursed or blessed with the privilege of mentality, can feel it only by a deliberate effort of will, and therefore cannot feel it at all. The feeling is antiquarian, or aesthetic, or nostalgic; it is a feeling contrived and imposed, never immediate and incontrovertible. No localisation of the God-mystery is possible any more.

The relation of the Church to the peasant is a past relation; it endures only as an anachronism. And the Church, like the peasant, is slowly disappearing from the world. The relation of the Church to an intellectual Catholic like Magnus was an utterly different thing, mental, forced and spurious. In the conversation between the two men the issue is defined. Lawrence feels and knows that he is superior to the peasant and Magnus is not. The peasant is superior to Magnus simply because he lacks the intellectual complacency of which Magnus was so proud. It is not the lack of mentality that makes the peasant superior; in that he lacks mentality he is indeed Magnus' inferior, but when that mentality is corrupted by complacency, by the persuasion that it is supreme, then the lack of it becomes a virtue by comparison. Lawrence is superior to the peasant, because he has mentality, and because his mentality is not corrupted by complacency. He says to Magnus:

" And if I think myself superior to the peasant, it is only that I feel myself like the growing tip, or one of the growing tips of the tree, and him like a piece of the hard, fixed tissue of the branch or trunk. We're part of the same tree: and it's the same sap."

" Why, exactly! Exactly! " cried Magnus. " Of course! The Church would teach the same doctrine. We are all one in Christ — but between our souls and our duties there are great differences."

It is terrible to be agreed with, especially by a man like Magnus. All that one says, and means, turns to nothing.

Though Magnus was in himself an inadequate representative of the Church, as a spokesman he is adequate. The communion of souls is not the communion that Lawrence desired and strove for. He wanted a communion of souls, also; but what he meant by a man's soul was utterly different from what the Church, or Magnus, meant by it. For Lawrence, when he was true to his own vision, a man's soul was the man in his wholeness, in the integrity of his achieved and total being — not that spiritual element which is in opposition to the physical and openly or tacitly denies the physical, but the unity born of the acknowledgment of both. The Church was right in the great days when it asserted the spiritual against the physical, because in those days the co-equality of the spiritual was not acknowledged. The victory of the Church was then a victory for Man. But now the other scale has tipped the beam. It was no longer the physical which overwhelmed the spiritual, but the spiritual was crushing the physical. The Church made absolute and eternal a momentary and necessary assertion. Therefore it is rejected, ignorantly but instinctively by the unthinking masses, in full consciousness by Lawrence. What was wisdom once is wisdom no longer; because there is no absolute wisdom; there is wisdom for the moment and the age.

What the Church was once to the mass of mankind, something must be to the mass of men to-day. There must be a new and different Church, with its new and different evangel; there must be new prophets, new leaders. Not " great negators like Lloyd George or Lenin or Briand," whose power is based upon a lie — the lie of the equality of men. These are the time-servers, the demagogues, men whose travesty of power depends on filling the deluded masses with the conceit of their own equality. " I don't believe," says Lawrence to Magnus, " that the lower classes can ever make life whole again, till they *do* become humble like the old peasants, and yield themselves to real leaders." Lawrence felt that he was one; and he might have been one.

Such were the thoughts in his mind as he looked down from Monte Cassino. There in the railway below, with the socialistic and anarchic railwaymen, was the modern world — industrialism, democracy, communism, fascism.

And here above . . . we were in the Middle Ages. Both worlds were agony to me. But here on the top was the worst: the past, the poignancy of the not-quite-dead past.

" I think one's got to go through with the life down there — get somewhere beyond it. One can't go back," I said to him.

" One can't go back." This was the realisation from which Lawrence was suffering so intensely at Monte Cassino. His ways of escape were being cut off. As there was no return to the pre-Christian world, so there was none to the Christian: neither paganism nor the Church offered a way out. The past was dead, and the way to the future lay " through the life down there," which was agony. No wonder he felt " as if his heart had once more broken." He didn't know why, he says. But we know why. Monte Cassino was a crucial experience. He stared nakedly into his own destiny. He came down from the mountain, broken-hearted, and crossed back to Capri.

There on the steamer I sat in a bit of sunshine, and felt that again the world had come to an end for me, and again my heart was broken. The steamer seemed to be making its way away from the old world, that had come to another end in me.

It was after this I decided to go to Sicily.

II

SICILY AND SARDINIA

*C*OELUM *non animum mutant qui trans mare currunt.*
Lawrence would have denied the truth of Horace's sentence.
He asserted that different countries changed the very constitution of his blood. If it was so, indeed — how could he
know? — and not a form of emphatic asseveration of his
quick imaginative response, then his soul was more independent of the physical body than he believed it was, for
it is certain that Lawrence's soul was not much changed by
his constant voyaging. In each new place the story was the
same. At first enchantment, then disillusion. The inward
hunger seems to be satisfied; then the pangs of yearning
are felt again.

So with Sicily, where he settled himself at Taormina.
He was enchanted with the new-old Grecian world.

In early April I went with my wife to Syracuse for a few days:
lovely, lovely days, with the purple anemones blowing in the
Sicilian fields, and Adonis-blood red in the little ledges, and the
corn rising strong and green in the magical, malarial places, and
Etna flowing now to the northward, still with her crown of snow.
The lovely, lovely journey from Catania to Syracuse, in spring,
winding round the blueness of that sea, where the tall pink
asphodel was dying, and the yellow asphodel like a lily showing
her silk. Lovely, lovely Sicily, the dawn-place, Europe's dawn,
with Odysseus pushing his ship out of the shadows into the blue.

Whatever had died for me, Sicily had then not died: dawn-lovely Sicily, and the Ionian Sea.

We came back, and the world was lovely: our own house above the almond trees, and the sea in the cove below. Calabria glimmering like a changing opal away to the left, across the blue, bright straits, and all the great blueness of the lovely dawn-sea in front, where the sun rose with a splendour like trumpets every morning, and rejoicing like a madness in this dawn, the dawn which is Greece, which is me.

It recalls the fancy with which Rupert Birkin charmed Ursula Brangwen, of a lovely silent world with no human beings in it, for Sicily, like the Alban Mountains, proves to be a place where every prospect pleases and only man is vile. In the late summer, from August to mid-October, Lawrence went north into Germany, where he wrote *Fantasia of the Unconscious* amid the trees of the Black Forest, at Ebersteinburg. Of that book we shall speak presently. Let him settle his account with Sicily first. He returned from Germany to Taormina in mid-October 1920. He had scarcely arrived, when he must move again, this time to Sardinia, but anywhere away from " these maddening, exasperating, impossible Sicilians, who never knew what truth was, and have long lost all notion of what a human being is." Etna is at the bottom of it, he says in *Sea and Sardinia*. " Unless a man is very strong, she takes his soul away from him and leaves him not a beast, but an elemental creature, intelligent and soulless. Intelligent, almost inspired, and soulless, like the Etna Sicilians." But when we come to think of it, there is no Etna in the Alban Mountains, where the people were also soulless and malevolent; and there is no Etna in Cornwall, where the people were also malevolent and soulless. The truth seems to be that Etna has very little to do with it. The simple fact is that Lawrence did not like soulless people at all.

That was a pity, for he felt he ought to like them. He wanted to like them; in theory, it was necessary he should like them. But in fact, he just did not. And that was awkward, so awkward that he is rather shy of confessing it. As, for example, when he admits that the Sicilians are " maddening, exasperating, and impossible "; then he feels he must withdraw. " Let me confess in parenthesis that I am not at all sure that I don't really prefer these demons to our sanctified humanity." The Lawrence who is not at all sure is not the Lawrence in his habit as he lived; he is the Lawrence whom Lawrence would like to be, but unfortunately is not. " Ugh! those Sicilians! " says the actual Lawrence, though the ideal and demonic Lawrence tries to put his hand over his mouth. In his first transport of enthusiasm for the Sardinians, which lasts till the end of his first day's journey in the island, he believes them to be open and downright — in fact, the " noble savages " whom so many idealists and romanticists before Lawrence have hoped to find. The socialism of the Sardinian railwayman, even, is the socialism of the simple savage, utterly unlike the socialism of the Sicilian. The Sicilian is " much too old in our culture to swallow Socialism whole: much too ancient and ruse not to be sophisticated about any and every belief. He'll go off like a squib; and then he'll smoulder acridly and sceptically even against his own fire. One sympathises with him in retrospect. But in daily life it is unbearable."

What it comes to is this: that the actual Lawrence was a man to whom in daily life it was unbearable that his surrounding human beings should be less human than himself. They had to be as tender, as sensitive as he was himself, or he began to suffocate. Theoretically, he had no use for the Christian virtues, but since in fact he possessed most of them in abundance, he was difficult to satisfy. His mind and heart were hopelessly at odds with one another. His mind did the " sympathising in retrospect " with the " non-human, ancient-souled " Sicilians; the heart by which he worked in daily life found them unbearable.

Of course, he was always ashamed of his heart. It tells him that the Sicilians are " suave and completely callous." But it must not be indulged. In the train, as he goes to Palermo, on the way to Sardinia, the little girl servant of a couple of stupid Sicilians is sick. Her master and mistress ignore her; their only visible concern is that she should not be sick over them. Particularly since the little girl has a charming, virginal face, Lawrence and his wife are concerned for her. But that is an unworthy feeling, and Lawrence pulls himself up. " Their naturalness," he says, " is unnatural to us. Yet I am sure it is best. Sympathy would only complicate matters and spoil that strange, remote, virginal quality." In short, it is best to be one of the suave and completely callous demons; but, unfortunately, Lawrence cannot stand their company.

✍

Perhaps in no single book of Lawrence's is this inward uncertainty and division more naively exposed than in *Sea and Sardinia*. At the first contact, escaping from the suave and callous demons of Sicily, he is enchanted with the Sardinians. At Cagliari, at the Scala di Ferro, the people seem " warm and good-natured, like human beings "; at Mandas, one day's journey northwards, they " still seem to have the downright mind." The native costume rouses him to raptures. " How fascinating, after the soft Italians, to see these limbs in their close knee-breeches, so definite, so manly, with the old fierceness in them still! " In the rest of Italy, in the rest of the world, " The hardy, indomitable male is gone." Here, in Sardinia, " men don't idealize women . . .

here they don't make those great leering eyes, the inevitable
yours-to-command look of Italian males. . . . Give me the
old salty way of love! " It is almost bewildering, to remember that a few months before, in *The Lost Girl,* he was
celebrating the Italian male, with his soft yearning yellow
eyes, in the person of Cicio. Then the Italian male was the
very perfection of masculinity; now, he is nothing, worse
than nothing, with " his great leering eyes." Off with the old
love, and on with the new. " I love my indomitable coarse
men from mountain Sardinia for their stocking-caps and
their strange animal-bright stupidity." But we have learned
to be very wary of Lawrence's enthusiasm for " animal-
bright stupidity "; it does not last. The men of Cornwall
had it, the men of Pescocalascio had it, the men of Sicily
had it, but it did not save them. Probably, in the case of the
Sardinians, it is not the animal-bright stupidity, but the
costume which kindles him. It wakes in him " a great heart-
yearning for something I have known " — not in actuality,
but in some former incarnation — " and which I want back
again." " Give us back," he cries again, " the scarlet and
gold, and devil take the hindermost." The distinctive, national costume is, indeed, for him not merely a present
delight to the eye, but a symbol of a revulsion against democratic uniformity and a mechanic civilization. Unfortunately, in the Sardinians themselves it does not represent
such a revulsion; they have not passed beyond democratic
uniformity, they have not reached it. They are beneath, not
beyond, the civilization which is as necessary to Lawrence
as to any other man who has inherited it.

By the end of forty-eight hours from having set foot on
Sardinian soil he is in a fury of rage at the foulness and
squalor of his bedroom at Sorgono. He had expected so much
of Sorgono and he found so little that he was consumed
with rage. The old jeering contrast, for which by now one

would have imagined him at least prepared, devastates him once more. " Real fresh wonder-beauty all around. And such humanity! " Half the brief journey over, and the Sardinian human-being is finished for Lawrence. On the way to Nuoro, in the motor-omnibus, the scales fall finally from his eyes.

The people crowd around — and many of them in very ragged costume. They look poor, and not attractive: perhaps a bit degenerate. It would seem as if the Italian instinct to get into rapid touch with the world were the healthy instinct after all. For in these isolated villages, which have been since time began far from any life-centre, there is an almost sordid look on the faces of the people.

Yet not more than a dozen pages before he had been " rather wishing " that the motor-omnibus had never been introduced into Sardinia, and that the country would lapse back into inaccessibility again. But these " hardy indomitable males," who flourish in their inaccessible mountains, turn out on closer contact to be savage and sordid and repulsive, like the landlord of the Risveglio at Sorgono. It is the men who are in closest contact with mechanical civilization who are kind and generous and human — the omnibus-drivers, the travelling merchants, even a disreputable pedlar like the *girovago*. Lawrence stops at a lovely mediaeval village, Orosei, and tries to buy bread. The people are horribly rude to him, and he laments Orosei over the wonderful — " yet there it is with a few grumpy inhabitants who won't even give you a crust of bread. And probably there is malaria — almost sure. And it would be hell to have to live there for a month." Further on, at Siniscola, he meets the same rudeness in the waiting-woman of the inn. " It is not meant to be offensive: yet it is so. Truly it is just uncouthness. But when one is tired and hungry. . ." Involuntarily to the mind comes: " I was hungry, and ye gave me to eat

. . . naked, and ye clothed me." It is the Christian tenderness which Lawrence requires. But when one of the
omnibus-men gently says of the uncouth savages at the
Sorgono inn that they are " ignorant," they don't *know* any
better, Lawrence is furious. There you are: that is the
modern Italian spirit — " endless pity for the ignorant. It
is only slackness." What would not be slackness would be
to fling a bottle at the head of the innkeeper. Excellent it
may be in theory, but why did not Lawrence himself begin
the good work of reform?

و

Sea and Sardinia is a lively, and often a lovely book, but
it seethes with weak and childish contradictions. Lawrence's
right hand does not know, or seems not to know, what his
left hand is doing. No doubt he would reply that he wrote as
he felt, and he felt as he wrote. If the feelings are inconsistent and even mutually destructive — well, it was so. It is
a poor defence, for one of the most precious elements of that
humanity which Lawrence desires to find in men is the
resolve to make one's thoughts and emotions harmonious.
To desire contradictory things is childish and petulant, less
than human. Lawrence, naturally, was well aware of it. He
rejected the peasants at Monte Cassino because " they had
no idea, no sustained emotion "; he knew the necessity of
these two things. But in *Sea and Sardinia* he makes no attempt himself to achieve them.

Behind its bewildering inconsequence lies the fact that
Lawrence is burking a vital decision. This decision, which
he is avoiding, has its objective and subjective forms; inevitably, because it is really vital. Objectively, it is the
dilemma which caused him such agony of soul at Monte
Cassino. He could not return to the past; he could not go

forward with the life that is. Yet he must " go through with the life down there — get beyond it." And the first step towards that bitter progress had been simply to escape once more — to Sicily. Sicily was the way of life, for a few months; it failed. Then Sardinia; it failed. These blessed countries which seemed to offer a more or less total escape from " the life down there " contain no human beings. And Lawrence found them intolerable. The question that stared him in the face at Monte Cassino stared him in the face again; and no more than before did he want to answer it. For whichever way he answered it a surrender, a sacrifice was demanded.

The question was this: Did he really accept, or did he really reject, modern life — life into which, fitfully and weakly, but yet finally, the spirit of love has entered? If he really rejected it, and chose to return to a condition of life more primitive, pre-mental, pre-Christian, would he abide by the consequences, would he accept the sordidness, the malevolence, the uncouthness of it? Actually, he would not abide by the consequences. They horrified and disgusted him. But neither would he accept modern life. That also horrified and disgusted him. He did not want to " go through with it." Now, manifestly, to accept modern life in any sense in which such acceptance was possible for Lawrence could not mean to cease from seeking to change it. Lawrence was essentially a prophet and a reformer. The only acceptance that could reasonably be required of him was that he should accept the facts of the situation, and offer remedies which were possible or at least conceivable. And this acceptance, of the limitations of the actual, *was* required of him; it was required of him that he should restrain his thought within the limits of the possible.

Lawrence could not bring himself to do that. He would not accept the essentials of the human situation as it existed in the world or in himself. He wanted to run with the hare and hunt with the hounds; to be able to extol the pre-mental as an ideal, and to denounce it as experienced fact. And this objective situation reflected an inward irresolution. Lawrence was actually permeated with the Christian virtues: he was tender, sympathetic, loving to an extreme degree. But mentally he was in a condition of violent reaction against these " spiritual " virtues; he wanted to be " a hardy and indomitable male," and he was always trying to dream himself into the part. He looks at his Sardinian mountaineers with their women and cries " Give me the old salty way of love! " whereas in fact the old salty way of love was quite impossible for him. In other words, he could not accept the fact of his own nature. He wanted to be a different man, and quite forgot that if he had been the " hardy and indomitable male " of his dreams, he would have been quite devoid of that exceptional human sensitiveness, that " more than ordinary organic sensibility " which made him precious to his fellowmen.

Just as in himself he could not be rid of this excessive hankering after a form of masculinity which he did not possess, and could not have possessed except by the loss of the other rarer qualities which were the very man; so in his imagination of the world he could not put away the hankering after bygone forms of life. He could not give up his dream. In a moment of clarity, as at Monte Cassino, he sees that there is no going backward; but he cannot accept the fact. He wants to go back, and as far as it is humanly possible, he will go back — to Sicily, to Sardinia. The callousness of the one, the squalor of the other, is intolerable.

Where now shall he look for a way of life that will satisfy him? That is the real object of his restless search — a country where he can feel himself profoundly at one with his fellow-men, where he can be whole, and be part of a whole. We can prophesy with certainty that the country will never be found. For the desires in himself that it has to satisfy are contradictory. Unless he will make himself a whole, he will never find the whole of which he can be a part.

Ᏸ

For the moment there is a pause. Italy, Sicily, Sardinia — all have failed. The rainbow begins to shine over America, and Lawrence has conceived the idea that he will make his way round the world. Europe is finished now, as England was finished; but the ways and means of leaving it are not yet forthcoming. In a page of *Sea and Sardinia* Lawrence takes stock of the position.

One begins to realise how old the real Italy is, how man-gripped and how withered. England is far more wild and savage and lonely in her country parts. Here since endless centuries man has tamed the impossible mountain side into terraces, he has quarried the rock, he has fed his sheep among the thin woods, he has cut his boughs and burned his charcoal, he has been half-domesticated even among the wildest fastnesses. This is what is so attractive about the remote places, the Abruzzi, for example. Life is so primitive, so pagan, so strangely heathen and half-savage. And yet it is human life. And the wildest country is half-humanised, half brought under. It is all conscious. Wherever one is in Italy, either one is conscious of the present, or of the mediaeval influences, or of the far, mysterious gods of the early Mediterranean. Wherever one is, the place has its conscious genius. Man has lived there and brought forth his consciousness there and in some way brought that place to consciousness, and, really, finished it. The expression may be Proserpine, or Pan, or even the strange shrouded gods of the Etruscans or the Sikels, none the less it is an expression. The land has been humanised through and through: and we in our own tissued consciousness bear the results of this humanisation. So that for us to go to Italy and to *penetrate* into Italy is like a most fascinating act of self-discovery — back, back, back, down the old way of time. Strange and wonderful chords awake in us, and vibrate again after many hundreds of years of complete forgetfulness.

And then — and then — there is a final feeling of sterility. It is all worked out. It is all known: *connu, connu!*

This Sunday morning, seeing the frost among the tangled, still savage bushes of Sardinia, my soul thrilled again. This was not all known. This was not all worked out. Life was not only a process of rediscovering backwards. It is that, also: and it is that intensely. Italy has given me back I know not what of myself, but a very, very great deal. She has found for me so much that was lost, like a restored Osiris. But this morning in the omnibus I realise that, apart from the great rediscovery backwards, which one *must* make before one can be whole at all, there is a move forwards. There are unknown, unworked lands where the salt has not lost its savour. But one must have perfected oneself in the great past first.

If we judge Lawrence by Remy de Gourmont's dictum that the whole effort of a sincere man is to make his personal impressions into universal laws, Lawrence was a prodigy of sincerity. But really there seems no reason why men, in order to become whole, must first have perfected themselves in the great past in Lawrence's particular way. No doubt it is a good way, and no doubt an imaginative realisation of the past out of which we come is necessary to a fully developed consciousness; it is a means to self-knowledge: but Lawrence's particular method of attaining it demands a mobility, a lack of entanglement in ordinary responsibilities which few men possess. If to be free from domestic ties, and to have a means of livelihood which can be exercised in any place, are an indispensable condition of being whole most men must resign themselves to permanent incompleteness.

But this is only another example of Lawrence's habit of false generalisation. The significance of his words lies elsewhere: in his declaration that the move forwards must be taken in a land which is unknown — unknown, that is, in Lawrence's particular sense, a land which has not been mastered by the human spirit, nor given expression by a human culture. Such lands are few: no part of the East will satisfy this condition. There is Australia, there is America. It is to those lands that Lawrence in spirit was now turning. Perhaps, I do not know (for I had no correspondence with him at this time), he had already formed the resolution to journey to America by way of Australia.

What was in his mind? I think nothing less than to be the founder of a culture in one of these " unknown," not yet humanised lands: to be the Moses, the law-giver, who should bring its soul to consciousness. An exorbitant dream, it will surely seem to some; and yet, I think, no one who really knew Lawrence and has some faith in the creative human spirit would look on his dream as in itself fantastic. I can only say that Lawrence was the most remarkable man I have ever known; and if it be true, as I believe it is true, that individual men have changed the current of human destiny, then there was no manifest reason why Lawrence should not have been such a man. If the Mahatma Gandhi can convulse and revivify an empire, then on the surface at least there was no reason why Lawrence should not give laws to a people.

On the surface, no reason at all. Those who dismiss Lawrence's dream as fantastic and savouring of megalomania are simply lacking in imagination. But beneath the surface, there was a very certain reason why the dream should remain only a dream. Lawrence was completely divided between love and hatred. He was impatient of his fellow-men, and he was impatient of any sacrifice of his own freedom.

A leader of men must be tolerant, and he must subdue himself to his followers; he is the head of a body, and he must never forget the body, by which and in which alone he has his being as a leader. This essential and instinctive self-submission was completely alien to Lawrence's nature. He was impatient of himself; how could he be patient of others?

The dream was destined to remain a dream. Lawrence was not the stuff of which the leader of men is made. But at this moment I am sure the dream haunted him. Perhaps it was a dream of being a leader in America. America had received his novel *Women in Love* almost with enthusiasm; it could not yet be even published in England. The reception of *Women in Love* in America was his first taste of popular success, and it was to remain his greatest " success " to the end. His publisher in America was eager to have more of his work, ready for anything he would write. It was directly to an American audience that Lawrence accordingly addressed a full statement of his own beliefs. *Psycho-Analysis and the Unconscious* and *Fantasia of the Unconscious* were published in America in 1921 and 1922, years before they were published in England. *Fantasia of the Unconscious* was written in Germany in the summer of 1920, before the journey to Sardinia.

III

FANTASIA OF THE UNCONSCIOUS

LAWRENCE'S *Fantasia of the Unconscious* is his greatest book; and, absolutely, it is a great book. I have read it many times since he first sent it to me in the spring of 1923. Then I read it with an instant quickening of the life that is within; and every time I have read it since, the same sense of instant quickening has returned. I cannot doubt that it will be a fountain of life for many years to come, and to generations yet unborn.

Obviously, it grew out of his shorter book, *Psycho-Analysis and the Unconscious*. Whether it was a direct and immediate continuation of that little book I cannot say. I do not know precisely when *Psycho-Analysis and the Unconscious* was written. *Fantasia of the Unconscious* was written in the mid-summer of 1920, and I imagine the smaller book was written shortly before that.

The importance of these books, which are really one, is two-fold. They are a deliberate statement of his philosophy; and they are an essential commentary on his imaginative work. In the preface to the *Fantasia,* written after the book was finished, he adds " one last weary little word."

This pseudo-philosophy of mine . . . is deduced from the novels and poems, not the reverse. The novels and poems come unwatched out of one's pen. And then the absolute need which

one has for some sort of satisfactory mental attitude towards oneself and things in general makes one try to abstract some definite
conclusions from one's experiences as a writer and as a man. The
novels and poems are pure passionate experience. These " polly-
analytics " are inferences made afterwards from the experience.

That is not quite clear. But by saying the novels and the
poems are pure passionate experience Lawrence meant that
the essential substance of them was his own immediate experience. Lawrence's work was, indeed, almost wholly autobiographical. There was a certain amount of artistic trans-
position, of the kind which we showed in *The Rainbow* and
in *Women in Love,* and occasionally, as perhaps in *The Lost
Girl,* the situation and characters may have been partly invented: but that was exceptional. The " pure passionate experience " of which he speaks in his preface does not include
that passionate exercise of the disinterested imagination in
the creation of human characters which is probably the
perfection of the art of literature. It is not that Lawrence
was incapable of it; though I do not think his capacities
were very great. Certainly he seldom cared to make use of
them. At bottom, he was not interested in art.

That is generally held to have been his shortcoming; he
was not enough of " the artist." I hold, on the contrary, it is
a proof of his eminence. He really did tower by a head and
shoulders above his contemporaries by this very recognition
that the necessary conditions of great " art " are lacking in
our age. Unless society is an organic unity, in which the
artist feels and knows himself spiritually secure, the undis-
turbed concentration of his artistic faculty upon the created
object is impossible. The necessary condition of great art is
that the artist should be able to take elemental things for
granted. The artist needs to serve an authority which he
acknowledges to be greater than himself, whether it be God

or King or both together; he does not question the powers that be. Then, and then alone, is he free to be an artist, with all his heart and all his mind and all his soul. These conditions do not exist to-day, and they will not exist for a long time to come. The artist to-day finds no spiritual authority which he instinctively acknowledges. If he acknowledges any it is the authority of Art itself, which is mere wordy nonsense. Art is not an authority, it is the means by which authority may be revealed and expressed. So that the artist who is conscious enough to be capable of great art is inevitably involved in the endeavor to discover or to create the authority without which his activity as artist is either trivial or anarchic.

Lawrence intuitively grasped the situation; he understood it better than any other artist of his time. He gave up, deliberately, the pretence of being an artist. The novel became for him simply a means by which he could make explicit his own " thought-adventures," the poem a means for uttering immediate experience. His aim was to discover authority, not to create art. Therefore to criticise him for not doing what he never intended to do is stupid; and it implies an inability to rise to the level of Lawrence's own comprehension. To charge him with a lack of form, or of any other of the qualities which are supposed to be necessary to art, is to be guilty of irrelevance. Art was not Lawrence's aim. It might have been, if the world had been different. To say or to imply that it ought to have been his aim, is to reveal oneself ignorant of the fundamental necessities which Lawrence knew.

Much better " art " has been produced by Lawrence's contemporaries; books better shaped, novels more objectively conceived, poems more concentrated. Beside Lawrence's work they seem frigid and futile. It is simply that they are not commensurate with our deep needs of to-day.

Our modern art is all obviously, irremediably minor. And it must necessarily be minor, so long as its aim is to be art. There is, and always will be, a place for minor art; but to produce it is not the function of a major soul. Lawrence was a major soul.

Hence the supreme importance in the work of one who is known by externals chiefly as a writer of novels and poems, of two books which are neither of these things. In actual fact, Lawrence was neither a great novelist nor a great poet: probably he had the gifts necessary for preëminence in both kinds, but the times in which he lived, the struggles in which he was involved, were such that he was compelled to use those gifts for other ends. That he recognised the compulsion where others did not is simply evidence of his superiority over them. But he was not a great artist. He was a prophet, a psychologist, a philosopher, what you will — but more than any other single thing, the great life-adventurer of modern times.

∽

Fantasia of the Unconscious is his gospel. Its first section (for so we must regard *Psycho-Analysis and the Unconscious*) begins quietly with a radical criticism of the psycho-analytical theories of Freud. What is " the unconscious " in reality, Lawrence asks? Is it something which is pre-conscious and pristine, or is it the place or condition in which exist desires stimulated by the mind but rejected by the moral consciousness? Is a repression a repressed passional impulse, or is it an idea which we suppress and disown? The question is of real importance, for if " the unconscious " of Freud is really the substrata of consciousness, then we must accept the fact of an insuperable division in ourselves. Consciousness *must* repudiate this Freudian unconscious, and the Freudian theory that by bringing the content of the unconscious into consciousness we liberate and annihilate these suppressed desires is false. All that can be done, if the Freudian theory is true, is deliberately to indulge the outlawed desires that lurk in the unconscious; and consciousness must rebel against this degradation. The last state is worse than the first. " This motivizing of the passional sphere from the ideal," says Lawrence, " is the final peril of human consciousness. It is the death of all spontaneous creative life, and the substituting of the mechanical principle."

Lawrence knows something of this peril; he encountered it in the experience recorded in *Women in Love*. The imagined consummation of Rupert and Ursula belonged precisely to this order. And at this point in his argument the accent of personal experience is plainly to be heard. Consider the example which he gives:

A man finds it impossible to realise himself in marriage. He recognises the fact that his emotional, even passional, regard for his mother is deeper than it ever could be for a wife. This makes him unhappy, for he knows that passional communion is not complete unless it be also sexual. He has a body of sexual passion which he cannot transfer to a wife. He has a profound love for his mother. Shut in between the walls of tortured and increasing passion, he must find some escape or fall down the pit of insanity or death. . . . And so the incest-motive is born.

There is the situation that underlay *Sons and Lovers,* and whose effects persisted long afterwards in the situation that underlay *Woman in Love.* What I have experienced, says Lawrence, is an extreme case of a condition now general. " Incest is the logical conclusion of our ideals, when these ideals have to be carried into passional effect." That is his way of saying that the demand for love made by the modern

mother upon the modern son, or the modern father upon
the modern daughter prematurely and viciously stimulates
the child's passional nature, and so incapacitates it from
entering into a true sex-relation. Further, even if, by the aid
of psycho-analysis, a modern man realises his condition, the
problem remains: the talk of " sublimation " is nonsense.
" We have still to find some way out. For there we are, all
of us, trapped in a corner where we cannot, and simply do
not know how to fulfil our own natures passionally."

It is easy to object that Lawrence is generalising his own
peculiar case, and it is certainly true that for the majority
of men the problem is not so painful nor so urgent as it was
for him. But it seems to me that his view of the modern
situation is fundamentally true. The extremity of his own
case made him more keenly aware of the elemental problem.
We may not suffer from a " mother-fixation " as he did,
though even that is far more frequent than we ordinarily
allow; we may not have become the victims of " idealism "
in precisely the same way as he: but that " idealism " is, in
one form or another, the real canker of our modern life is
surely evident.

We need to be clear as to what Lawrence means by
" idealism." He uses the word at once in a larger and narrower sense then the ordinary. It is larger, in that " idealism " means for him not merely the supremacy of the ideal,
but of the idea; it is narrower, in that it means the assertion
of the supremacy of the idea in the passional sphere. Thus
the triumph of the basic principles of psycho-analysis is a
triumph of " idealism," in Lawrence's sense of the word, for
those principles assert that the way to health is to become
completely conscious of the sex-impulse within us. And
these principles are now become a common-place of psychol-
ogy and education. He would be reckoned positively ante-
diluvian who did not subscribe to the doctrine that the veil

of mystery surrounding sex must be lifted for the modern child. Sex-hygiene and birth-control are among the first articles of every modern social creed; and the exploitation of conscious sex the favoured theme of every advanced and successful modern novel. As Lawrence says, there is a great fascination in a completely effected " idealism," that is, in a completely achieved mental consciousness of our own natures. To this fascination the modern world is succumbing; this is, indeed, the distinguishing mark of the modern world — that which makes it modern.

Lawrence was more deeply involved in this process than any other man. It is quite wrong, totally mistaken, to conceive of him as a sort of primitive emergence. He belonged, completely, to the modern world and its " idealism "; the intensity of his revulsion against it is the index of the completeness of his identification with it. Where he differed from the vast majority of intellectuals and " idealists " was that his ultra-sensitive organism was early aware of the fearful perils that lay along this seemingly inevitable road of complete mentality. He was, in this, a truly prophetic man. The whole of his life, the whole of his work, was a struggle to overcome his own mental " idealism." This struggle, like the struggle of any heroic soul, was forced upon him by the necessities of his nature; it was essentially his own struggle: but it was a struggle on our behalf. Even when he seems most absolutely to deny his fellow-men, he is fighting for them. Even that deliberate effort to escape from his own spirituality which we have described as perversion, when it is regarded with true imaginative comprehension, appears as an effort to explore the way for us. Ultimately, in all he did, Lawrence was a hero — the hero of our time.

In *Fantasia of the Unconscious*, however, he makes his great step forward. He no longer struggles to escape from his spirituality; he accepts his destiny (which is ours) as a fully conscious being. Not less, but more consciousness, is the solution; we must "go through with it." We have to learn, by pushing on to the completion of consciousness, how and where to be unconscious. To the mental consciousness itself this must necessarily be a contradiction in terms; but Lawrence does not expect that he and his similars will be positively renewed: they cannot finally escape their own conditioning. What he and they can do is to assert or reassert the fundamentals of a true science of life in order that coming generations may profit by it. The fruits of our bitter wisdom shall be that the children's teeth are set on edge no more.

In his two books on the unconscious he applies himself to this great work. It is the culmination of his life-work; his incomparable legacy to the future. "We do know this much," says Lawrence towards the end of the second chapter of *Psycho-Analysis and the Unconscious,* "that the pushing of the 'ideal' to further lengths will not avail us anything." Alas, that we do not know it, even yet. But this realisation is the basis of Lawrence's wisdom. If we have not attained it, then the essence of Lawrence's work must be without meaning for us. From this realisation he begins.

We have actually to go back to our own unconscious. But not to the unconsciousness which is the inverted reflection of our ideal consciousness. We must discover, if we can, the true unconscious, where our life bubbles up in us prior to any mentality. The first bubbling life in us, which is innocent of any mental alteration, this is the unconscious. It is pristine, not in any way ideal. It is the spontaneous origin from which it behoves us to live.

The true "unconscious" for Lawrence is the primordial principle of life. It cannot really be generalised. It is mani-

fest only in individuality; indeed, it is individuality. Take
it back to the simplest and most primitive form of life we
know — a single cell — and life and individuality are inseparable. In this sense, life and individuality and the unconscious are interchangeable terms. " By the unconscious
we wish to indicate that essential unique nature of every
individual creature, which is, by its very nature, unanalys-
able, indefinable, inconceivable. It cannot be conceived, it
can only be experienced in every single instance." Although
for his purposes Lawrence restricts it here to living things,
there is plenty of evidence that he admitted this essential
unique nature in everything; but it is certainly not our business to tie up the loose ends of his ontology, or to point out
the resemblances between his axioms and Aristotle's. His
immediate meaning is clear. The unconscious, he admits, is
an awkward word; " soul " would be better, but the word
" soul " has been vitiated by the idealistic use. It is the
" holistic principle " of Smurs. " The unconscious brings
forth not only consciousness, but tissue and organs also."

The " unconscious " cannot be mentally known, but only
experienced. This mode of experiencing the unconscious in
living creatures outside ourselves Lawrence calls " dynamic
objective apprehension." In our day we have gradually come
to call it " imagination." By its means, " a man in time adds
on to himself the whole of the universe, by increasing pristine
realisation of the universal," that is, a realisation of the
universal in and through the individual. But this is a particular form of experiencing; it belongs to what Lawrence
distinguishes as the upper centres.

This matter of upper and lower centres is radical in Lawrence's exposition of the unconscious as it exists in the human being. The lower centres are primary; he locates them
in the sympathetic plexus and the voluntary ganglion. I
suppose, though I do not know, that his physiology of the

nervous system is mistaken. I have never troubled to en-
quire; for the point to be seized is that it does not matter
whether Lawrence has correctly located his centres or not.
The locating may be quite arbitrary, but the psychological
distinctions he is making are real. There is in the new-born
child an utterly pre-conscious mode of experience, and this
mode of experience is dual. There is an urge towards identification with the mother, and an urge of resistance away
from her: towards merging, and towards individuality. Lawrence says they proceed from the sympathetic plexus and
the voluntary ganglion respectively. That may be true or
false; but the important thing is that these two primary
urges exist, and that their polar antinomy is life itself: and,
further, that the kind of " consciousness " which they manifest is wholly subjective.

After our long training in objectivation and our epoch of worship
of the objective mode, it is perhaps difficult for us to realise the
strong, blind power of the unconscious on its first plane of activity.
It is something quite different from what we call *egoism* — which
is really mentally derived — for the ego is merely the sum-total
of what we conceive ourselves to be. The powerful pristine sub-
jectivity of the unconscious on its first plane is, on the other hand,
the root of all our unconsciousness and being, darkly tenacious.
Here we are grounded, say what we may. And if we break the
spell of this first subjective mode, we break our own main root
and live rootless, shiftless, groundless.

What Lawrence is driving at here is that this immediate
subjective relation between two individuals which is historically and genetically the foundation of consciousness, is
never superseded except at the cost of a vital impoverish-
ment. Basically, a full human life is always, as it is in the
beginning, an affair of *two* individuals united in a subjective
polar antinomy. The changing over, in the man, from the

mother to the wife, or in the woman from the father to the husband, does not alter the mode of the relation, " darkly subjective."

Next, historically, come into play the two upper centres — the sympathetic plexus in the breast, the thoracic ganglion in the shoulders. Here the unconscious experience takes on an objective mode; but this objectivity is also pre-mental. Here, Lawrence's exposition is rather confusing. Of this objective mode of unconscious experience he says, " Psychically, it is basic objective apprehension. Dynamically, it is love, devotional, administering love." For Lawrence, these upper centres of the thorax and the shoulders are the home of " spiritual " love; in the sympathetic plexus is centred " the blissful sense of ineffable transfusion with the beloved, which we call love, and of which our own era has perhaps enjoyed the full," in the ganglion the objective apprehension of the beloved as other — " objective knowledge as distinct from objective emotion." It is difficult, but I think his meaning is intelligible. This objective spiritual love-knowledge is what is traditionally called " contemplation," what Keats called " speculation," what Lawrence says we have gradually come to call " imagination ": that delightful dwelling on the sheer individuality of the object in and for itself, without desire and without anxiety. The objective spiritual love-emotion is what is called love, the motion of the " heart " towards utter union with the beloved person or object. It may be that Lawrence is right in calling them two complementary modes of the same level of experience; but it would not have occurred to me, nor is it in accordance with the mystic tradition or with truth itself, to call the objective knowledge of spiritual love pre-mental. But that is no great objection. Terminology is difficult; and the point is that " contemplation," or " imagination," is non-intellectual. Lawrence himself points out that objective

spiritual love-knowledge is the mystical apprehension —
the means of " the progress to infinity in modern, male
mysticism."

These then are, in Lawrence's view, the four elements of
the true unconscious: two on the objective spiritual plane,
two on the subjective sexual. Each has to be nourished and
brought to perfection, and perfect equilibrium between them
all maintained. This is the real business of life. And the
elemental knowledge which makes possible this fulness of
life has been forgotten.

The amazingly difficult and vital business of human relationship has been almost laughably underestimated in our epoch. All
this nonsense about love and unselfishness, more crude and repugnant than fetish-worship. Love is a thing to be *learned,* through
centuries of patient effort. It is a difficult, complex maintenance of
individual integrity throughout the incalculable processes of inter-
human polarity. Even on the first great plane of consciousness,
four prime poles in each individual, four powerful circuits possible
between two individuals, and each of the four circuits to be established to perfection and yet maintained in pure equilibrium with
all the others. Who can do it? Nobody. Yet we have all got to do
it, or else suffer ascetic tortures of starvation and privation or of
distortion and over-strain and slow collapse into corruption. The
whole of life is one long, blind effort at an established polarity
with the outer universe, human and non-human; and the whole of
modern life is a shrieking failure. It is our own fault.

We have in all this practically lost sight of the unconscious; and that was inevitable, because Lawrence's real aim
has been to give an anatomy of the human being, more adequate than the old division into Body, Mind, Soul, and —
vague and elusive appendix — Spirit. This he has done. It is
not complete. Mind has to be settled; but the foundations of

the self are well and truly laid. Manifestly they are the foundations of consciousness. What Lawrence has been engaged in is establishing the fact that " the vast bulk of consciousness is non-cerebral," or at least, non-intellectual; in other words, that intellectual mentality is a subsidiary mode of experience. The difficulty, as ever in these vital investigations, is the difficulty of language. Intellectual mentality, in the abstract and conceptual mode, has so strong a hold of us to-day that we are always tempted to believe that what cannot be clearly expressed in abstract and conceptual language has no reality. If we are still the victims of this delusion — and no delusion is more widespread among serious men to-day — then *Psycho-Analysis and the Unconscious* will appear nonsense to us. In fact, it is sanity itself. But, obviously, if we are still the unconscious victims of the tyranny of mind, we shall resent Lawrence's effort to emancipate us from that tyranny. The chief, the most vital centres of human experience, he says and demonstrates, are non-intellectual. And we should note well this, as being true in itself and characteristic of Lawrence in a moment of calm, that of the four vital and non-intellectual centres which he distinguishes, two are " spiritual " and two are " sensual." He holds the balance quite evenly between the " spiritual " and the " sensual " man. We have to be fully developed in both modes to be full men. What he insists upon, rightly, is that the " spiritual " mode is not intellectual.

We may connect the wisdom of Lawrence with the wisdom of Keats, if only to drive it home. Keats, in his letter on Soul-Making, accepts the traditional distinction of man into Body, Heart, and Mind. Body corresponds to Lawrence's sensual centres, Heart to his spiritual centres. " The Heart," says Keats, " is the Mind's Bible, the text from which it sucks its identity," and by this profound submission the

Mind becomes a Soul. " Yes," Lawrence would reply, " that is true, but only half the truth. Body no less than Heart is the Mind's Bible; the sensual centres no less than the spiritual." And Keats would have agreed and been grateful to him for this new clarity which did not deny, but only completed, his own insight. Both saw clearly that Mind was only an instrument. It was the means by which — in this matter of individual self-achievement — Body and Heart, the sensual and the spiritual centres, attained to their own self-expression; the means by which the true equilibrium of the fourfold being could be attained and know itself as existing.

So much for *Psycho-Analysis and the Unconscious*. We pass to the *Fantasia*. Part of it — the earlier part — is in the main a re-statement of the principles laid down in *Psycho-Analysis*. Equilibrium, harmony, between the four centres is the goal. The danger is in allowing any one of them to become dominant. This occurs when the Mind identifies itself with one of these four centres, or one of these two modes, instead of being the delicate unconsciousness of them all. Again, it is hard to find language for expression. The Will is involved; and what, and where, is the Will? The Will, in the four-fold being, is really the pre-mental conscience, the exquisite principle of internal self-adjustment — the *vis vitae*. But with the appearance of Mind, claiming authority as an autonomous and sovereign faculty, the Will becomes subservient to the tyrant. It endorses and enforces the Mind's decisions, and diverts the energy of life into the favoured centre, or the favoured mode; it starves and impoverishes the other centres. In our day, the Will, acting as the accomplice and henchman of the Mind, has exalted the sympathetic upper centre of spiritual love-emotion, and abased not merely the two lower sensual centres but its own complementary and opposite voluntary centre of spiritual love-knowledge.

In our day, most dangerous is the love and benevolence ideal. It results in neurasthenia, which is largely a dislocation and collapse of the great voluntary centres, a derangement of the will (i.e. of the pre-mental, spontaneous will). It is in us an insistence upon the one life-mode only, the spiritual mode. It is a suppression of the great lower centres, and a living of a sort of half-life, almost entirely from the upper centres. Thence, since we live terribly and exhaustively from the upper centres, there is a tendency now towards phthisis and neurasthenia of the heart. The great sympathetic centre of the heart becomes exhausted, the lungs, burnt by the over-insistence on one way of life, become diseased, the heart, strained in one mode of dilation, retaliates.

Physiology may be sceptical of this, but as a piece of life-knowledge it is sound. Physiology can only tell us that phthisis is due to the operations of the tubercle bacillus; as to why and when the bacillus operates it can tell us nothing. My experience confirms Lawrence's knowledge. That Lawrence himself died of phthisis, at the same age as Spinoza and of the same disease, is significant. In modern times no man has been more wonderfully developed in the upper spiritual centres than Spinoza, whose vision of the world *sub specie aeternitatis* is the perfection of objective spiritual love-knowledge. Keats, who acknowledged the Heart but left out the Body, died of phthisis. Tchehov died of it. Katherine Mansfield died of it. Lawrence died of it. Alas, that wisdom cannot save her dearest children. Lawrence knew what was wrong; he could point out the way for future generations to put it right: but he could not avert his own destiny. He was the spiritual lover who knew the doom that overtakes spiritual love. Thinking of his destiny, he writes:

Let us beware and beware and beware of having a high ideal for ourselves. But particularly let us beware of having an ideal for our children. So doing, we damn them. All we can have is wisdom. And wisdom is not a theory, it is a state of soul. It is the state wherein we know our wholeness, and the complicated, manifold nature of our being.

It is for the creation of a new generation that the *Fantasia* was really written; to save children from being bullied and warped and destroyed by the vicious ideal. The men and women to whom Lawrence addresses himself cannot be saved in their own lives any more than Lawrence himself could be saved. But life can be saved. We cannot ourselves have life in its fulness, but we can have life-wisdom; we can restore life to those who come after us. The *Fantasia* is radiant with life-wisdom.

And, of course, it is saturated through and through with Lawrence's own experience. It is the book of the wisdom drawn by a great man from his own intense life-experience. Let us take one single chapter, on " Parent Love." It will do as well to begin with as any other, for the *Fantasia* is an organic, living whole, and the whole is implicit in any of its parts.

∾

When Lawrence wrote the *Fantasia* he was thirty-five. We prick up our ears, therefore, at a paragraph which begins: " When a man approaches the beginning of maturity and the fulfilment of his individual self, about the age of thirty-five, then is not his time to come to rest."

On the contrary. Deeply fulfilled through marriage, and at one with his own soul, he must now undertake the responsibility for the next step into the future. He must now give himself perfectly to some further purpose, some passionate purposive activity. Till a man makes the great resolution of aloneness and singleness of

being, till he takes upon himself the silence and central appeasedness of maturity; and *then,* after this, assumes a sacred responsibility for the next purposive step into the future, there is no rest.
The great resolution of aloneness and appeasedness, and the further
deep assumption of responsibility in purpose — this is necessary
to every parent, every father, every husband, at a certain point.
If the resolution is never made, the responsibility never embraced,
then the love-craving will run on into frenzy, and lay waste the
family. In the woman particularly, the love-craving will run on to
frenzy and disaster. . . .

"Usually, she turns to her child," Lawrence continues.
Now he is passing from his experience as man to his experience as child. We remember the charge he brought against
his father as long ago as *Sons and Lovers,* that "ultimately,
he would not take responsibility." Responsibility, in the
fuller sense in which Lawrence himself proposes to take it,
and indeed is taking it now in the writing of this book — the
responsibility "for the next purposive step into the future,"
his father could not have been expected to take. But in
reality, simply to take real responsibility for his wife and
his children is enough; it is, fundamentally, the same responsibility. Lawrence's father should have taken it for his
actual children, as Lawrence, the childless man of genius,
takes it for all the children of the world — the children that
are his by imagination and adoption.

"The unhappy woman beats about for her insatiable
satisfaction, seeking whom she may devour. And usually,
she turns to her child." Here is Lawrence's own history.
He tells it now again with the insight of maturity, swiftly, in
naked essentials.

Here she provokes what she wants. Here, in her own son who
belongs to her, she seems to find the last perfect response for which
she is craving. He is a medium to her, she provokes from him her

own answer. So she throws herself into a last great love for her son, a final and fatal devotion which would have been the richness and strength of her husband and is poison to her boy.

Poison. A strong and bitter word, with which there is nothing to compare in *Sons and Lovers*. But when Lawrence wrote that book, he believed that it was in his power to liberate himself, and to enter life new and whole. He knows better now. "As a matter of fact, a man never leaves his first love, once the love is established."

Parents are the first in the field of the child's further consciousness. They are criminal trespassers in that field. But that makes no matter. They are first in the field. They establish a dynamic connection between the two upper centres. . . . They establish this circuit. And break it if you can. Very often not even death can break it.

Inevitably, says Lawrence, this criminal stimulation of the spiritual love-centres in a child awakens the sensual centres into activity. No matter how much the parent may consciously repudiate the idea, no matter how deeply and genuinely abhorrent the notion may be, this is the result.

Then see what happens. If you want to see the real desirable wife-spirit, look at a mother with her boy of eighteen. How she serves him, how she stimulates him, how her true female self is his, is wife-submissive to him as never, never it could be to a husband. This is the quiescent, flowering love of a mature woman. It is the very flower of a woman's love: sexually asking nothing, asking nothing of the beloved, save that he shall be himself, and that for his living he shall accept the gift of her love. This is the perfect flower of married love, which a husband should put in his cap as he goes forward into the future in his supreme activity. For the husband, it is a great pledge and a blossom. For the son also it seems wonderful. The woman now feels for the first time as a true wife might feel. And her feeling is towards her son.

And then what? The son gets on swimmingly for a time, until he is faced by the fact of actual sex-necessity. He gleefully inherits his adolescence and the world at large, without an obstacle, mother-supported, mother-loved. Everything comes to him in a glamour, he feels he sees wondrous much, understands a whole heaven, mother-stimulated. Think of the power which a mature woman thus infuses into her boy. He flares up like a flame in oxygen. No wonder they say geniuses mostly have great mothers. They mostly have sad fates.

And then? — and then, with this glamorous youth? What is he actually to do with his sensual, sexual self? Bury it? Or make an effort with a stranger? For he is taught, even by his mother, that his manhood must not forego sex. Yet he is linked up in ideal love already, the best he will ever know. . . . You will not easily get a man to believe that his carnal love for the woman he has made his wife is as high a love as that he felt for his mother.

There is Lawrence's history; and he is resolute to do his part in order that it shall not happen again. It is the fathers and the mothers who are the cause of the evil. The fathers fail the mothers, because they will not assume purposive responsibility; the mothers fail the fathers, because they are unwomanly, cold and untender: and the children are devastated by the diverted and perverted love.

ᘓ

Once more, it is easy to say that Lawrence is generalising an intensely individual life-history. And once more I reply that it is intensely individual only by its extremity; and further, that this extremity is the cause of the fierce clarity of Lawrence's insight into the central issues. Lawrence was abnormal; his experience was abnormal. But if we think we can put him aside with the word, then our obtuseness shrieks to heaven. It is the abnormal men from whom we have to learn. They, and they alone, have something of import to teach us. Every man from whom humanity has learned how to make a real step forward into the future has been an abnormal man. He has been abnormal because he belongs to the future, because he was himself the soul of the future.

Lawrence was the future; as much of it as we are likely to get in our time. Vital issues were tried out to a conclusion in him; the stress of suffering their resolution devoured and destroyed him. In so far as we understand the order of his significance, therefore, we understand also that it is impossible to *judge* him. His total being is all equally significant, because of the order to which he belongs. No truly significant man was ever significant in parts alone, for the significance of the parts gives significance to the parts which are not significant. Which may be nonsense, but is also truth. It follows therefore that if, at any point in the description of Lawrence which is this book the language of judgment is used, it is used only as a means of discourse. A symbolic and prophetic man *cannot* make mistakes; all that he is and does is his destiny. Which is, I take it, more or less what St. Paul meant when he declared that spiritual things must be spiritually discerned. For the Lawrence who matters, the real and only real Lawrence, is the Lawrence who is discerned by what he himself called " basic objective apprehension in the spiritual mode." It is true that any man, dead or alive, genius or fool, might conceivably be the object of spiritual apprehension; but only conceivably, as we might imagine him visible to the eye of an omniscient God. What we really mean by a man of genius is that he is a man who has raised himself to the status of an object of spiritual knowledge for his fellow-men. He expresses himself, he gives us the clues to his own apprehension, he convinces us in a thousand ways that he is worth apprehending, and above all he strives to make his total being apprehensible, to make himself capable of being *experienced*. When a man has been able to do this, then he cannot make mistakes: he is completely validated.

That, I hold, is the necessary attitude towards Lawrence; the compelled acknowledgment of the order to which he belonged. This is, as it were, the background of our understanding of him. But against this final background we make other discriminations, belonging to another order. We have, for example, clearly to recognise the import of the personal experience which is the core of the *Fantasia*. How clearly he presented it to his own consciousness, I cannot tell, but indisputably Lawrence's aim was so to alter the conditions of life that an emergent personality like his own should be impossible. He is saying, with candour and passion, that the conditions which produced him were radically wrong, and that he ought never to have been produced as he was. In other words, if Lawrence's message is ever accepted, there will be no more Lawrences. I believe from my heart that he would have accepted that implication without a pang if it had been brought home to him; nor, indeed, do I really doubt that at this moment he had accepted it. But the implication must never be forgotten. " He flares up like a flame in oxygen. No wonder they say geniuses mostly have great mothers. They mostly have sad fates." Behind that is a bitter self-knowledge. And the bitterness flashes out in odd places, as when he tartly adds at the end of his magnificent chapter on " Education," that he detests the clockwork Kant, or the petit-bourgeois Napoleon, or " even Jesus." " They were all failures." " Like myself," he might have added. Or again, more strikingly, when at the end of a " Litany of Exhortations," he turns with a jagged irony upon himself after he has uttered the yearning of his most secret soul.

Learn, learn, learn the one and only lesson worth learning at last. Learn to walk in the sweetness of the possession of your own soul. And whether your wife weeps as she takes off her amber beads at night, or whether your neighbour in the train sits in your coat-bottoms, or whether your superior in the office makes supercilious remarks, or your inferior is familiar and impudent . . . say to yourself: " My soul is my own. My soul is with myself, and beyond implication." And wait, quietly, in possession of your own soul, till you meet another man who has made the choice, and kept it. Then you will know him by the look on his face: half a dangerous look, a look of Cain, and half a look of gathered beauty. Then you two will make the nucleus of a new society — Ooray! Bis! Bis!!

The sudden turn jars, jars horribly; and it continues to jar until we realise that Lawrence himself is jarred, and jarred more deeply. That second man who should make the nucleus of a new society he never found, and it was impossible that he should ever find him. That extreme conditioning which made his marriage so agonising isolated him also ultimately from men. He was in reality incapable of that communion in purposive activity which he so ardently desired. The land which he saw from his Mount Pisgah was one which he himself was debarred from entering. The cause why the vision was so clear to him, and the cause why he himself could not attain it were the same cause. We need but barely return to it now; and, after all, it is implicit — indeed explicit — in the personal core of the *Fantasia*. No matter how clearly he saw why marriage must be for him unsatisfying, because his love had been taken by his mother and not even her death could restore it for him to give his wife, his clarity of self-knowledge could not change the situation. It was adamantine. Therefore, it followed implacably, that in his own life he could never know that absolute fulfilment in marriage which he knew and proclaimed to be the essential condition of man's purposive activity with men.

When the sex passion submits to the great purposive passion, then you have fulness. And no great purposive passion can endure long unless it is established upon the fulfilment in the vast majority of individuals of the true sexual passion. No great motive or ideal or social principle can endure for any length of time unless based on the sexual fulfilment of the vast majority of individuals concerned.

Thus the general proposition. These are the two great motives in human life, the sexual and the creative — " the desire of the human male to build a world." It is a re-statement, with a different emphasis, of the creative antim-ony propounded in *The Crown,* six years before — the rain-bow that is arched between consummation in the darkness and consummation in the light. And behind the general re-statement, as always, the personal history.

I think it is terrible to be young. The ecstasies and agonies of love, the agonies and ecstasies of fear and doubt and drop-by-drop fulfilment, realisation. The awful process of human relationships, love and marital relationships especially. Because we all make a very, very bad start to-day, with our own idea of love in our head, and our sex in our head as well. All the fight till one is bled of one's self-consciousness and sex-in-the-head. All the bitterness of the conflict with this devil of an amiable spouse, who has got herself so stuck in her own head. It is terrible to be young — But one fights one's way through it till one is cleaned: the self-consciousness and the sex-idea burned out of one, cauterized out bit by bit, and the self whole again, and at last free.

The best thing I have known is the stillness of accomplished marriage, when one possesses one's own soul in silence, side by side with the amiable spouse, and has left off craving and raving and being only half one's self. But I must say, I know a great deal more about the craving and raving and sore ribs, than about the accomplishment. And I must confess that I feel this self-same " accomplishment " of the fulfilled being is only a preparation for new responsibilities ahead, new unison in effort and conflict, the effort to make, with other men, a little new way into the future and to break through the hedge of the many.

It was bravely and wisely said. Nevertheless, behind it all lurks the secret unsatisfiedness that is constant in Lawrence. And, in a sense, it can be simply explained. For a man who believed so passionately in marriage as Lawrence, to be married and childless was a disaster; and it must have filled him with misgivings, to find that the simple seal of fulfilment in marriage was denied him — and to know that it was he, not his wife, that was incapable. How far, how terribly far, he was from " the hardy indomitable male " of his dreams! How insecure was his own place in the basic life of the world! How precarious was that necessary fulfilment in marriage, on which his creative mind must always build!

In reality, his proclamation of final fulfilment in marriage was a farewell to marriage. He turns to children and to the future; but the children are of the spirit, not of the flesh. He fulfils his desire magnificently, in the spirit; he completes himself splendidly, in the spirit. But he, being what he is, must be haunted by the thought that it is a " compensation." The plane on which that word has finality is not ultimate: ultimately " compensation " is the source of all the spiritual riches of the world. The orphan Jesus creates a Father-God for centuries and nations of men. The childless Lawrence begets a new generation of children. But the simple human hunger remains; he is denied that living thing on which in fact he could put forth the complete love that he can never give to a woman, the living counterpart of that wonderful child on which in imagination he poured forth that love so richly and so wisely.

Thus, inevitably, the desire to pour forth that love endures. In his dream, it is the brother who shall receive it, the brother with half a look of Cain, half a look of gathered beauty in his face — the angel-devil brother who will go forth with him to make all things new. And he does not exist, he cannot exist: for he is Lawrence himself. Once try to make his dream a reality, and it vanishes. For the man, if he existed, would *be* fulfilled in marriage. If he were not, Lawrence could not abide him; and if he were, he would not have the love which Lawrence feels. He could not return it. And in his heart Lawrence knows it, and it jars him terribly. " We two will make between us the nucleus of a new society," he says in his dream to his brother. " Ooray! bis! bis!! " grins the waking man. He is alone, and will be alone until his death.

All this and more is behind the *Fantasia,* and all this helps to make it as strange and abrupt a book as it is a wise and beautiful one. It has the gathered beauty; and it has the look of Cain — both together. It is the perfect expression, and the perfect portrait of Lawrence: it utters the paradox of the man completely — the man who sees and knows, but cannot be, who sees and knows, because he cannot be. In it, more simply and directly than in any other of his books, he confesses the longing of his heart.

Our leaders have not loved men; they have loved ideas, and have been willing to sacrifice passionate men on the altars of the blood-drinking ever-ash-thirsty ideal. Has President Wilson, or Karl Marx, or Bernard Shaw ever felt one hot blood-pulse of love for the working man, the half-conscious, deluded working man? . . . Never.

And me? There is no danger of the working man ever reading

my books, so I sha'n't hurt him that way. But oh, I would like to save him alive, in his living, spontaneous, original being. I can't help it. It is my passionate instinct.

I would like him to give me back the responsibility for general affairs, a responsibility which he can't acquit, and which saps his life. I would like him to give me back the responsibility for the future. I would like him to give me back the responsibility for thought, for direction. I wish we could take hope and belief together. I would undertake my share of the responsibility, if he gave me his belief.

" Our leaders have not loved men." If it is not evident by this time that Lawrence did love them, it never will be. " A leader who loved men " — to be this was his dream. And his dream will come true, as the dreams of great prophets always come true — but not in their life-times nor in the warm immediacy for which they yearn.

One might write, it seems, for ever concerning the *Fantasia;* its riches are inexhaustible, its wisdom radical and revolutionary, and it is, to all intents and purposes, utterly neglected. If men and women read it, they are perhaps moved by its vehemence and vivacity, they say perhaps: " What a wonderful book! " and straightway they forget it. They go on in the same old way as though it had never been written; they adhere, in their inertia and ignorance, to the same old system which is decaying about them. They are not changed at all. It has been to them only one more titillation, one more sensation, one more turn in the eccentric performance of a " genius " on the modern literary stage.

But I hope and I believe that a generation will arise to whom it will be a direct quickening of the soul. From it the warm life will pour into their veins. They will read, and they will act. What will prevent them from acting, if once they understand? The essential demands of the *Fantasia* cannot indeed be easily fulfilled, but their fulfilment does not depend on anything save the inward willingness and deep resolve of the individual man and woman. Society can be regenerated from within; new cells can grow within the outworn body of the social organism, isolated at first, yet gradually growing into vital connection with each other, until first one and then another piece of new living tissue is created, and at last the whole made new.

At bottom the message of the *Fantasia* is perfectly simple. We may be as sceptical as we like concerning the plexuses and planes with which the book begins, or concerning the cosmology with which it ends. This last is only a language of expression for the central truth that " there is only one clue to the universe: that is the individual soul within the individual being." In other words, be a whole man, and the universe itself will be incorporate with you, because it will have its meaning in you. To be whole, we must tear down the idea and the ideal from their throne; for the truth is not that the Word was made Flesh but that Flesh is made the Word. The idea and the ideal must grow out of the individual life, not be imposed upon it. And this is not to deny the idea and the ideal; they too are forms of life. To deny them sovereignty is not to deny their proper validity. They are not nothing, because they are not supreme. " We must live by all three, ideal, impulse, and tradition, each in its hour. But the real guide is the pure conscience, the voice of the self in its wholeness, the Holy Ghost."

To break the vicious circle of our own inward distortion, by which our children are distorted — a distortion caused by the deliberate thrusting of the fixed ideal into the delicate process of the pristine, individual human life — this is what Lawrence calls upon us to do. If we cannot make ourselves whole — and we cannot — by reason of our hypertrophied mentality, we can know why and how we have become what we are; and by that knowledge we can save our children from the woes that have befallen us. We can stand aside, and let them *be:* not negatively let them be, but positively let them *be*. And if that distinction is meaningless to any reader of this book, let him read the *Fantasia*. If it is still meaningless, then let him not trouble his head with this book, or with Lawrence, any more.

IV

AARON'S ROD

IN Aaron Sisson, the name-character of *Aaron's Rod,*
Lawrence imagined the friend and brother who should form
with him the nucleus of a new society; whose failure to
manifest himself jarred Lawrence so deeply. Lawrence himself is in the book. He is Rawdon Lilly. And Aaron is his
friend of his dream. That he is and will remain a dream,
Lawrence half recognises by leaving the final outcome un-
decided. In the last chapter Lilly calls upon Aaron to yield
himself up to him; if he is to be Lilly's friend, he must accept
Lilly as his leader. The argument of the *Fantasia* is reas-
serted. " Men," says Lilly to Aaron, " must submit to the
greater soul in a man for their guidance; and women must
submit to the positive power-soul in man for their being."

" You'll never get it," said Aaron.
" You will when all men want it. All men say they want a leader.
Then let them in their souls *submit* to some greater soul than
theirs. At present, when they say they want a leader, they mean
they want an instrument, like Lloyd George. A mere instrument
for their use. But it's more than that. It's the reverse. It's the deep,
fathomless submission to the heroic soul in a greater man. You,
Aaron, you have the need to submit. You, too, have the need
livingly to yield to a more heroic soul, to give yourself. You know
you have. And you know it isn't love. It is life-submission.
And you know it. But you kick against the pricks. And perhaps

you'd rather die than yield. And so, die you must. It is your affair."

There was a long pause. Then Aaron looked up into Lilly's face. It was dark and remote — seeming. It was like a Byzantine eikon at the moment.

" And whom shall I submit to? " he said.

" Your soul will tell you," replied the other.

There the book ends. Whether Aaron will submit or not, we do not know; nor what would have happened if he had submitted. What is certain is that Aaron is the chosen one. In him, Lawrence came nearest to drawing the actual features of his dream-friend. The relations of Gerald Crich to Rupert Birkin, of Kangaroo to Richard Somers of Ciprian to Ramon — each in its several kind an attempt to realise the imagined relation of man to man — are none of them so near, nor so persuasive in their reality. We must look closely into Aaron.

The first and the last thing that strikes us about Aaron is that he is extraordinarily like Lawrence, or like Lilly. Lawrence confesses it. " The two men had an almost uncanny understanding of one another, like brothers. They came from the same district, the same class. Each might have been born into the other's circumstance. Like brothers, there was a profound hostility between them. But hostility is not antipathy." Naturally they come both out of mining villages in the Midlands. Lilly is a writer, Aaron a flute-player. Aaron, in the crucial moments of his positive and complete thinking, utters himself through music, on his flute, and Lawrence the author translates his meaning into words. Lilly has the gift of fluent word-utterance, of which Aaron is often impatient or even contemptuous. It is an admirable arrangement, technically and otherwise.

Further, Aaron has made, of his own independent motion, the crucial decision that Lawrence demanded of his brother in the *Fantasia*. He is aware of his own central aloneness. The story begins with his final revolt against his wife's unconscious determination that he shall submit to " the sacred priority of woman." He will not submit, he will not yield himself to be enveloped in her all-beneficent love. He leaves his wife, leaves his children. He meets Lilly, he falls ill in London and Lilly cares for him, as a wife would care for her husband; and finally he follows Lilly to Italy. There, apart from Lilly, in a strange country and a strange house, he realises the truth of his own nature.

He realised that he had never intended to yield himself fully to her or to anything: that he did not intend ever to yield himself to her or to anything: that his very being pivoted on the fact of his isolate self-responsibility, aloneness. His intrinsic and central aloneness was the very centre of his being. Break it, and he broke his being. Break this central aloneness, and he broke everything. It was the great temptation, to yield himself; and it was the final sacrilege. Anyhow, it was something which, from his profoundest soul, he did not intend to do. By the innermost isolation and singleness of his own soul he would abide though the skies fell on top of one another, and seven heavens collapsed.

It is the very language of the *Fantasia;* and we are not surprised that to express this realisation, Lawrence evokes his favourite image.

Having in some curious manner tumbled from the tree of modern knowledge, and cracked and rolled out from the shell of the preconceived idea of himself like some dark, nightlustrous chestnut from the green ostensibility of the burr, he lay as it were exposed but invisible on the floor, knowing, but making no conception; knowing, but having no idea. Now that he was finally unmasked and exposed, the accepted idea of himself cracked and rolled aside like a broken chestnut-burr, the mask split and shattered, he was at last quiet and free.

Ripe and apt, according to the doctrine of the *Fantasia*, to return to his wife and children, and convert her to the same ultimate realisation, in order that the perfect work of masculine creation, based on individual sex-fulfilment, may begin. But, for some reason, the women are left out of *Aaron's Rod*. Tanny, Lilly's wife, is remote in Norway; and before her voyage has shown no more sign than Aaron's wife of accepting the doctrine of submission to "the positive power-soul in man." Aaron's wife is behind in England, and he has apparently no intention of returning to her. The problem is simplified, out of all knowledge, by these convenient segregations.

Still, manifestly, Lilly has found his man. What is to happen between them? Aaron, possessing himself in his own central aloneness, does not intend "ever to yield himself up entirely to anything." Lilly has reached the same realisation, and made the same resolve. According to the programme, they are to form the nucleus of a new society. How are they to do it? The positive plans are vague, in fact precisely Lawrence's own plans. They consist of leaving Europe, which is worn out, and avoiding Asia — "I can't do with folk who teem by the billion," says Lilly. "Only vermin teem by the billion. Higher types breed slower." But the positive plans may be left aside for the moment. What is to happen between these two men? Each has reached his realisation; each is resolved never to yield himself entirely. Yet Lilly demands that Aaron shall yield to him.

No wonder the issue is left doubtful. Nevertheless, Lilly

tries to prepare the way for some solution of the impasse. Aaron discovers that he cannot be quite alone. " I can't stand by myself in the middle of the world and in the middle of people, and know I am quite by myself, and nowhere to go, and nothing to hold on to. I can for a day or two — but then, it becomes unbearable as well." Which is doubtless true, but awkward for Aaron as compared with Lilly. For Lilly has Tanny, and Aaron has not got his wife. He makes his confession in a conversation at which Lilly is present. Lilly replies:

" Can't one be alone — quite alone? . . . I don't mean like Simeon Stylites. I mean can't one live with one's wife and be fond of her: and with one's friends, and enjoy their company: and with the world and everything, pleasantly: and yet *know* that one is alone? "

What Aaron's reply to that would have been, we can only conjecture. In the story, Lawrence allows him no remark. The dice are loaded. Lilly is to be alone with his wife, Aaron to be alone without his wife. Since Aaron is the father of a family, and Lilly not, it seems it should be the other way about. But that would never do.

It would simplify matters greatly if both men left their wives finally, and not Aaron only. But that would fit neither with the doctrine of the *Fantasia*, nor with Lawrence's own situation. He, at least, *could* not leave his wife. So Aaron must leave his. For obviously one of them must leave his wife, or there would be no ultimate relation between the men; and, obviously, it cannot be Lilly, for he, for some reason not given in the book, but of which by this time we are not ignorant, cannot leave his wife. So Aaron must leave his wife, and Lilly remain with his; and since Aaron, having no woman any more, needs somebody, and Lilly, having no man, needs somebody, they are made for each other.

The solution, though Lawrence does not assert it plainly, is accordingly prepared.

But no! (Aaron muses) If he had to give in to something: if he really had to give in, and it seemed he had: then he would rather give in to the devilish little Lilly than to the beastly people of the world. If he had to give in, then it should be to no woman, and to no social ideal, and to no social institution. No! — if he had to yield his wilful independence, then he would rather give himself to the little, individual *man* than to any of the rest.

But surely we must ask: Why had Aaron to give in to anything? There is not, ultimately, the faintest distinction in soul-achievement between Aaron and Lilly. If Aaron had to give in to something, then we may be sure (whether or not it is apparent in the texture of the novel itself) that Lilly also had to give in to something. But to what? The end of this book may give an answer to that question. For the moment the seeming solution is that Aaron gives in to Lilly, and Lilly gives in to nothing — except his own Holy Ghost. It is as though on the last page Lawrence suddenly remembered that Aaron had a Holy Ghost also. It would have been simpler if he hadn't. We have to believe that Aaron's Holy Ghost would have told him to follow Lilly's. And we just can't believe it; neither could Lawrence himself.

Aaron's Rod is a truly subtle and ironic commentary on the unresolved inward division that lies concealed beneath the *Fantasia*. In the unimpeded freedom of the imagination, Lawrence is trying, in *Aaron's Rod*, to solve his personal problem. And he cannot solve it. He needs a man, and he needs a man of realisation like his own. He creates the man — Aaron Sisson. Sisson is a dream-Lawrence: Lawrence

without his physical weakness, but with his spiritual sensibility — Lawrence metamorphosed into "the hardy indomitable male " and yet still Lawrence. Everything, it seems,
is propitious for the perfect man-to-man relation. Yet Lawrence in his strange integrity discovers, though he will not
wholly admit, that it cannot be. His own isolated soul depends upon a woman, as his own realisation has come
through a woman. Aaron's realisation has come through
a woman, in the same way as Lilly's: therefore, he also,
in the same way as Lilly must depend upon a woman.
But no! he must depend upon Lawrence, and abjure
his woman for ever. And why? Because Lawrence needs
him. That is the final reason, and there is no other, why
Lilly is to be true to the principles of the *Fantasia* and
Aaron play them false. We are back to the old and heart-
breaking impasse of the end of *Women in Love:* where the
salvation of Gerald Crich lies in his becoming blood-brother
to Birkin first, and then, and only then, entering into a
permanent relation with a woman. And now as then an inward reluctance prevents Lawrence from asking himself
what woman would take a man who had submitted himself
utterly to Lawrence.

Let us be clear. There are two issues in the *Fantasia:*
one the impersonal issue, the other the personal. In the
first, Lawrence sees clearly. He sees clearly that the New
Jerusalem must be builded on a basis of true sexual fulfilment between achieved individual men and women; and that
the true creative relation between men must grow from
that strong root. But in the personal issue, it is impossible
that he should ever enter in to the New Jerusalem which
shines so clearly before his spirit. He, the living Lawrence,
is an unsatisfied man; he has not touched, and cannot touch,
that goal of true sexual fulfilment. His yearning for love needs
a man as well as a woman; and since that yearning for a man

proceeds out of unfulfilment with a woman, it cannot be satisfied; it demands more from a man than a man could ever give, if he were indeed a man. And nothing less than a man who is a man will do for Lawrence.

So Lawrence tries to escape this bitter conclusion. Lilly tries to convince Aaron, but really to convince himself, that whereas it is right that he should depend on a woman, it is right that Aaron should depend on a man.

" I don't go back on what I said before [says Lilly]. I do believe that every man must fulfil his own soul, every woman must be herself, herself only, not some man's instrument, or some embodied theory. But the mode of our being is such that we can only live and have our being whilst we are implicit in one of the great dynamic modes. We *must* either love, or rule. And once the love-mode changes, as change it must, for we are worn out and becoming evil in its persistence, then the other mode will take place in us."

It sounds well enough. But that plausible general statement that " we *must* either love or rule " does not at all cover the situation at the end of *Aaron's Rod.* When its duplicity is unfolded, it means two utterly different things: it means that Aaron must either obey a woman, or obey a man, and it means that Lilly must both rule a woman, and rule a man. And we repeat, there is no reason why, save Lawrence's personal need.

The personal issue obscures and distorts the impersonal. Words are changed and become deceptive by being passed from the one order to the other. " Power," which enters abundantly into the argument of *Aaron's Rod,* thus becomes quite double edged. It is very meet and right that men should recognise, and be submissive to, the magical and dynamic power that is sometimes manifest in men. To recognise power in another is to become powerful oneself. The recognition is the current that passes between the souls of two achieved individuals. But Lawrence's true conception of power was distorted by his personal need; it passed into a lower order, and became a magniloquent name for devouring personal possession of another man. Aaron is required to submit to the power in Lilly; to give him "the deep fathomless submission to the heroic soul in a greater man." Again, it sounds well. But what does it mean? It does not mean that those two shall go forth to found the nucleus of a new society in the terms of the *Fantasia*, for Aaron is required to abandon his wife and children. It means simply that Aaron shall follow Lilly as his body-servant, wherever Lilly's Holy Ghost may lead him. He is not to ask where and why the Holy Ghost of Lilly will lead. Says Lilly calmly:

"I am a vagrant really, or a migrant. I must migrate. . . . I know I must oscillate between North and South, so oscillate I do. It's just my nature. All people don't have the same natures . . ."

We are not surprised that "a deep disappointment began to settle over Aaron's spirit." "Then next year," Aaron asks: "What will you do?"

"Who knows? I may sail far off. I should like to. I should like to try quite a new life-mode. This is finished in me — and yet perhaps it is absurd to go further. I'm rather sick of seekers. I hate a seeker."

It may conceivably have been a temptation to Aaron to follow Lilly, whose fascination (which was Lawrence's fascination) impelled him powerfully, but it was manifestly his duty as a man, even according to Lawrence's own doctrine, to resist the temptation. Of ideal, and impulse, and tradition, which in their harmony make the Holy Ghost of a man, at most impulse could have spoken for submission:

Jack

Will the bird perish,
Shall the bird rise.

To the old raven, in
the act of becoming a
young phoenix

D H L

AN ENLARGED IMPRESSION OF A SEAL GIVEN
BY D. H. LAWRENCE TO THE AUTHOR
AT CHRISTMAS 1923, WITH THE
ACCOMPANYING NOTE

ideal and tradition assuredly, and perhaps the deepest impulse of all, would turn him aside from the discipleship in irresponsibility.

ᲪᲘ

But what Lawrence was asking for was not even a disciple, but simply a lover. He disguised it from himself, as he needed to do. But those who are responsive to the unconscious emotion no less than to the explicit thought of a book, cannot mistake the meaning of the beautiful chapter describing Aaron's illness in Lilly's little flat. The women are far away, the underlying tension of hostility that is always felt when Lawrence is describing a woman and a man together dissolves peacefully away. Lilly is blissfully happy looking after Aaron, with a more than wifely tenderness. Lawrence never drew a more life-like picture of himself than this whole description of Lilly.

He put on the kettle, and quietly set cups and plates on a tray. The room was clean and cosy and pleasant. He did the cleaning himself, and was as efficient and unobtrusive a housewife as any woman. While the kettle boiled, he sat darning the socks which he had taken off Aaron's feet when the flautist arrived, and which he had washed. He preferred that no outsider should see him doing these things. Yet he preferred also to do them himself, so that he should be independent of outside aid.

His face was dark and hollow, he seemed frail, sitting there in the London afternoon darning the black woollen socks. His full brow was knotted slightly, there was a tension. At the same time, there was an indomitable stillness about him, as it were in the atmosphere about him. His hands, though small, were not very thin. He bit off the wool as he finished his darn.

There is Lawrence in his habit as he lived. In this chapter, " Low-water Mark," he is enjoying a moment of imaginative peace and bliss. He is caring with exquisite tenderness for a man. Aaron's illness takes a serious turn. His influenza seems to have taken from him the will-to-live. The doctor complains to Lilly that he is sulking himself out of life.

" I think it depresses him partly that his bowels won't work. It frightens him. He's never been ill in his life before," said Lilly.

" His bowels won't work if he lets his spirit go, like an animal dying of the sulks," said the doctor impatiently. " He might go off quite suddenly — dead before you can turn round — "

Lilly was properly troubled. Yet he did not know what to do.

He tries in vain to rouse Aaron by speaking of the country and of gardens, which Aaron loved, by proposing that they should go into the country together as soon as Aaron is well. Then Lilly has his inspiration.

Suddenly Lilly rose and went to the dressing-table.

" I'm going to rub you with oil," he said. " I'm going to rub you as mothers do their babies whose bowels won't work."

Aaron frowned slightly as he glanced at the dark, self-possessed face of the little man.

" What's the good of that? " he said irritably. " I'd rather be left alone."

" Then you won't be."

Quickly he uncovered the blond lower body of his patient, and began to rub the abdomen with oil, using a slow, rhythmic circulating motion, a sort of massage. For a long time he rubbed finely and steadily, then went over the whole of the lower body, mindless, as if in a sort of incantation. He rubbed every speck of the man's lower body — the abdomen, the buttocks, the thighs and knees, down to the feet, rubbed it all warm and glowing with camphorated oil, every bit of it, chafing the toes swiftly, till he was almost exhausted.

Immediately, there is a change for the better in Aaron. There has been the crucial physical contact which was, for Lawrence, a necessary and essential part of a relation between man and man. When Aaron has slept, with Lilly watching by his side, he wakes refreshed, and they begin to talk. Lilly says that he is glad he has no children, though his wife wants children badly. He is glad, because it is " against his instinct " to add his quota to the mass of children in the world, and because when a woman has children, " she thinks the whole world wags only for them and her," and finally because: If childhood is more important than manhood, why live to be a man at all? " All of which is, of course, obvious special pleading. If the arguments were valid, the begetting of children would have to be left to sub-human men. The childless Lawrence would like to convince himself that it is due to his perfected manliness that he has no children. With this warped reasoning, Lilly leads on to his destination.

" Men have got to stand up to the fact that manhood is more than childhood — and then force women to admit it," said Lilly. " But the rotten whiners, they're all grovelling before a baby's napkin and a woman's petticoat."

" It's a fact," said Aaron. But he glanced at Lilly oddly, as if suspiciously. And Lilly caught the look. But he continued.

" And if they think you try to stand on your legs and walk with the feet of manhood, why, there isn't a blooming father or lover amongst them but will do his best to get you down and suffocate you — either with a baby's napkin, or a woman's petticoat. . . . That's why marriage wants readjusting — or extending — to get men on to their legs once more, and to give them the adventure again. . . . And can you find two men to stick together, without feeling criminal, and without cringing, and without betraying one another? You can't. One is sure to go fawning around some female, then they both enjoy giving each other away, and doing a new grovel before a woman again."

On this passage a voluminous commentary might be written. We must be content to note a few things. First, that

Lilly would have a better chance of convincing the unyield-ing Tanny that manhood was more than childhood if he had given her the children she wanted so badly. It is not easy for a man incapable of begetting children to convince a woman of his perfect manhood. Second, that Aaron's at-titude, though expressed in verbal agreement, hovers con-fessedly between " suspicion " and " amusement " at Lilly's doctrines. Thirdly, that there is nothing in the least " crimi-nal " in two men " sticking together " in the simple and straightforward sense of the phrase. And, fourthly, that, in spite of all the phrases, it is not Aaron but Lilly who ap-parently has " to go fawning round some female." In other words, Lilly wants a homo-sexual relation with Aaron to complete his incomplete hetero-sexual relation with Tanny. This he calls " extending " marriage. Other people might find another name for it.

ᔕ

It would be manifestly unjust, and manifestly ridiculous, to condemn Lawrence for this. Lawrence was what he was, and we accept him whole. But it is absolutely necessary to distinguish what Lawrence, as a living person, is de-manding, from what Lawrence, as a man of profound im-personal vision, declares to be necessary. What Lawrence is demanding in *Aaron's Rod* looks very like, but is very different from, what Lawrence declares to be necessary in the *Fantasia*. To be united impersonally in creative and pur-posive act on the basis of a true marriage fulfilment is one thing; to be homo-sexually united to a man of genius be-cause he finds it impossible to achieve sexual fulfilment in marriage is quite another. The former is, we believe, a true and universal ideal; the latter an individual indulgence, or an individual necessity. It is criminal to confuse them; but Lawrence wanted to confuse them. I do not believe that he confused them deliberately. He simply could not help it. Ultimately, he could not admit his own astonishing idiosyncrasy; he had to conceal it from himself, by representing it to himself as the universal constitution of a man. And this, in a sense, it is: for Man does need man, as deeply as he needs woman. But these universal needs in Lawrence assumed an extreme form: the intensity with which he felt them made him, on the impersonal and spiritual plane, a symbolic and prophetic man; on the personal and actual plane, they simply tore him asunder.

Most fearful of all, the intensity of these conflicting desires isolated him utterly in actual life. In spirit he was the friend and lover of all men, in life he could be the friend and lover of none. He could not enter into communion with a man or with men, in life. They did not " betray " him; they simply could not give him that for which, they knew instinctively, he was hungering. Aaron does not give it: Lawrence's crucial integrity prevents him from representing that he does. And in Aaron Lawrence created the only kind of man from whom he could, in imagination, have got what he needed. Aaron Sisson is an astonishing creation. He is Lawrence's dream-friend, and he embodies much of Lawrence's ultimate knowledge about himself. Aaron's suspicion of Lilly is Lawrence's suspicion of himself, Aaron's foreknowledge of Lilly is Lawrence's foreknowledge of himself. Says Aaron to Lilly in London:

" But what's the good of going to Malta? Shall *you* be any different in yourself, in another place? You'll be the same there as you are here."

" How am I here? "

" Why, you're all the time grinding yourself against something inside you. You're never free. You're never content. You never stop chafing."

Lilly dipped his potato into the water, and cut out the eyes carefully. Then he cut it in two, and dropped it in the clean water of the second bowl. He had not expected this criticism.

" Perhaps I don't," said he.

" Then what's the use of going somewhere else? You won't change yourself."

" I may in the end," said Lilly.

The conversation between the two men is marvellous. To those who are aware of the issue at stake, the self-mastery displayed by Lawrence in this lucid interrogation of himself is magnificent. The true greatness of the man is beautiful. Aaron sticks to his point. Lilly may roam the world, " but the man in the middle of him will not change," no matter what Lilly's hopes may be. " What's to be done then? " asks Lilly.

" Nothing so far as I can see. You get as much amusement out of life as possible, and there's the end of it."

" All right then, I'll get the amusement."

" Ay, all right then," said Aaron. " But there isn't anything wonderful about it. You talk as if you were doing something special. You aren't. You're no more than a man who drops into a pub for a drink, to liven himself up for a bit. Only you give it a lot of names, and make out as if you were looking for the philosopher's stone, or something like that. When you're only killing time, like the rest of folks, before time kills you."

Lilly did not answer. It was not yet seven o'clock, but the sky was dark. Aaron sat in the firelight. Even the saucepan on the fire was silent. Darkness, silence, the firelight in the upper room, and the two men together.

" It isn't quite true," said Lilly, leaning on the mantelpiece and staring down into the fire.

. . . " What else is there to it? " Aaron sounded testy.

" Why," said Lilly at last, " there's something. I agree, it's true what you say about me. But there's a bit of something else. There's just a bit of something in me, I think, which *isn't* a man running into a pub for a drink."

The phrasing is too simple for the issue. What is " running
into a pub for a drink " in the case of a man like Lawrence?
In the language of the *Fantasia*, is it the satisfaction of impulse alone among the three elements of impulse, ideal, and
tradition? Or is it obedience to that transcendent unity
which is born of all three elements, and consummates, but
does not consume them — the Holy Ghost? To the spiritual
vision of complete detachment, to satisfy impulse and to
obey one's Holy Ghost, are alike the following of one's
nature. We are all conditioned, and there is no escape from
our conditioning; but there is in potentiality, and there may
be in reality, that in us which is not conditioned — namely,
that final imagination which knows that we are conditioned:
the pure spirit. It is to this that Lilly turns in his struggle to
make plain to himself the element whereby he was not
simply a creature seeking immediate satisfaction — the bit
of something in him which wasn't a man running into a pub
for a drink. And rather strangely, considering his aversion
for the East, he puts it thus:

" I think a man may come into possession of his own soul at
last — as the Buddhists teach — but without ceasing to love, or
even to hate. One loves, one hates — but somewhere beyond it
all, one understands, and possesses one's soul in patience and
in peace — "

The pure doctrine of the spirit. But listen to Aaron's
challenge.

" Yes," said Aaron slowly, " while you only stand and talk
about it. But when you've got no chance to talk about it — and
when you've got to live — you don't possess your soul neither in
patience nor in peace, but any devil that likes possesses you and
does what it likes with you, while you fudge yourself and fray
yourself out like a worn rag."

And there the naked contradiction remains. It is all very well for Lilly to say, as he does, that " he doesn't care." He cared terribly. And it is all very well for him to say that he is learning to do it. The intimate substance of the book denies it. It is all very well to reassert the central doctrine of the *Fantasia.*

" I'm learning to possess my soul in patience and in peace, and I know it. And it isn't a negative Nirvana either. And if Tanny possesses her soul in patience and peace as well — and if in this we understand each other at last — then there we are, together and apart at the same time, and free of each other, and eternally inseparable. I have my Nirvana, and I have it all to myself. But more than that. It coincides with her Nirvana."

Good, good, we might say; but now, alas, we know too much. This seeming consummation is a dream. This seeming fulfilment in marriage is in reality a farewell to marriage. Impersonally, it is wisdom; personally, it is a confession of failure, and the turning of the love-hunger towards a man, in vain, always in vain.

And, as though Lawrence's thoughts were now turning upon themselves, like a squirrel in a cage, or as if in instant demonstration of the truth of Aaron's insight that he is " all the time grinding against something inside him," the conversation returns upon itself. Aaron once more admits that he himself asks only for immediate satisfaction — " to be amused " — and once more he challenges Lilly. Is he any different?

" No, I'm not very different. But I always persuade myself there's a bit of difference. Do you know what Josephine Ford confessed to me? She's had her lovers enough. ' There isn't any such thing as love, Lilly,' she said. ' Men are simply afraid to be alone. That is absolutely all there is in it: fear of being alone.' "

" What by that? " said Aaron.

" You agree? "

" Yes, on the whole."

" So do I — on the whole."

There we touch rock-bottom. There we have the answer
to the question why a woman is still indispensable to Lilly
when he has achieved his own Nirvana. Why should he require also a Nirvana in another person than himself? Why
not simply *be* alone? And the answer is that Lawrence could
not bear it. And now that he had found himself alone, now
that the relation with his wife was reduced to a nothing,
why turn to a man? The answer is the same. Neither in
marriage, nor out of it, could Lawrence bear to be alone. As
Lilly puts it:

" You learn to be quite alone, and possess your soul in isolation — and at the same time to be perfectly *with* someone else.
That's all I ask."

That was all he asked, indeed; and it was *quite impossible.*
It sounds wonderful. But it is a contradiction. Lilly is confusing the orders of human experience. He is asking for the
final detachment of spirit, and for the warmth of human
relation, *at the same moment,* and in the same order. In the
order of spirit, men and women are neither married nor given
in marriage but are as angels. Whether they are companioned
or lonely, childless or patriarchs, is utterly indifferent.
It simply is not true that spiritual self-possession, which is
spiritual self-surrender, depends upon fulfilment in marriage, or fulfilment in friendship. Still less does it depend
upon the other persons having achieved the same spiritual
self-possession. It depends on nothing save oneself.

Above all, you cannot be " perfectly *with* " anybody in
the order of pure spirit. In that order, you are just as " perfectly *with* " any created thing as you are with the wife of

your bosom. You are absolutely alone. The longing to be
" perfectly *with* " somebody belongs to a quite different
order — the human and personal order. It may conceivably
be satisfied, it may be disappointed; but spirit is neither
exalted by the success nor dismayed by the failure. Nor
does the indifference of spirit to our human and personal
destinies absolve us for one moment from the effort to live
well and truly. Man's first and final business is to make that
effort. His achievement of the isolation of spirit can never
release him from the obligation; he is involved and implicated in the process of life from his birth to his death, and
he must accept his responsibility.

Now it is true that spiritual detachment can co-exist with
fulfilment in marriage, or fulfilment in friendship. There is
no real contradiction between the acceptance of one's own
isolation in the spiritual order, and the avoidance of isolation in the personal order. To be alone in spirit, and not to
be alone in person are perfectly compatible; but to maintain
that not to be alone in person is the condition of being alone
in spirit is quite false. Lawrence is always pretending that
there is this essential connection. Spiritual isolation is, for
him, the outcome of a marriage struggle. " It is what you get
to," says Lilly to Aaron, " after a lot of fighting, and a lot of
sexual fulfilment." And that is simply untrue. What you get
to " after a lot of fighting and a lot of sexual fulfilment " is
what Lawrence has got to. He calls it " possessing his soul
in isolation;" but, as Aaron points out to him, it is a condition wherein " any devil that likes possesses you and does
what it likes with you." It is the old, insidious equivocation,
by which the exhaustion after conflict becomes the peace
which passeth understanding.

The struggle to reach a true married relation is one thing;
the process of achieving spiritual detachment quite another.
Lawrence confuses them. He cannot help it. He was con-

demned to fail to achieve a true married relation; and it was his failure, not his fulfilment in marriage, that brought him to this false semblance of spiritual detachment. It is not to be wondered at that he represented the outcome of his marriage-failure as a true marriage fulfilment. Nevertheless, it is a self-deception and a grave one, which will crumble to pieces as his work goes on. It is one more manifestation of that strange hybridization between spirituality and sensuality which is constant in Lawrence's work; and it leads, at this moment, to the truly preposterous demand that the woman also should find in this false spiritual detachment her true marriage-consummation.

Of course, Tanny rebelled, as Ursula rebelled before. She would have none of this convenient plan by which she was to be, as it were, paid-off with an unreal consummation, while her husband, having come to the end of his marriage, set about "extending" marriage to include a man. Lilly cannot understand her.

" Tanny's the same. She does nothing really but resist me: my authority, or my influence, or just *me*. At the bottom of her heart she just blindly and persistently opposes me. God knows what it is she opposes: just me myself. She thinks I want her to submit to me. So I do, in a measure natural to our two selves. Somewhere she ought to submit to me."

To the outside observer what Tanny resists is manifest. Her woman's instinct resents, and bitterly resents, Lilly's attempt to pay her in false or foreign coin. False spiritual currency is not legal tender in the personal and sexual realm. She has no use for a spiritual Nirvana; and she is the more hostile to this attempt to ring the changes on her because

Lilly has hitherto professed, with utter sincerity, to accept the primacy of the sexual. She has been cheated of her fulfilment; she will not be cheated again. She will not accept him as a leader, or as a man, still less will she accept as her wifely consummation the " spiritual " satisfactions that are proper to fallen angels. If he cannot give her fulfilment in her own order, let him at least acknowledge his dependence upon her, for that is absolute.

Tanny could believe in Lilly's ultimate independence, only if he had the courage to leave her, as Aaron has left his wife. Aaron knows that if he has not the courage to leave his wife on the vital issue of his own or her supremacy, he will succumb. So he leaves her, and saves his own integrity. But Lilly cannot leave Tanny, though the issue between them is the same. He can only make a forlorn attempt to have his love-desire fulfilled by a man. His fear of being lonely in the physical world is more powerful than the joy of being alone in the spiritual. In the final issue, therefore, he is bound to succumb to the woman's claim. It is more profound than his own, because in his secret soul he admits it, while she will never admit his in hers. From *Aaron's Rod* — the subtlest of all Lawrence's later books — we learn that he will never be able to maintain that supremacy of the spiritual over the physical, of the masculine-creative over the female-sexual, which he asserted in the *Fantasia*.

♌

The threads of the book are many, and they are intricately woven. And there is more of the essential Lawrence in this than any other of his novels. The writing is notable for its ease and power. It is, in every sense of the word, a great book. But the seeds of future decay are manifest in it. At the centre is the uncertainty of the divided soul. Every-

thing is doubtful. Lawrence has no confidence in his forthcoming journey, no confidence that he will find his friend, no
confidence in marriage, no confidence in himself. He has a
kind of half-belief that a miracle will happen: that with a
change of continent may come an elemental change in himself. But the driving impulse is negative — *n'importe où
hors du monde.* When that realisation is intolerable, he tries
to comfort his unbelieving soul with the hope that a new life-
mode may bring him peace. But what faith he really has,
has been declared in the *Fantasia;* it is a new generation of
men, which he will never live to see. For the rest, he speaks
" perhaps his greatest, or his innermost truth " through the
lips of Aaron.

" I don't want my fate or my Providence to treat me well.
I don't want kindness or love. I don't believe in harmony or people
loving one another. I believe in the fight and in nothing else.
And if it is a question of women, I believe in the fight of love,
even if it blinds me. And if it is a question of the world, I believe
in fighting it and having it hate me, even though it breaks my
legs. I want the world to hate me, because I can't bear the thought
that it might love me. For of all things love is the most deadly to
me and especially from such a repulsive world as I think this
is. . . ."

And if it is a question of men? At this moment Aaron's
thought is upon Lilly. Lilly was the " one fact that remained
unbroken in the débris of his consciousness." There was,
indeed, one other: Aaron's hatred for his wife. Hatred for
the woman, what for the man? Not love, of course. But
what? To fight the woman, to fight the world — that is the
programme. Why leave out the man?

It is very difficult. For how is Lawrence to say what he
means, when the word to express his meaning is taboo —
of all things most deadly? Not love, of course. The mode is
changed. The love-mode is exhausted, the power-mode be-

gins. " But, of course, there must be one who urges, and one who is impelled."

" Just as in love there is a beloved and a lover: the man is supposed to be the lover, the woman the beloved. Now, in the urge of power, it is the reverse. The woman must submit, but deeply, deeply submit."

But the woman just won't. Neither Lilly's Tanny, nor Aaron's Lottie, will play her allotted part. With the woman, it is a fight to the end.

Perhaps the man will give what the woman will not give. But what is required? Profound submission in the power-mode. But what is power? And to this vital question it is terribly hard to find an answer. We must gather up what clues we can.

Power is a mode, in which, as in the mode of love, there is an attractor and an attracted. Power is achieved, in the individual, by his not denying the Holy Ghost which is inside him, his own soul's self. But whether it is the power of the attractor, or the power of the attracted, that is thus achieved, Lilly does not tell us.

" You talk," says Aaron, " as if we were like trees, alone by ourselves in the world. We aren't. If we love, it needs another person than ourselves. And if we hate, and even if we talk."

" That's the point," says Lilly bewilderingly. " We've got to love and hate moreover — and even talk. But we haven't got to fix any of these modes." So that power is apparently after all, not a mode which can replace the love-mode. It co-exists with it. Behind the accidents of the love-mode, as it were, exists the substance, which is power. Beneath my states of emotion endures my inviolable and secret self. This inviolable and secret self may be an attractor, or an at-tracted. Lilly is to be the attractor, Aaron the attracted. The reason why never appears; it is a datum. But even given this submission of Aaron's inviolable self to Lilly's in the power-mode, they are evidently as free, or indeed as bound as ever, to go on loving and hating one another as before. Aaron will love and obey Lilly, or he will hate and obey him; but he will obey. And what will he obey? Lilly's "soul in its dark motion of power and pride." And what will he obey with? Presumably his own "soul in its dark motion of power and pride."

That is the one solution to the agonising problem of human relations which Lawrence now has to offer. The relation of man to woman is now become secondary, irrelevant, negligible. The woman will not accept the power-mode as a reality, nor Lawrence as a man of power. Lottie rejects Aaron, Tanny rejects Lilly, in the power-mode: the more utterly because neither woman will admit its existence. A new generation of women is required. But between man and man it may be possible. Lawrence only half-believes it. *Aaron's Rod* leaves Aaron completely uncommitted. But this is the one way out that Lawrence spies, or dreams. With woman, the fight; with the world, the fight; with the chosen man, perhaps, an ultimate and unbreakable bond, beyond love or hate, a bond of profound submission of one man's Holy Ghost to another. This fundamental theme is treated hastily in *Kangaroo*, more deeply in *The Plumed Serpent*. In those books Lawrence tries to find whether his solution is indeed a solution.

Or should we say rather, whether his way of escape is indeed a way of escape. For, behind it all, as we have perhaps sufficiently showed, is his desire to escape from the bondage and the devastating scepticism of woman — of woman who will not accept him as man. In Aaron Sisson he

presents himself without his own haunting disabilities.
Aaron is Lawrence made fully man, a man who has made
the complete answer to the woman's call. He represents
Lawrence's effort to prove to himself that even if their
relations were perfect on the animal and sensual plane, still
the woman would deny his ultimate authority. It is not his
shortcoming, not the fact that he is not "the hardy and
indomitable male," which is the cause of his failure to gain
the woman's submission. It is an impersonal resistance.

Impersonal, but perhaps not eternal. Lilly-Lawrence half-
believes; Aaron-Lawrence is sceptical. Says Lilly:

"Whatever else happens, somewhere, sometime, the deep power-
urge in man will have to issue forth again, and woman will submit, livingly, not subjectively."

"She never will," persisted Aaron. "Anything else will happen,
but not that."

"She will," said Lilly, "once man disengages himself from the
love-mode, and stands clear. Once he stands clear, and the other
great urge begins to flow in him, then the woman won't be able to
resist. Her own soul will wish to yield itself."

"Woman yield — ?" Aaron re-echoed.

"Woman — and man too."

This is the final issue in *Aaron's Rod,* and in the rest of
Lawrence's novels. Really, the conclusion is foregone; for
the power-urge has (by hypothesis) already begun to flow
in Lawrence, and still the woman does not yield. But perhaps, runs the thought in his mind or the dream in his soul,
the power-urge needs to be established as a circuit between
two men before it is really manifest. Man joined eternally
to man, in the bond of the Holy Ghost, and leaving recalcitrant woman behind — this may be the foundation of the
New Jerusalem.

Meanwhile, without his man, but with his woman, he
goes forth to explore the other life-modes.

THE ROAD TO AMERICA

THE *Fantasia* was first published in America, and addressed primarily to an American audience. Somewhere at the back of Lawrence's mind was the hope that America would accept him as a leader, and the intention that the *Fantasia* should be used as his gospel. In a poem, " The Evening Land," written in Germany at the same time as the *Fantasia,* he confesses his divided mind with regard to America.

> Shall I come to you, the open tomb of my race?
> I would come if I felt my hour had struck.
> I would rather you came to me.

He is afraid of America, afraid first of the machine-American, next of the boundless ideal love. But he is self-cajoled by his sense of the presence there of something which carries him where he wants to be carried ("or don't I? ") — " beyond what we call human."

> Nobody knows you.
> You don't know yourself.
> And I, who am half in love with you,
> What am I in love with?
> My own imaginings?

For a long while already Lawrence's imagination had been at work on America, above all on the America of the

Redskin and the Aztec. I remember that in the early years of the war, when his mind was set on escaping from the horror of England and Europe, he was engrossed in Prescott and in Crèvecoeur — a book which I bought for a shilling and passed on to him. " I would have loved the Aztecs and the Red Indians," says Lilly to himself in *Aaron's Rod*. " I know they hold the element in life which I am looking for — they had living pride." The American races — and the South Sea Islanders — the Marquesans, the Maori blood. That was the true blood. It wasn't frightened. That represents very much the upshot of Lawrence's reading and his imagination, by the end of the war. At that moment it was impossible for him to go to America: he had not the money. And later, when it was possible, he hesitated. There is much hesitation on the matter in *Aaron's Rod*. Something in him was sceptical of his own imagination; something, plainly manifest in *Sea and Sardinia,* reluctantly acknowledged that he found the human indispensable in spite of all his longing to be carried " beyond the human." Lawrence during all his life would have bitten his tongue out rather than confess that what he wanted was more love: he preferred to say aloud and to persuade himself that of all things the one he hated most was love. If he had said " of all words," it might have been true. He was a man who did not find enough love in the world. He was a disappointed lover of humanity: and he always found it bitter indeed to face that simple truth about himself.

He became adept at cheating himself with words. Half of what he meant by the " power-mode," which was to replace the " love-mode," would have been more truthfully conveyed by the frank admission that what he wanted was a new mode of love; the other half by the admission that what he wanted was a new mode of hate. The desire for love is manifest in *Aaron's Rod*. Yet Lawrence half-persuaded himself that the new mode was, in fact, an old mode: that it had existed among the Aztecs, and the Red Indians, and the South Sea Islanders, and even among the subtle Etruscans, whom his imagination made soul-brothers of the Aztecs.

In the beautiful poem " Cypresses " he gives voice to his nostalgia for the Etruscans, of whose life-mode the " vicious, dark cypresses " are to him the sole remaining monument. The Romans said that the Etruscans were evil, and obliterated them; but Lawrence regrets them.

> For oh, I know in the dust where we have buried
> The silenced races and all their abominations
> We have buried so much of the delicate magic of life.

It is the same nostalgia that took hold of Lawrence so powerfully in Cornwall, for the " dark sensual magic " of a forgotten mode of life. This mode of life — which Lawrence at different times imagined to have been achieved and enjoyed by the Etruscans, the Egyptians, the Aztecs, the dark Iberians — was the fulfilment of many yearnings, and contained many elements. It is bewilderingly multiform. It was the home of the mystery " beyond the phallic," of deliberate yet mindless sensuality between man and woman and, still more, between man and man; of the worship of the death mystery; of human blood-sacrifice; of the mode of " power "; of death to the " spiritual "; of many other things. But, I think, above all else it was a realm where Woman could not enter without putting off for ever her female nature: a realm where children are neither begotten, nor born, and the great female demand upon the male is never made.

Lawrence was absolutely divided between the love of life

and the love of death; between the desire to escape utterly from life, and the longing to bring into being a more perfect life. This contradiction finds a momentary resolution in the *Fantasia,* where the more perfect life after which he labours involves his own obliteration. In the New Jerusalem, there should be no Lawrences: he dies that men may live. But for the most part this resolution is impossible for him. The inward division of the unfulfilled man breaks out again: the desire for death and the desire for life fly apart again. The glamour of the pre-mental, death-seeking, hate-loving world of his imagination is upon him again.

But he cannot present the reality of himself to himself in these naked terms. He must convince himself that the will to escape and the will to go through with it are really the same. His voyage is not a flight, but an expedition of discovery. He is a pioneer looking for a new life-mode. He is going to America to find it. But what he means by America is something totally different from what ordinary men understand by the word: it has nothing to do with the perfectly mechanised civilisation which the word generally connotes. America is the country of the Red Indian and the Aztec; both of whom the America we know has utterly denied.

> Evil, what is evil?
> There is only one evil, to deny life.
> As Rome denied Etruria
> And mechanical America Montezuma still.

So ends the poem " Cypresses." One need hardly point out the self-deception. Not to deny life, in this sense, would mean that every manifestation of life must be maintained in existence. True, Lawrence has declared (in the *Fantasia*) that he does not believe in evolution; but in a succession of catastrophes and creations. But that alters nothing. For within each creative cycle life-denial is necessary to life. Nature is red in tooth and claw, and so is humanity. Life-denial is the very process of life. And further, if it is evil that the palefaces should deny the life of the Aztecs or the Redskins, why is it not evil that the Aztec blood-sacrificers should deny the life of their victims?

The contradiction is hopeless, and the cause is manifest. The nostalgia for mindlessness and death, for the escape from consciousness, and for communion and comradeship in the mindless world, is upon Lawrence again. He feels bitter that the Aztecs, whom "he would have loved," and with whom he might have lived in this communion of mindlessness, are no more. Yet perhaps, he dreams, something remains; perhaps even mechanical America at his summons will cease to deny Montezuma; perhaps he can reveal to America its own deep desire for that which he desires. Thither he will go.

But before he departed from Taormina and from Europe, he wrote some beautiful poems contained in *Birds, Beasts and Flowers*. They make it clear to us what it was in himself that he desired to escape, and they declare it more nakedly than he has declared it before. The chief of these poems is the brief sequence: *Tortoises*. They are very remarkable poems. They are remarkable, first, because of the extraordinary tenderness which Lawrence feels towards the tortoises. It is as though the passion of love which he would not suffer himself to feel, or at least to express, for mankind, or for an individual woman, had to find an outlet. He was safe in loving a baby tortoise; the baby tortoise could not love him back. So Lawrence lavishes his tenderness upon the little creature, " the invincible forerunner "; who cannot respond.

Alone, small insect,
Tiny bright-eye,
Slow one.

No poems of Lawrence's are to me more beautiful than these
to the little tortoise; and none more pathetic in their full
implication.

But the crucial significance of the tortoise poems lies
elsewhere. Of course, Lawrence completely humanises his
tortoises, though he would have rejected the imputation with
disdain. He would call it " blood-tenderness " that he feels
towards them; in fact, it is wonderful imaginative love.
But what fascinates him and most deeply arouses his sympathy, is the tortures of sexual desire which he imagines
the tortoise to endure. The tiny invincible forerunner grows
to tortoise-manhood. Lawrence watches him scuffling beside
his female, persistent, unsatisfied, humiliated.

And how he feels it!
The lonely rambler, the stoic, dignified stalker through chaos,
The immune, the animate,
Enveloped in isolation,
Fore-runner.
Now look at him!

How the description fits the achieved and lonely soul of
Lawrence, " immune, enveloped in isolation, forerunner "!
Lawrence knows nothing whatever of what a tortoise feels.
The chasm of the " other dimension " is between them eter-
nally. But he does know what one particular man feels.

Alas, the spear is through the side of his isolation.
His adolescence saw him crucified into sex,
Doomed, in the long crucifixion of desire, to seek his consumma-
tion beyond himself.
Divided into passionate duality,

He, so finished and immune, now broken into desirous frag-
    mentariness,
Doomed to make an intolerable fool of himself
In his effort towards completion again.

In poem after poem of this sequence the theme returns.
" Sex, which breaks up our integrity, our single inviolability,
our deep silence." The woman pities the female-tortoise.
How the male pesters and torments her! " How much more
is *he* pestered and tormented! " Lawrence replies. Not only
the tortoise, but the goat and the ass — all suffer the crucifixion of sexual desire. For the ass:

> He fell into the rut of love.
> Poor ass, like man, always in rut.
> The pair of them alike in that.
> All his soul in his gallant member,
> And his head gone heavy with knowledge of desire
> And of humiliation.

There is, in all these poems, a profound resentment against
the compulsion of sex upon the male. Only the point of view
of the male — if it can be called the point of view of *the*
male — is considered. It is the male alone who bears the
cross, who is humiliated, whose integrity is violated. He, so
complete and immune is his isolation, is torn in sunder by
desire.

> Born to walk alone,
> Fore-runner,
> Now suddenly distracted into this mazy side-track,
> This awkward harrowing pursuit.

We are reminded of Rupert Birkin's sudden outburst in
Women in Love. " On the whole he hated sex: it was such a
limitation."

This fierce and burning resentment is almost startling,

because Lawrence seldom gave it such naked expression as in these poems, and we fall imperceptibly into the habit of thinking that because Lawrence was so constantly concerned with sex, he loved it. The very vehemence of his concern, on the contrary, should have put us on our guard. At bottom it is a fetter which he longs to shake off. Knowledge of desire, for him and for the ass, is knowledge of humiliation; and he has the intense hatred felt by the mediaeval monk against this humiliation and the cause of it — Woman. Love really *is* hatred for him.

This is behind the sheer detestation of woman which underlies *Aaron's Rod*. The longing to escape from the love-mode is the longing to escape from the bondage to woman, from the bondage to woman so agonisingly felt by the unsatisfied and unsatisfying man. And, whatever else the new life-mode which he is seeking will contain, we may be certain of one thing, that the basic union will be the union between men, and that the woman will be brought into complete subjection. The brave will have his squaw; but the business of life will be done with men and men alone. The squaw's sole function is to answer the call of the male, and to be satisfied when he tells her she should be satisfied. She herself must do no calling. Above all, she must never criticise his manhood.

This is the main element in the paradisal life-mode of the Redskin and the Aztec, of which Lawrence sets himself to discover the vestiges in *Studies in Classical American Literature*. The great ideal is announced in the essay on Fenimore Cooper, in the very phrases of the *Fantasia* which it completely repudiates.

What did Cooper dream beyond democracy? Why, in his immortal friendship of Chingachook and Natty Bumpo he dreamed the nucleus of a new society. That is, he dreamed a new human relationship. A stark, stripped human relationship of two men,

D. H. LAWRENCE

IN THE MARKET-PLACE AT OAXACA 1926

deeper than the deeps of sex. Deeper than property, deeper than fatherhood, deeper than marriage, deeper than love. So deep that it is loveless. The stark, loveless, wordless unison of two men who have come to the bottom of themselves. This is the nucleus of a new society, the clue to a new world-epoch. It asks for a great and cruel sloughing first of all. Then it finds a great release into a new world, a new moral, a new landscape.

It is improbable that Fenimore Cooper did dream this, and probable that he would have been aghast at Lawrence's assertion. Cooper certainly took the relation between man and man more easily, as he took the relation between man and woman more easily, than Lawrence. But there is no doubt at all that Lawrence was dreaming it, now. He fathers his desire on to Cooper, just as he fathered his new life-mode on to the Etruscans or the Aztecs, in order that it should have less of the appearance of his own personal dream. Besides, he would like to convince the Americans that his desire is native to them. They have only to be aware of their own tradition, to make their land a home for him.

But this declaration of the dream and the desire has a further importance. It gives, or seems to give, some answer to the perplexing problem left unsolved at the end of *Aaron's Rod*: the problem, Why should Aaron's Holy Ghost submit to Lilly's, and not Lilly's to Aaron's? Lawrence now tells us something more.

Natty and the Great Serpent are neither equals nor unequals. *Each obeys the other when the moment arrives.* And each is stark and dumb in the other's presence, starkly himself, without illusion created. Each is just the crude pillar of a man, the crude living column of his own manhood. And each knows the godhead of this crude column of manhood. A new relationship.

We have put the crucial sentence in italics. It would have made things easier if Lilly could have spoken so plainly to

Aaron. But, at that time, it scarcely occurred to Lilly that also he should be called upon to make submission to "the heroic soul" of Aaron. This particular essay on Cooper was evidently written when Lawrence had actually arrived in America. Can it be (one might wonder) that the former dream of leadership has suffered abatement in the democratic air? The answer is No. In the last hiding place of his soul, Lawrence does not want to lead at all; or if to lead, to lead but one man, and be led by him. Leadership, power — these are only the names he gives to the relation with a man for which he hungers. He cannot call it the love which "passes the love of women," because the word is forbidden him. But he is the same man still who in his first book declared that his friendship with a man was "more perfect than any love he had known since."

Let me not be misunderstood. I believe, and very deeply, that Lawrence *was* a leader, or rather that in generations to come he will be found to be a leader. But he was not at all a leader in the mode which he dreamed. He was, or will be, a leader in the mode which, with his lips, he utterly repudiated. He was a leader after the fashion of the man who leads because he suffers, who leads because he is crucified. "I, if I be lifted up, will draw all men unto me." This was the mode in which Lawrence was destined to become a leader. And he lifted himself up. The inexorable compulsion was upon him of uttering himself, of exposing himself, as perhaps no man has been uttered and exposed before. One is aghast at the completeness of his self-revelation: aghast and awed and finally overcome with a passion of love and reverence for that which he was. His escapes, his disguises, his repudiations, his denials — these are all part of the man — the form of his prayer that the cup might pass from him.

We shall return to *Studies in Classical American Literature*. Now for a time we must follow him in his journeying. He left Italy in the spring of 1922 to reach America by way of Australia. He avoided India, for India might have understood him too well; but he touched at Ceylon, and, I believe, stayed there some little time. At any rate he wrote a poem in Kandy; it describes a procession of elephants passing before the Prince of Wales — "that tired remnant of royalty up there, whose motto is *Ich dien*." And Lawrence persuades himself that the reason why the great night festival of homage fell, or seemed to him to fall, into frustration, why the mighty elephants were, or seemed to him to be, dejected, was that beasts and men alike had come to pay homage to a Prince indeed, to hear the majestic summons: *Dient Ihr!* "Serve me."

Instead of which, the silent, fatal emission from that pale shattered boy up there:
Ich dien.

Lawrence's imagination puts a momentary spell upon us. We shake it off and remember that *Ich dien* was the motto also of the Black Prince at Cressy, of Prince Harry at Agincourt. Still, it is true that royalty — or English royalty — is drudge to the public, though it is unlikely that the elephants found more delight in going on their knees before the great Aurungzebe himself than before the Prince of Wales. And it is true also, I believe, that it is for men, if not for elephants, "good as a draught of cold water to bow very, very low to the royal." But not for one moment do I believe that the Sinhalese mahouts felt "the silent fatal emission." The Prince of Wales, in his tiredness and his languor, was truly royal to them.

It was Lawrence's advised European soul that felt the disappointment. Royalty meant nothing to him; he could not respond any longer. Royalty was only a romantic dream for him, and if in fact the Prince of Wales had been a berserk, Lawrence would not have responded to his royalty. To the man, no doubt, for Lawrence always did respond to a man: but to the Prince, never.

I wish they had given the three feathers to me;
That I had been in the pavilion, as in a pepper-box aloft and alone,
To stand and hold feathers, three feathers above the world,
And say to them: *Dient Ihr! Dient!*
Omnes, vos omnes, servite.
Serve me, I am meet to be served,
Being royal of the gods.

Lawrence might have remembered that in a world where royalty is truly royal, prophets are nobodies, and geniuses content, nay positively exalted, to be the very least of the gentlemen of the bedchamber. He should have been a little more grateful to this age of democracy, which, with all its manifest and crying iniquities, had this at least to its credit, that it suffered him to be what he was. A more violent, or more royal, age would have allowed him shorter shrift.

Significant, too, that the romantic dream of temporal majesty should have allured him when he was as near as he ever dared to come to India — the one country in the whole world where perhaps he might have been a leader in virtue of the qualities he really possessed, not those he merely dreamed of possessing. In India, it seems, the spiritual man is revered for the spirit that is in him.

But he passed India by and went on to Australia. I believe that he stayed some weeks in Western Australia before going on to Sydney. During those weeks he met a lady — a nurse in an up-country hospital — who showed him a novel she had written. Lawrence was impressed by it, and promised to re-write it, and find a publisher for it. It became *The Boy in the Bush*. It is, as we shall see, an important document in Lawrence's soul-adventure; but it cannot be understood except as a sequel to the novel of Australia that is wholly his own, namely, *Kangaroo*.

AUSTRALIA

KANGAROO is a chaotic book. It has many passages of great descriptive beauty, but internally it is a chaos. It is also the last of Lawrence's novels in which he himself appears as the chief character. This for obvious reasons. The internal chaos of *Kangaroo* is the internal chaos of Richard Lovat Somers, who is Lawrence. It is impossible that he should be a character any more. He is exploded in fragments. Nothing in his being, at the end of the book, is more important than anything else.

Not that Lawrence cares to put it precisely in that way, though he is, on occasion, ruthless enough with himself to do that. But for the most part he represents his nihilism in the form of an apotheosis of all his contradictory elements. Every impulse is a " God." Somers attracts people, becomes involved with them, gives friendships, swears allegiance, withdraws, lets them down, behaves with utter irresponsibility; and every time it is a " God " whom he obeys. It looks, and feels, like blasphemy, even to his own religion.

Lawrence felt it himself. If there is any God in the book, it is Somers himself; and he makes a poor one. The purpose, the inscrutable purpose, divine or human, which seemed to hold Lawrence's former embodiments together and to make Birkin, and Sisson, and Lilly men in whose life- and thought-adventures we are agonisingly interested, as though some

issue of deep and present import to ourselves were being
decided in them — this purpose seems slowly to fade out of
Somers in the course of *Kangaroo*. In his actual self he
seems to shrink physically, to dwindle; and, curiously
enough, this impression is not a trick of the reader's imagination. Lawrence himself suddenly begins to throw emphasis
on Somers' smallness and slightness. He is called, more than
once, " little Richard," and the name sticks in the memory.
We feel that Lawrence had suddenly become conscious of
his own physical frailty. He is losing physical significance,
in his own eyes.

That phrase, " losing significance," sums up better than
another, the total effect of *Kangaroo*. As the sly and smiling
and cynical Cornishman, Jaz, says at the end to Somers,
when he has decided to leave Australia and go to America,
" Why, Mr. Somers, seems to me you just go round the world
looking for things you're not going to give in to. You're as
bad as we folk." Somers will not have it. The blow to his
pride he cannot accept, because it is given by another man.
He does give in, he claims. He gives in " to the Lord God
Almighty — which is more than you do." Since Somers
himself is the sole interpreter of His oracles, it seems un-
reasonable to deny that Jaz does the same. But Somers does
deny it. And not only does he claim to surrender to the Lord
God Almighty; he claims to do more than this.

" And another thing," said Richard. " I won't give up the flag
of our real civilised consciousness. I'll give up the ideals. But not
the aware, self-responsible, deep consciousness that we've gained.
I won't go back on that."

In isolation it is impressive; but by the time we reach the
end of *Kangaroo,* we are doubtful whether it means anything at all. We suspect that the self-responsible consciousness may be, like " God," a synonym for Somers; and that

obedience to the Lord God Almighty, and not giving up the flag of the self-responsible consciousness, mean exactly the same thing: Somers will be obedient to Somers, and Somers will keep the flag of Somers flying. It is enough. That is, indeed, his mission and his destiny.

∽

I do not know whether there was anything in Lawrence's actual experience in Australia to correspond, even remotely, with the main events of *Kangaroo*. Certainly, Kangaroo himself, the impassioned and unmarried idealist, is an invention; he is a symbol, who makes no impression of human reality upon us. He is the means by which Lawrence tries to decide, in his imagination, whether he would lead or help to lead a nation. Kangaroo is already a leader of a kind of Fascist organisation. His object is to create a new society based on the love between man and man. His movement is wholly a man's movement, and its inspiration is the ideal of comradeship — a sort of powerfully organised Whitmanism. Kangaroo offers Somers a place of leadership in this movement, and a relation of comradeship to himself. On the other side, Struthers, the leader of the revolutionary socialists, a bitter exponent of the class warfare which is anathema to Kangaroo, also offers Somers a place of responsibility in his movement. Somers is drawn to both, particularly drawn to Kangaroo, to whom he actually promises allegiance, then withdraws, then promises allegiance again, and backs out finally. The rejection of Struthers' offer is less difficult.

But long before he is actually involved with these central men, Harriet, the woman, has seen the process beginning in Somers' growing intimacy with Jack Calcott, their next-door neighbour in Sydney, who turns out to be one of Kangaroo's lieutenants. In this book, the woman has grown far larger than before. As Somers has decreased, she has increased. The effect is not deliberate; but now for the first time in the sequence of self-recording novels we have the definite impression not of the man and woman as equals, though antagonists, with the man seeking to lead, but of the woman as a tolerant, and kindly, but rather cynical mother, humouring a wayward child. Harriet knows the whole history before it is even begun. Why must Somers begin involving and implicating himself with men again? Why should he not simply settle down with her, in this marvellous new country, quite alone and be happy? And Somers answers:

" Because I feel I *must* fight out something with mankind yet. I haven't finished with my fellow-men. I've got a struggle with them yet."

Harriet asks him what struggle, and why? And he cannot answer. He *doesn't* like people, she tells him. He always turns away from them and hates them. " Yet like a dog to his vomit you always turn back. And it will be the same old game here again as everywhere else." All he does, she says, is to delude himself about a lot of twopenny little people, and hate them and himself afterwards, and fall back finally on her.

He was silent. He heard all that she had to say: and he knew that as far as the past went, it was all quite true. He had started off on his fiery courses: always, as she said, to fall back rather the worse for the attempt, on her. She had no use at all for fiery courses and efforts with the world of men. Let all that rubbish go.

All he has to say in his defence is that he still has the longing to make the attempt, and would she wait until the longing is exhausted? Tolerantly, with a sort of pitiful tenderness, she says she supposes she'll have to.

" You see," he said, " I have the roots of my life with you. But I want, if possible, to send out a new shoot in the life of mankind — the effort man makes forever, to grow into new forms."

She looked at him. And somehow she wanted to cry, because he was so silly in refusing to be finally disappointed in his efforts with mankind, and yet his silliness was pathetic, in a way beautiful. But then it *was* so silly — she wanted to shake him.

" Send out a new shoot then. Send it out. You do it in your writing already! " she cried. " But getting yourself mixed up with these impudent little people won't send any shoots, don't you think it. They'll nip you in the bud again, as they always do."

He pondered this also, stubbornly, and knew it was true. But he had set his will on something, and wasn't going to give way.

" I want to do something with living people, somehow, somewhere, while I live on the earth. I write, but I write alone. And I live alone. Without any connection whatever with the rest of men."

" Don't swank, you don't live alone. You've got *me* there safe enough, to support you. Don't swank to me about being alone, because it insults me, you see. I know how much alone you are, with me always there keeping you together."

And again he sulked and swallowed it, and obstinately held out.

Never before had Lawrence touched this pitch of ruthlessness with himself. The candour of the confession is wonderful, but the confession itself terrible. It is made again, and still more impressively, a little later in the book, when Jack Calcott has told Somers some of the details of Kangaroo's organisation and his plans, and sworn him to secrecy. He is not to tell his wife: this is a man's business. Jack Calcott, who is a good deal of " the hardy indomitable male " in fact and not in dream, has no trouble whatever in keeping his affairs from his charming wife. Quite otherwise with Somers. Harriet asks, and he will not tell her. She resents the exclusion, and at the end of the day he finds her with tears in her eyes.

At once his heart became very troubled: because after all she was all he had in the world, and he couldn't bear her to be really disappointed or wounded. He wanted to ask her what was the matter, and to try and comfort her. But he knew it would be false. He knew that her greatest grief was when he turned away from their personal human life of intimacy to this impersonal business of male activity for which he was always craving. So he felt miserable, but went away without saying anything.

It was tender-hearted and lovable in Somers; but an unsuspecting reader of his books would have imagined that this problem was settled long ago: that, indeed, it was not a problem at all. The strong and lonely man of the *Fantasia* was to go about his impersonal male creative activity in complete independence of the woman, and the woman would be satisfied, more than satisfied, fulfilled with a completeness of fulfilment she could attain by no other way. But all this, we now realise, was a wish-fulfilment. In actual life it is far different. But how far different not even the most advised reader would have guessed without the further evidence of *Kangaroo*.

Somers recounts a dream. It is a recurrent dream. It may not have been an actual dream of Lawrence's; but it fits too close to his circumstances not to convey an intimate personal experience. If it is not a dream he dreamed, it is a dream he imagined he ought to have dreamed — a dream " of a woman, a woman he loved, something like Harriet, something like his mother, yet unlike either, a woman sullen and obstinate against him, repudiating him."

The Somers of the dream was terribly upset. He cried tears from his very bowels, and laid his hand on the woman's arm saying:

" But I love you. Don't you *believe* in me? Don't you *believe* in me? " But the woman — she seemed almost old now — only shed a few bitter tears, bitter as vitriol, from her distorted face, and bit-

terly, hideously turned away, dragging her arm from the touch of
his fingers; turned, as it seemed to the dream-Somers, away to the
sullen and dreary, everlasting hell of repudiation.

The woman is Woman; the face, Somers says, is the face
not only of his mother and his wife, but of his sister, and
girls he had known when young. And it is terrible and fearful to him.

Two women he had loved down to the quick of life and death:
his mother and Harriet. And the woman in the dream was so
awfully his mother, risen from the dead, and at the same time
Harriet, as it were, departing from this life, that he stared at the
night-paleness between the window-curtains in horror.

"They neither of them believed in me," he said to himself.
Still in the spell of the dream, he put it in the past tense, though
Harriet lay sleeping in the next bed. He could not get over it.

And he is afraid of his dream. He was a great enemy of
dreams, for in his private life his dreams were like devils.
He tried to comfort himself with the thought that they were
weaknesses which he had overcome in his waking consciousness, come to assail him in sleep, when he was off his guard.
Really, the dream was evidence that he had overcome the
weakness. So he argues with himself; but the fear abides.

But what is the weakness? What is it that he is afraid
of? One would almost say the vengeful spirit of Woman,
for the whole strange passage gives one the sense of a
man haunted by the Furies: the impression is far stronger
than that given by the next words of explanation. There is
real *terror* in the fear.

He had an ingrained instinct or habit of thought which made
him feel that he could never take the move into activity unless
Harriet and his dead mother believed in him. They both loved
him: that he knew. They both believed in him terribly, in per-

sonal being. In the individual man he was, and the son of man, they believed with all the intensity of undivided love. But in the impersonal man, the man that would go beyond them, and with his back to them, away from them into an activity which excluded them, in this man they did not find it so easy to believe.

"Not so easy" is less than the truth: evidently, impossible is the word. And who is this Lawrence — this impersonal Lawrence — in whom the two women of his life find it impossible to believe? Briefly, he is the independent Lawrence: and the reason why it is impossible for them to believe in him is that they know, quite simply and finally, that he does not exist. As Lawrence in childhood depended on his mother, so now in manhood he depends upon his wife. His mother knew it, his wife knows it. Nay more, after a long and fearful struggle to be free, he is lapsing now back into the condition of child in relation to his own wife. She is big and warm and comforting, and he is "little Richard." He is creeping back to her. He is about to disappear as individual and independent man even from the world of his own imagination: his own novels will know him no more.

The doom is horrible to him. He loathes it; and he hates Woman by whom it is imposed upon him. The Woman he can love must be dead; living Woman he hates. And in a strange poem written in New Mexico a few months after *Kangaroo* was written — "Spirits Summoned West" — he makes the confession. He calls to him over the ocean the spirits of the women " he had loved and told to die." He is safe with the spirits of women,

> Women who were gentle
> And who loved me
> And whom I loved
> And told to die.

"And told to die," in order that he might love them, who could not love them living. Living, he hated them; they engulfed him, they put aside with deadly and intimate knowledge his pretensions of separateness, they did it without knowing what they were doing, instinctively, and were perplexed by his revulsions and his hatred, which sprang from his weakness, not their crime. Says Lawrence truly:

> I didn't tell you to die, for nothing.
> I wanted the virgin you to be home at last
> In my heart.

None the less this would-be perfect love of Woman is an escape from Woman; an absolute separation made between the living and instinctive woman whom he hates, and the spiritual woman whom he can love.

This does not mean that the poem is not a beautiful poem. It is very beautiful indeed, and it utters the deep, intolerable and final yearning of Lawrence's heart, for a manhood that should not be torn asunder and crucified by sex, for a life in which his integrity should not have been broken up by the torment of desire, for that resurrection in which there is neither marriage, nor giving in marriage. How strange it seems to the mere outward reader of Lawrence's writings that this should have been the deepest yearning of his heart, to be as an angel in heaven!

It is pitiful and tragic that at this moment in his life Lawrence had not the courage to take the mortal leap, and separate himself finally from woman. If he could have had the final courage of his own isolation, how different the remaining story might have been! Instead of being shattered into fragments, he might have been a perfect unity, a universal man actively by achievement, not passively by destiny. The moment had come when he, like his great forerunner, was called upon to say: "Woman, what have I to do with thee? " And he could not say it. By failing in this, he forfeited ultimately the belief of men and women alike. They can believe in him, henceforward, only personally; in the impersonal man they cannot, and will not, believe. He could not pay the price of his final integrity.

In the terms of Somers' confession in *Kangaroo,* Lawrence's fatal weakness is that his woman must believe in him, impersonally, or he cannot go forward. And the woman cannot believe in him, impersonally, while she knows that he depends upon her belief in him. It is impossible. The choice is before him now, and he cannot escape. If he tries to postpone the choice, he has chosen. Either he must tear himself finally free from his dependence upon the woman, and decide, once for ever, in his soul that it does not matter whether she, or any woman, or any man, believes in him. Or he must resign all hope of going forward any more. Not to go forward for such a man is to go backward.

Lawrence could not do it. He could not tear himself free. He could not be finally alone. We may say: he could not believe *in himself.* And indeed he could not. But no man ultimately believes in himself, of himself. To believe in oneself is to have surrendered oneself. And this Lawrence could not do. He could not leave go. He clung to the woman. He could not believe in himself without ceasing to cling to the woman; he could not cease to cling to the woman without believing in himself. There is a vicious circle; there is no way out. But this is eternally the situation of the human soul on the verge of its own death and resurrection. Then nothing but the courage of a final loneliness will avail. A man must plunge into death, expecting nothing, hoping nothing, with only the knowledge that he can endure the deep inward division no longer. He must choose, and he must

228 SON OF WOMAN

choose death, rather than a life that is no life. If he chooses
death, life will come. Lawrence chose life, and death came
instead.

∽

And the first signs of approaching death are unmistakable
in *Kangaroo*. Implicit in it all is a surrender not to any God,
but to the woman. She now contains him wholly, in the
sure knowledge that all his efforts towards an impersonal
activity with men will fail, and that all his talk about it in
the last resort is " swank." Her knowledge is instinctive,
unreasoned. She does not need to argue it, she simply knows
that a man who is dependent upon her as he is dependent
cannot enter into an impersonal activity with men. It is a
craving in him, the inevitable counterpart of, and reaction
from, his craving for her. Let him conquer that craving,
tear it out of himself by the roots, and she will believe in
him impersonally. Till then she cannot, neither can any
woman, nor any man.

The real substance of *Kangaroo* is Somers' continual
evasion of his own evasion, the continual endeavour to
represent it to himself as a positive significance. When
friendship is offered, he withdraws. He does not know why
he withdraws; he simply feels that he shrinks away. *C'est
plus fort que lui.* Therefore it is a God who draws him back.
He deceives himself, if God is more than a word. It is the
absence and denial of the God within him which draws him
back: the fear that his own ultimate weakness may be
exposed, that the man will know him as the woman knows
him, as one who cannot be alone, and therefore cannot be
trusted.

" When it comes to doing anything," says Jack to Somers
at the end, " you sort of fade out, you're nowhere." It is
pitiless, and it is true. Somers, at the crisis, has faded out.

" No, we don't mind," Jack continued. " It's quite right, you haven't let us down, because we haven't given you a chance. That's all. In so far as you've had any chance to, you've let us down, and we knew it."

Richard was silent. Perhaps it was true. And he hated such a truth.

He well might hate it, well might be intolerably pained by " the contempt of the confident he-man for the shifty she-man." How could Jack understand his nature and his torment? But there it was. All the king's horses and all the king's men couldn't put Somers together again. He himself does his best. It is the cause, he says to himself, the cause in which he does not believe; he doesn't believe in Kangaroo's aims. But the issue has been decided long before there is any question of Kangaroo's ultimate aims, before Somers has even met Kangaroo. It is decided when Jack offers his comradeship.

He half wanted to commit himself to this whole affection with a friend, a comrade, a mate. And then in the last issue he didn't want it at all. The affection would be deep and genuine enough: that he knew. But — when it came to the point he didn't want any more affection. All his life he had cherished a beloved ideal of friendship — David and Jonathan. And now when true and good friends offered, he found he simply could not commit himself even to simple friendship. The whole trend of this affection, this min-gling, this intimacy, this truly beautiful love, he found his soul just set against it. He couldn't go alone with it. He didn't want a friend, he didn't want loving affection, he didn't want comradeship. No, his soul trembled when he tried to drive it along the way, like Balaam's Ass. It did not want friendship or comradeship, great or small, deep or shallow.

It took Lovat Somers some time before he would really admit and accept this new fact. Not till he had striven hard with his soul did he come to see the angel in the way; not till his soul, like Balaam's Ass, had spoken more than once. And then, when forced to admit it, it was a revolution in his mind. He had all his life had this craving for an absolute friend, a David to his Jonathan, Pylades to his Orestes: a blood-brother. All his life he had secretly grieved over his friendlessness. And now at last, when it really offered — and it had offered twice before, since he had left Europe — he didn't want it, and he realised that in his innermost soul he had never wanted it.

Yet he wanted *some* living fellowship with other men; as it was he was just isolated. Maybe a living fellowship! — but not affection, not love, not comradeship. Not mates and equality and mingling. Not blood-brotherhood. None of that.

What else? He didn't know. He only knew he was never destined to be mate or comrade or even friend with any man. Some other living relationship. But what? He did not know. Perhaps the thing that the dark races know: that one can still feel in India: the mystery of lordship. . . .

We need not follow Somers into the new elaboration of his dream, nor even into the actual terms of his argument with Kangaroo. It is abundantly clear that the issue is not impersonal; it is personal, and it is decided before Somers has met Kangaroo. The Kangaroo episode, in itself not very convincing, is irrelevant to the inward argument of the book. Lawrence definitely says so.

Before Somers went down to find Jack and to be taken by him to luncheon with the Kangaroo, he had come to the decision, or to the knowledge that mating and comradeship were contrary to his destiny. He would never pledge himself to Jack, nor to this venture in which Jack was concerned.

The book is at an end before it is well begun. Really, it was at an end long before this, in the conversation between Somers and Harriet which we have quoted. " I have to be the only man as well as the only woman," she says. There is nothing more to say.

௮

The true interest in the book, apart from its passages of magical description — the interest of what Lawrence called the " thought-adventure " of his writing, lies in the manner in which he will, because he must, evade the ultimate admission. He admits much — terribly much; but he cannot admit that his final surrender to the Woman, and his final rejection of the man, are the same. He does not even admit, in his consciousness he *cannot* admit, that he has finally surrendered to the Woman. He can only admit that he has finally rejected the man; and rejection is too strong a word for what he does. He shrinks away from the man. So much, and no more, he admits in his consciousness.

His excuse is an excuse that now is wearing thin. It is that he cannot bear " love," or " mingling," or " intimacy." But our memories rebel; we cannot forget that in *The White Peacock,* in *Women in Love,* in *Aaron's Rod,* it was precisely the " mingling " and " intimacy " with a man which he craved — the physical contact, the absolute of naked touch, the blood-brotherhood: it could never be intimate enough.

We may leave it at that, and watch Somers at his work of hiding from himself. He withdraws from the men, from the men themselves, and from their activities.

What did he want with guns and revolvers? Nothing. He had nothing to do with them, as he had nothing to do with so much that is in the world of man. When he was truly himself, he had a quiet stillness in his soul, an inward trust. Faith undefined and indefinable. Then he was at peace with himself. Not content, but peace like a river, something flowing and full. A stillness at the very core. . . . Somers realised that he had a fright against being swept away, because he half-wanted to be swept away; but that now, thank God, he was flowing back. . . . Some men, some women must stay by their own inmost being, in peace, and without envy. And there in the stillness listen, and try to know, and try to obey.

We have heard it before, in the *Fantasia,* and there, we remember, the achievement of this inward peace was but the prelude to the creative activity with men, the founding of the nucleus of a new society. Now it has come to be the refuge from the creative activity with men. But our hands are not required to demolish this Elysium. Somers will do it himself, and immediately.

But poor dear Richard, he was only resting and basking in the old sunshine now, after the fray. The fight would come again, and only in the fight would his soul burn its way once more, to the knowledge, the intense knowledge, of his " dark god." The other was so much sweeter and easier, while it lasted.

Fight? But what has the fight been? As far as we can see, only the struggle back from the threat of friendship with men, of immersion in the affairs of men. This is hardly a fight, and in any case there is to be no more such " fighting." And, again, who is this new " dark god " of whom in this " fighting " he gains this intense knowledge? " Dark gods " we have met before in Lawrence's work, but this is a new one, of whom we must know more.

We must wait for the knowledge. To the moment of " inward peace," inevitably succeeds a long period of black hatred, when Somers felt " just generally diabolical, for no reason at all." Then he explains it to himself. He has not been keeping the inward connection with Harriet.

It is one of the deepest realities in life. When a man and a woman truly come together, when there is a marriage, then an unconscious vital connection is established between them, like a throbbing blood-circuit. A man may forget a woman entirely with his head, and fling himself with energy and fervour into whatever job he is tackling, and all is well, all is good, if he does not break

that inner vital connection which is the mystery of marriage. . . .
Now in this revolution stunt, and his insistence on " male " activity, Somers had upturned the root-flow, and Harriet was a
devil to him — quite rightly — for he knew that inside himself he
was devilish.

What kind of " male " activity, we must ask, would leave
this inward connection with the woman unbroken? And the
answer, we fear, is any kind of male activity that is not
male: and the only activity we can think of that satisfies
these necessary conditions is the imagination of a male
activity — to sit down with Harriet and imagine that she is
not there.

Or, to put it in our former terms, this male activity which
will not break the connection must be one that Harriet believes in; and since it is now accepted that Harriet cannot believe in any of Somers' male activities, there is no
male activity in which Somers can possibly indulge which
will not break the inward connection between them. The
vicious circle closes round him again. And again, Somers
admits it: he tears away the verbiage of his own previous
" explanation."

Him, a lord and master! How could one believe in such a man!
If he had been naturally a master of men, general of an army, or
manager of some great steel-works, with thousands of men under
him — then, yes, she could have acknowledged the *master* part
of the bargain, if not the lord. . . . Whereas . . . he had absolutely nothing but her. And that was why, presumably, he wanted
to establish this ascendancy over her, assume this arrogance.

So speaks Harriet. And there seems to be no way out at
all. He can prove that he is a lord and master, that he has
power, only by being ready to leave her, and he cannot do it,
and because he cannot do it he is, in verity, neither a lord
nor a master.

∽

The impasse is absolute, to normal eyes. But Somers has still a solution. It is the new "dark God," of whom he told us so little, and so obscurely, before.

He did not yet submit to the fact which he *half*-knew: that before mankind would accept any man for king, and before Harriet would ever accept him, Richard Lovat, as a lord and master, he, this self-same Richard who was so strong on kingship, must open the doors of his soul and let in a dark Lord and Master for himself, the dark god he had sensed outside the door. Let him once truly submit to the dark majesty, break open his doors to this fearful god who is master, and enters us from below, the lower doors; let himself once admit a Master, the unspeakable God: and the rest would happen.

After which Lawrence adds a nursery rhyme: "The fire began to burn the stick. . . ." Which can be interpreted only as meaning that this last "dark God" is too much even for Lawrence. He cannot really believe in him.

This "dark God" appears again: indeed he haunts the second half of *Kangaroo*. He is Lawrence's final refuge. We must try to look upon him face to face. In his debate with himself after he has refused Struthers' offer, Somers begins by re-asserting the belief with which we are now familiar. The foundation of a new society will be the new sacred bond between men, beyond the family, "the new passion." But, he says, human love and trust are perilous; they always break down. Human beings *can't* absolutely love one another. Yet love is the greatest thing between human beings. Yet it is impossible. "Each man *does* kill the thing he loves, by sheer dint of loving it. Is love then just a horror in life? " And Somers replies to himself:

" Ah no. This individuality which each of us has got and which makes him a wayward, a wilful, dangerous, untrustworthy quantity to every other individual, because every individuality is bound to react at some time against every other individuality, without exception — or else lose its own integrity; because of the inevitable necessity of each individual to react away from every other individual, at certain times, human love is truly a relative thing, not an absolute. It *cannot* be absolute.

" Yet the human heart must have an absolute. It is one of the conditions of being human. The only thing is the God who is the source of all passion. Once go down before the God — passion and human passions take their right rhythm. But human passion without the God-passion always kills the thing it loves. . . . With no deep God who is the source of all passion and life to hold them separate and yet sustained in accord, the loving comrades would smash one another. . . . Any more love is a hopeless thing, till we have found again, each for himself, the great dark God who will sustain us in our loving one another. Till then, best not play with more fire."

But who can believe that there *is* a dark God who will sustain us in loving one another? That Lawrence needs something to sustain him in loving woman or man is abundantly clear, just as it is clear that in him the passion of " love " is of such a nature that it does kill the thing it loves. Love, in him, " presupposes a corpse."

Because his love is inordinate, not a strength but a weakness, because in it there is no final detachment at all, unless it be the detachment wrought by death, or the chasm between the human and the non-human, Lawrence flees from it. Yet the fearful craving remains. Now in his need he invents the new " dark God " who shall enable him to love without killing or being killed. There is no such " dark god "; unless he is Death himself. Death will detach us from the beloved, whether we will or no. And Lawrence's fevered imagination, seeking an issue from his hopeless imprisonment, seeks a condition of death without being dead. He has not had the strength to die, by tearing himself away from the woman; to die in actual life is beyond his powers. He can only imagine a death.

The new " dark God " is this imagined death, that is no death. That is what he is essentially. All kinds of other elements are heaped into him to make him real — " the first dark ithyphallic God," the vertebral consciousness of the great whales, and other similar things. He is almost, but not quite, imposing. But he is too Protean. When he has become " the vertebral interplay between men," and when we are assured that this " vertebral interplay is the root of all our living," it is time to call a halt. What does this " vertebral interplay " amount to? It is, we are told, the " vertebral emanations " which gave Napoleon his power. What do they give Richard Somers, in his crucial interview with the sick Kangaroo?

Poor Richard, he went away almost blinded with stress and grief and bewilderment. Was it true what Kangaroo had said? Was it true? Did he, Richard, love Kangaroo? Did he love Kangaroo and deny it? And was the denial just a piece of fear? Was it just fear that held him back from admitting his love for the other man?

Fear? Yes, it was fear. But then did he not believe also in the God of fear. There was not only the God of love. To insist that there is only one God, and that God the source of love, is perhaps as fatal as the complete denial of God, and of all mystery. He believed in the God of fear, of darkness, of passion, and silence, the God that made a man realise his own sacred aloneness. If Kangaroo could have realised that too then Richard felt he would have loved him, in a dark, separate, other way of love.

So " the dark God " is simply the endorsement of Somers' impulses. The " God of power " becomes the god of fear. One must obey the God of fear. But why call him a god? Only that Somers may believe that an impulse he cannot resist is irresistible. What hope can there be of communion with other men in the service of such a " God " ? What he cannot resist, other men can and do. His " God " can never be theirs. Yet this is the dark God who was to sustain men in loving one another; now he sustains Somers in escaping from love.

The chaos is irremediable; the self-deception manifest. The impulses that Somers cannot resist are irresistible and divine. And, of course, there is a sense in which it is salutary for a man to say to himself once for all: " I am what I am, and finally I am not responsible." The last step in the progress of a human soul is to surrender all responsibility for himself; it is upon God, or the Unknown, or Life, and he can only be what it is his destiny to be. But the moment we admit so much, we must admit that all men are like ourselves: they also are not responsible. The God that has made me, has made them also.

This Somers cannot and will not admit. The God is in him, but not in other men. He serves the God, and they do not; whereas the God he serves is some God that all men serve: only they do not call it God, or call it service.

Instead of Somers saying simply to himself: " I am afraid. In the last issue I cannot enter into this bond of love with men which I desire. Something fails within me," he says: " I cannot enter into this bond of love with men, because I am the servant of the dark God, and they are not. If they were also servants of the dark God, then I could love them, in the dark, separate, other way of love."

It is self-delusion. They serve the dark God every whit as much as he. They follow their natures, as he does; they are capable of loving him, he is not capable of loving them. It is a bitter tragedy, for his capacity and need to love is so much greater than theirs. Still, why not admit that these things are so, and not otherwise? Why delude oneself with the dream that there is a dark realm where love is possible, only it is not love?

The answer to that question is that Lawrence must delude himself, if he is to live. If he were not still to delude himself, he must die. He must give up all hope of the one thing needful to him — namely, love. Somewhere, somehow, he must invent a Heaven where love is possible to him. And the kingdom of the dark God is now that place.

But the place does not exist; of it he knows nothing. Its God is simply the power that has made him what he is. He rhapsodises about it; he makes it into an imaginative solace for his own incurable distress. He calls it " the greater mystery of the dark God beyond a man, the God that gives a man passion, and the dark unexplained blood-tenderness that is deeper than love, but it is so much more obscure, impersonal, and the brave, silent blood-pride, knowing his own separateness, and the sword-strength of his derivation from the dark God." The words are impressive, but they mean something simple: a love which is love *and* hate. " To meet another dark-worshipper," he sighs, " that would be the best of all meetings." Yet within a dozen lines he acknowledges that he has met one: Jack, with the light in his eyes and the grin on his face, after killing three men with an iron bar in the fight at the Socialist meeting. Then Somers was just horrified. And to explain why this meeting with a dark-worshipper was unsatisfactory, he tells us that " that was killing in the name of love." The dark god was not invoked, by name.

When the deeds of the dark God are really done, Somers is horrified. Once make the dark God a reality, and Lawrence would flee to the mountains to escape him, or have recourse to any quibble to avoid acknowledging him. The man who suffered pangs of remorse from throwing a block of wood at a snake is not the man to take the smallest hand in a blood-sacrifice. The darkness of his dark God is an imaginative indulgence. In so far as he is a God at all, he is the God of love. But since the desire for love cannot be satisfied in life, he is the God of Death. What darkness he has is the darkness of death.

$$\backsim$$

The effort to solace himself with the imagination of the dark God will next absorb him. The dark God is as divided as himself. On the one hand, he is ruthless, powerful, cruel, bloody, full of hate and death — the last metamorphosis of " the hardy indomitable male." He will be celebrated in *The Boy in the Bush* and *The Plumed Serpent* — books in which Lawrence himself does not appear. On the other hand, as an actual reality, he is simply the power that has made Lawrence as he is, a now utterly divided man: veritably, a chaos — a man who, determined never to lose his soul, has lost it perdurably. And he knows it. At the end of *Kangaroo*, he stands on the sea-shore, and drifts into indifference.

" Far-off, far-off, as if he had landed on another planet, as a man might land after death. Leaving behind the body of care. Even the body of desire. Shed. All that had meant so much to him, shed. All the old world and self of care, the beautiful care as well as the weary care, shed like a dead body. . . .

" Why have I cared? I don't care. How strange it is here, to be soulless and alone."

" Why do I wrestle with my soul? I have no soul."

Clear as the air about him, this truth possessed him.

" Why do I talk of the soul? My soul is shed like a sheath. I am soulless and alone, soulless and alone. That which is soulless is perforce alone."

This is not the core of inward stillness which Lawrence once thought he had found; it is not anything beyond the flux of circumstance and mood. On the contrary it is a complete lapse into the flux, a final denial of all detachment, of all possibility of detachment; the utter reversal of the great word of Jesus that " he who loses his soul shall find it." Lawrence had not lost his soul; it had been taken from him, because he clung to it. He has demanded that every element of himself shall be valid, that his contradictory desires shall have equal dignity; he has declared that everything in himself is God, and claimed a total apotheosis. Therefore his everything is become a nothing, his totality a nullity, his integrity a disintegration.

Back to Harriet, to tea. Harriet? Another bird like himself. If only she wouldn't speak, talk, feel. The weary habit of talking and having feelings. When a man has no soul, he has no feelings to talk about. He wants to be still. And " meaning " is the most meaningless of illusions. An outworn garment.

Harriet and he? It was time they both agreed that nothing has any meaning. Meaning is a dead letter when a man has no soul. And speech is like a volley of dead leaves and dust, stifling the air. Human beings should learn to make weird, wordless cries, like the animals, and cast off the clutter of words. . . .

No home, no tea. Insouciant soullessness. Eternal indifference. Perhaps it is only the great pause between meanings. But it is only in this pause that one finds the meaningless of meanings — like old husks which speak dust. . . .

And among the things which have no meaning are Somers himself, and his " dark god." Things happen, and there is an end. The " dark god " is only the last desperate attempt to give himself a meaning, a significance; and the last thing to which the " dark god " prompts him is a denial of all meaning, all significance. It was inevitable, for on the shoulders of the " dark god " he has laid all the burden of his own self-evasion. The " dark god " is his self, in all the nakedness of its own inward division; he is the endorsement and perpetuation of that division, the consecration of his own self-decreed meaninglessness, his chosen dissolution. The god has left him now, as Hercules left Antony: the god who is very God of very God, who lives in man, and in man alone, and lives in him so long as man seeks his own inward unity. He claims to have found another; but his other god is no god at all, he is only the denial of the possibility of God.

This god without feet or knees or face. This sluicing, knocking, urging night, heaving like a woman with unspeakable desire, but no woman, no thighs or breast, no body. The moon, the concave mother-of-pearl of night, the great radium-swinging and his little self. The call and the answer without intermediary. Non-human gods, non-human human beings.

" Non-human gods, non-human human beings." Such is the end of *Kangaroo*. The gods made for the man, not the man by the gods. The human being weary of his own humanity, disowning it finally, and deifying only that which remains when the humanity of which he is weary is cast away. Therefore, Lawrence can be no more a character in his own books: that which holds the man together is gone, and as the god has departed from him, so must he depart from the world of his own imagination. He cannot conceive himself any more.

٩

The Boy in the Bush is a strangely beautiful book. It is so largely because Lawrence did not have to create it. He could clothe his collaborator's story in an added glory of flesh and blood, and pour out the riches of his imagination upon the given theme. But someone else planted; it was Lawrence who gave the increase. If Lawrence had written it alone, it would have been a far poorer book than it is. With the burden of foundation removed from him, he was free to make it an amazingly rich one.

I would give much to have a sight of the manuscript of

The Boy in the Bush before Lawrence began to re-write it. If it still exists I hope it will be published; it would be a priceless document. But without that actual evidence, it is easy to see what is Lawrence's own addition. In the main, it amounts to this: that Lawrence saw in Jack Grant, or his collaborator's first draft of Jack, a chance to realise his own imagination of what he might have been. More and more, as the book goes on, he makes of Jack the figure of his dreams. Jack is a servant of " the dark god," he is " a lord of death," he is triumphant over woman. Not for Jack the hateful knowledge that he is dependent on and contained by a woman; not for Jack the hateful knowledge that no man will look upon him as a lord and master; not for Jack the hateful knowledge that he clings to life. Jack is the super-man, the conqueror of woman and man and death alike, the rebel triumphant. Above all, Jack has conquered the division between the natural and the spiritual man, which has conquered Lawrence; conquered it, that is, as Lawrence dreamed it might be conquered.

And when the flame came up in him, tearing from his bowels, in the sudden new desire for Monica, this was his spiritual body, the body transfigured with fire. And that steady dark vibration which made him want to kill Easu — that was his spiritual body. And when he had hit Easu with his broken left hand, and the white sheet of flame going through him had made him scream aloud, leaving him strange and distant, but superconscious and powerful, this, too, was his spiritual body. The sun in his right hand and the moon in his left hand. When he drank from the burning right hand of the Lord, and wanted Monica in the same fire, it was his body spiritual burning from the right hand of the Lord. And when he knew he must destroy Easu, in the sheet of white pain, it was his body spiritual transfigured from the left hand of the Lord. And when he ate and drank and the food tasted good, it was the dark cup of life he was drinking, drinking.the life of the

dead ox from the meat. And this was his body spiritual commun-
ing with the sacrificed body of natural life: like a tiger glowing
at evening lapping blood. And when he rode after the sheep
through the bush, and the horse between his knees went quick and
delicate, it was the Lord tossing him in his spiritual body down
the maze of living.

That is eloquent; but there is a generation of men for
whom life does not consist wholly in taking a woman, and
killing one's enemy, and eating and drinking, and riding
after sheep. Perhaps it would have been a good thing if the
generation of men to which Lawrence pre-eminently belonged
had never been born. But it is there; and for it there is no
way of escape from the spiritual, simply by denying it. That
is what Lawrence would like to do and cannot do; that is
what he makes Jack Grant do.

But Jack is, essentially, all that Lawrence is not — the
hardy indomitable male to the perfection of his dream, who
takes women and leaves them, fights his enemy to the death,
and society till he drops. He is a man who can and does stand
alone. But, simply as the hardy indomitable male, he would
not be very interesting to Lawrence: so that he has to be endowed with all kinds of qualities which are incongruous with
himself, but do most patently belong to Lawrence, and in particular to the Richard Lovat Somers of *Kangaroo*. He has
Somers' inordinate craving for intimacy; and Somers' inordinate revulsion from his own craving. He has, more
strangely still, Somers' comprehensive repudiation of the
modern world, which, in a barely educated boy of eighteen in
the late eighties of the last century, is miraculous.

He really didn't want his fellow-men. He didn't want that
amiable casual association with them which took up so large a
part of his life. It was a habit and a bluff on his part. Also it was
part of his nature. A certain real amiability in him, and a natural

kindly disposition towards his fellow-men combated in him with a repudiation of the whole trend of modern human life, the emotional, spiritual, ethical and intellectual trend. Deep inside himself he fought like a wildcat against the whole thing. And yet, because of a naturally amiably-disposed, even benevolent nature in himself, he took any casual individual into his warmth, and was bosom friends for the moment. Until, inevitably, after a short time the individual betrayed himself a unit of the universal trend, and Jack recoiled in anger and revulsion again.

Which is perfect truth of Somers, but really incredible in Jack Grant. In fact, Lawrence has very hard work to make Jack Grant sufficiently rebellious. Somers can do a great deal of talking; and Jack Grant, towards the end, when Lawrence has fairly got hold of him, does far more than is humanly probable. But since Jack Grant, by hypothesis, does not move in the world of ideas at all, it is difficult to make his rebellion manifest. Lawrence achieves this by the curious expedient of making him want two wives at once. (Apparently, at the end, he is to have also a third, and to blossom out as a full-fledged trigamist.) And we are given to understand that in making this demand openly, Jack is perfectly right: he is obeying the " dark God." That is very perplexing, superficially, to those who remember that Somers, who is the great servant of the " dark God," is an impassioned monogamist. But only superficially. Lawrence, we have learned by now, was a monogamist in spite of himself. Through Jack Grant he takes his revenge on the woman " in whom his life is rooted." But I cannot help thinking that Jack Grant's polygamy must have been astonishing to his original creator, Lawrence's collaborator. She must have rubbed her eyes to discover that she had given birth to a monster.

All kinds of queer things happen to Jack Grant. He has two perfect friends, Tom and Lennie, shy and mistrustful boys who come to adore him. Loyalty in friendship could go no further than Tom and Lennie take it. Jack Grant has in them a gift from the gods. But quite suddenly, for no reason at all, Jack discovers that they don't love him at all for what he is, but for what they want him to be. As for him as he is, " they think he ought to be destroyed." This again is quite true of Somers and his friends, or of what Somers thinks about himself and his friends; but it is completely incongruous with anything we are told of Jack, or Tom, or Lennie. Again Jack has to fit the new pattern, though he is made a monster in the process.

Strange, indeed, are his metamorphoses, and they must needs be strange, since in Jack Grant must be combined all that Somers would like to be, with all that Somers is. Seeing that Somers is what he is because he is not what he would like to be, Jack Grant finally becomes a chimaera: the hardy indomitable male with Lawrence's psychological revulsions and Lawrence's imaginative satisfactions. In nothing is this so apparent as in Jack's repeated determination to be one of " the Lords of Death." The Halls of Death, the Lords of Death — these phrases return again and again in Jack's thoughts or on his lips. They are the last phrases to haunt the mind of the real Jack Grant. But they did haunt Lawrence's mind.

Jack knew his Lord as the Lord of Death. The rich dark mystery of death, which lies ahead, and the dark sumptuousness of the halls of death. Unless Life moves on to the beauty of the darkness of death, there is no life, there is only automatism. Unless we see the dark splendour of death ahead, and travel to be lords of darkness at last, peers in the realms of death, life is nothing but a petulant, pitiful backing, like a frightened horse back to the stable, the manger, the cradle. But onward ahead is the great porch of entry into death, with its columns of bone-ivory. And beyond the porch is the heart of darkness, where the lords of death arrive home out of the vulgarity of life, into their own dark and silent domains, lordly, ruling the incipience of life.

For all its seeming magnificence this is nothing more than rhetorical self-consolation. If the lords of death rule the incipience of life, why then is life so vulgar? *N'importe où, hors du monde* is the motive of this rhetoric. Lawrence is weary of life, he is beaten by it: Death is the place where he can imagine himself triumphant. Which is well enough; but unfortunately he proposes to live — even to go to America " which does not attract him." So that somehow he has to contrive the imaginative anticipation of heroic and glorious death, with a knowledge of his own determination to live. This difficulty is overcome by the Protean " dark God," whose darkness is conveniently ambiguous: it is either the darkness of non-mental life, or the darkness of death, or both together. These two darknesses are not the same darkness, any more than a live snake is the same as a dead one. But Lawrence at this moment wanted to confuse them. He wanted to console himself with the thought of a victory in death, and with the thought that he might have it by not dying. He wanted in this, as in other vital matters, to eat his cake and have it. As he wanted to be alone, and not to be alone, to be womanless and to be married, to love and to deny love, so he wanted to be dead and not to be dead. It is all-too-human, but less than heroic. We do not demand of little men that they shall be heroic. Of Lawrence we do.

The strange dusky road of the years, where you go with your head up and your eyes open and your spine sharp and electric, ready to fight your man and take your woman, on and on down the years, into the last black embrace of death. Death that stands grinning with arms open and black breast ready. Death, like the last woman you embrace. Death, like the last man you are fighting with. And he beats you. But somehow you are not beaten if you are a Lord of Death.

Death, at this moment, was the only solution for Lawrence; and he could not take it. He could neither " die into life " nor die out of it. He elected to live. Living, he could not remain stationary. Since he could not go on, he must begin to decline. He must begin that " pitiful backing, like a frightened horse, back to the stable, the manger, the cradle." He must begin to surrender the ground he has striven to conquer.

PART IV

I

AMERICA

IN the autumn of 1922, Lawrence went to America. He came from Sydney, crossing the South Seas, touching at New Zealand and the islands, to San Francisco. Very quickly he went down through California and to New Mexico. The immediate sequel was *Studies in Classical American Literature,* in their final form.

He had said at the end of *Kangaroo,* that he was going " to a country which did not attract him." He had confessed, as long ago as *Aaron's Rod,* that he had no particular belief in his going there. But at the same time he had confessed his dream: he would have loved the Aztecs and the Red Indians — and the Marquesans, the Maori blood. That is his fantasy; his fantasy of an earthly paradise. Mechanical America horrifies him. His disillusions come quick. The Polynesian fantasy is annihilated in the course of a single journey from Sydney to San Francisco. By the time he writes his essay on Herman Melville, he is utterly repelled by the Polynesians: he finds he is separated from their " inchoate, saurian softness," by the old familiar gulf of the " other dimension." Only the Aztecs remain as a possible living embodiment of his paradisal fantasy. And, naturally, he has not very much faith in their reality.

There remains to make the best of white America: not, of course, in the sense of accepting white American civilisation. Making the best of America means reshaping America in accordance with his dream, becoming for America the prophet of its unknown destiny. That is appearance; deeper down the intention is to make white America the symbol of himself, the paradigm of his own hungering and uneasy reality.

The first necessary identification is easy. The white Americans came to America; Lawrence has come to America. Therefore they came with the same motive, driven by the same impulse. " They came largely to get *away* — that most simple of motives. To get away. Away from what? In the long run away from themselves. Away from everything. That's why most people have come to America and still do come. To get away from everything they are and have been." And the next identification follows easily. According to Lawrence white America was and is fundamentally in rebellion against the European consciousness, the worship of the " ideal." Its rebellion is manifest in the very extremity to which it has carried the worship of the " ideal." This deliberate superficial reverence covers an unconscious inward determination to destroy the " ideal." When the process of destruction is over, the new thing will be born. Thus America is the promised land, in which the process which Lawrence believes to be at work in himself, will be vastly accomplished. Therefore, white America may become the "living homeland " for which he pines. At the very beginning of the book he confesses his yearning. Freedom is an illusion.

Men are less free than they imagine; ah, far less free. The freest are perhaps least free. Men are free when they are in a living homeland, not when they are straying and breaking away. Men are free when they are obeying some deep, inward voice of religious belief. Obeying from within. Men are free when they belong to some living, organic, believing community, active in fulfilling some unfulfilled, perhaps unrealized purpose.

Which is, of course, profoundly true. But how it is to be reconciled with Lawrence's perpetual mobility is not evident. Not that we can fairly charge him, in this, with seeing the better and choosing the worse course. He could truly say that he had found no such living, organic, believing community, and that he was condemned to be an exile and a wanderer in spite of himself. And now, for a moment, he was trying to create an imaginative earthly paradise in white America.

ᔕ

This is the theme, so far as it has a central theme, of *Studies in Classical American Literature:* the old dream of the new society. Let us take the individual of this new society first. The newness of the new man will be that he will obey his own Holy Ghost. In the early pages of the *Studies* there is a great deal about the Holy Ghost. Since following him at work in Richard Somers, we have conceived a deep suspicion of the Holy Ghost. We try once more to put a handful of salt on the tail of this Protean and most undovelike bird. " The next era is the era of the Holy Ghost. And the Holy Ghost speaks individually inside each individual, always, for ever a ghost. There is no general manifestation. Each isolate individual listening in isolation to the Holy Ghost within him." Then, unexpectedly, we learn that the Holy Ghost is " the thing which prompts us to be real, and not to push our cravings too far." Then, "it is the multiplicity of Gods within us make up the Holy Ghost "; and we remember that Somers' fear of admitting love was a God, and Jack Calcott's murderous fury was a God. Then, the Holy Ghost is man's fortress against woman: " unless a man fiercely obeys his Holy Ghost, his woman will destroy him." Then, the Holy Ghost teaches you when to change from mental to non-mental consciousness. Then, "the real human soul is the Holy Ghost, and believes in the Holy Ghost." And finally, "a thing you sincerely believe in cannot be wrong, because belief does not come at will. It comes only from the Holy Ghost within."

It would be utterly unworthy to make play with these logical contradictions. But there is in all this something of infinitely greater import than a contradiction, or a thousand contradictions. Contradictions are necessary to the utterance of living truth. But here is a lie. Let us put it as simply as we can, by means of an instance from this same book. In the essay on *Two Years before the Mast*, Lawrence castigates Dana for feeling physically sick when the captain strings up Sam and flogs him; he is still more furious at the seaman John for protesting. In flogging Sam, the captain was obeying his Holy Ghost. In protesting, the seaman John was not obeying his Holy Ghost. In being sick, in "refusing the blood contact of life," Dana was not obeying his Holy Ghost. Why not? Who is Lawrence to judge the workings of the Holy Ghost in another man? What presumption to pronounce for the Captain, and against Dana and Seaman John! And what a lie! For we remember that at the end of *Kangaroo*, Somers realized that Jack Calcott "wanted to give him a thrashing" — an obvious manifestation of the Holy Ghost in Jack Calcott. But "the thought was horrible to Richard Lovat, who could never bear to be touched physically." Touched physically, mind you, not thrashed or flogged. Yet now, in the essay on Dana, he has the hardihood to say: "In my opinion there are worse insults than floggings. I would rather be flogged than have most people 'like' me." And, presumably, in all this self-deception, Lawrence is obedient to his own Holy Ghost. His Holy Ghost has prompted him to cheat himself at will concerning his own nature.

The fact is that Lawrence is now doomed, beyond all possible escape, to betray his Holy Ghost. The conception of an ultimate and infallible self is a true one; it is true that it is man's duty never to violate his own integrity. But Lawrence *must* now violate his own integrity even in word; he must pretend to beliefs in which he does not believe: and he must pretend that this violation of his own integrity is obedience to his own Holy Ghost. It is inevitable. Lawrence is involved in a lie, and he cannot escape save at a price he cannot pay. He will *not* accept himself; he must pretend to be other than he is. It is inevitable, but that inevitability is discerned and asserted by the spirit, to which Lawrence appears *sub specie aeternitatis*. We do not live on that plane, or in that order; on the plane and in the order in which we live, Lawrence's offence is unforgivable. He is betraying himself, and he is betraying his fellow-men.

The result of this violation of his own integrity is that the new world to which he pretends to lead us is a chaos. A society based on such obedience to the Holy Ghost as his would be a million times more hideous than the society in which we live. It would be a lawless anarchy, where murder and rapine would range at their own sweet will. Lawrence, if he had dared really to imagine it, would have recoiled from it in horror, as from a nightmare. But he does not dare. The same final reluctance which prevents him from acknowledging his own inward chaos, prevents him from acknowledging the mightier chaos which would ensue if men were to follow him. He dares not acknowledge it, as he dares not look calmly into himself; but he cannot avoid a premonition of the disaster which awaits him. At the end of his essay on Melville, he cries in frenzy:

We are doomed, doomed. And the doom is in America. The doom of our white day.

Ah, well, if my day is doomed, and I am doomed with my day, it is something greater than I which dooms me, so I accept my doom as a sign of the greatness which is more than I am.

Melville knew. He knew his race was doomed. His white soul, doomed. His great white epoch, doomed. Himself doomed. The idealist, doomed. The spirit doomed. . . .

Oh God, oh God, what next, when the *Pequod* has sunk?

She sank in the war, and we are all flotsam.

Now what next? Who knows?

It is a cry of frenzy, and a wail of anguish; and it is terrible to hear.

The more terrible, because the torture which wrings it from Lawrence is the torture of an inward lie. Melville himself denies it, denies it utterly. Whatever Melville's last works — *Pierre* and *Clarel* and *Billy Budd* — may mean, they are not shrieks of anguish and of doom. But Melville did not know the war. He knew war. And, in any case, the war, in itself, was not different from any other evil, it was the fact of suffering and of death, its magnitude made it more naked, that is all. Human wisdom, the ultimates of human love and human courage, did not have to wait for the war before they could be finally proved. Man can only suffer, and be annihilated, and be reborn. It is not the war which has broken Lawrence into fragments, or made men flotsam. Lawrence himself has proved it: he surmounted the war. *The Lost Girl*, the *Fantasia, Aaron's Rod* even — what were these but evidence that his spirit was strong enough to survive and triumph over the wounds of the war? The faith which the war killed in him was a false faith, which needed to be killed in him and every man.

It is no use his blaming the war: it is only another self-deception. If he says, as he seemed to say in " The Nightmare," that the war turned his love of men into hatred, again he deceives himself. It was he who suffered his love to be so changed. He may be a great man, he is a great man, but he has not passed beyond the wisdom of Jesus: " Father, for-give them, for they know not what they do." He has not reached it. He loathes Jesus, he cannot away with him; but that is because he needs must loathe a man with finer courage than his own. It needs more courage, far more courage, to love your enemy than to hate him. Better hate him than pretend to love him — that is true; and let Law-rence be thanked for saying it. But there is a love of one's enemy which is beyond all pretence; a love that is born of the annihilation of love. This love Lawrence does not, and will not, know. He cries:

Nowadays society is evil. It finds subtle ways of torture, to destroy the life-quick, to get at the life-quick in a man. Every possible form. And still a man can hold out, if he can laugh and listen to the Holy Ghost. But society is evil, evil, evil, and love is evil. And evil breeds evil more and more.

Love is not evil. That is a lie; and it is a denial of the Holy Ghost within. The best, the finest, the most precious element that was in Lawrence was his love; it is because of that, and ultimately because of that alone, that he will be remembered. But he was afraid of it, always afraid of it. That was no foolishness, or cowardice, to be afraid of love: for his capacity for love was mighty and overwhelming. Love is a fearful thing; as a man's capacity for love, so is his capacity for suffering. Therefore love is a terribly lonely thing, for nothing is more lonely than suffering. It was the loneliness of the suffering which is love which Lawrence could not endure. Always he fled from it, and always to the woman. Woman for him was never an object of love, always a refuge from love. It was so from the beginning.

Therefore he hated woman. Woman was for him always the symbol and witness of his own cowardice: Eve, the tempter, the seducer of man from his own integrity. " All our human unhappiness," he cries in this book, " *viennent de ne pouvoir être seuls*. As long as man lives he will be subject to the yearning of love or the burning of hate, which is only inverted love." This is the cry of that " crucifixion into sex," which he lamented so bitterly. But the " crucifixion into sex " was true of himself alone. Neither men, nor women, are crucified into sex if they love each other. But, for Lawrence, sex was a crucifixion: it was the irreparable violation of his integrity, the sacrifice of his love. He loathed the sexuality which he seemed to glorify; but the strength to depart from it he did not possess.

All this is manifest in his essay on Hawthorne. *The Scarlet Letter* is to Lawrence one of the greatest allegories in all literature. It is to him an allegory of the destruction of man by woman. The bias of the essay comes with a shock to those who are not prepared. Dimmesdale is seduced by Hester; by taking her, or rather by her taking him, " he has lost his manliness, fallen from his integrity as a minister of the Gospel of the Spirit."

She had dished him and his spirituality, so he hated her. . . . The women make fools of them — the spiritual men. And when, as men, they've gone flop in their spirituality, they can't pick themselves up whole any more. So they just crawl, and die detesting the female, or the females, who made them fall.

De se fabula narratur. Lawrence does not say, in so many words, that he is a spiritual man, and this is what has befallen him; yet he scarcely conceals it. He announces, as a simple and manifest truth, that all men are divided in this

great matter of sex against themselves. This is " the cross "
of humanity.

The mind and the spiritual consciousness of man simply *hates*
the dark potency of blood acts; hates the genuine dark sensual
organisms, which do, for the time being, actually obliterate the
mind and the spiritual consciousness, plunge them in a suffocating
flood of darkness. You can't get away from this.

On the contrary, we can get away from it: but only through
simple love. Lawrence himself cannot get away from it; that
is the trouble; and that is why he ranges himself on the side
of Dimmesdale, and identifies himself with him. Lawrence's
attitude is that of the Christian ascetic; but since he is a
Christian ascetic who has succumbed to the woman, who
has had to realise that woman is necessary to him, it changes,
superficially but not essentially, to the attitude of the Oriental polygamist. Again, the manner in which Lawrence reveals himself is startling. Hawthorne happens incidentally
to say that Hester " had in her nature a rich, voluptuous,
oriental characteristic — a taste for the gorgeously beautiful." Lawrence takes up the phrase, and wrests it to a sense
it does not bear, simply in order to rid himself of his thought.

" A voluptuous oriental characteristic " — that lies waiting
in American women. It is probable that the Mormons are the fore-
runners of the coming real America. It is possible that men will
have more than one wife in the coming America. That you will
have again a half-oriental womanhood, and a polygamy.

Do not be deceived. This is not a simple speculation about
the future of the United States. The coming America is, in
this book, the realisation of Lawrence's dreams of what
ought to be. Lawrence is dreaming the same dream as Jack
Grant in *The Boy in the Bush* — patriarchs and polygamy,

when " the women *choose* to experience again the great submission." And this dream of polygamy is simply the reverse
of Christian asceticism; both alike express the basic *fear*
of the woman. She must be held in submission; for her
desire is to destroy men.

Unless a man believes in himself and his gods, *genuinely;* unless
he fiercely obeys his own Holy Ghost; his woman will destroy
him. Woman is the nemesis of doubting man. She can't help it.

Again, our memory revives. We remember that Richard Somers could not believe in himself, unless Harriet
believed in him. We cannot think that Lawrence is very
different. How is he then to believe in himself and his gods,
genuinely?

Alas, it is not possible; and it is not the woman's fault.
She cannot help knowing her man subtly, she cannot help
knowing that finally he does not believe in himself. The
simple fact that he cannot leave her is enough. The prophet
of isolation and integrity and the Holy Ghost cannot exist
without the woman; the prophet of polygamy cannot exist
without one particular woman; the prophet of flogging cannot bear to be physically touched. All these things she
knows. How can she believe in him as prophet, when he
prophesies these things? Or in the Holy Ghost which
prompts him to prophesy them? These are to her the foibles
and waywardness of a child. And the more " fiercely " he
insists on this obedience to the Holy Ghost, the less of belief will she have in him. It is not her fault. As Lawrence
himself asserts, belief does not go by choice. It would be a
denial of her Holy Ghost if she were to believe in him. She
cannot, she must not, believe in him: so she destroys him.

It begins to be clear why *The Scarlet Letter* is to Lawrence the profoundest of all allegories: it is the allegory of
himself. His vehemence betrays him at every point.

Unless a woman is held, by man, safe within the bounds of belief, she becomes inevitably a destructive force. She can't help
herself. . . . Let a woman loose from the bounds and restraints
of a man's fierce belief, in his gods and in himself, and she becomes a gentle devil. She becomes subtly diabolic. The colossal
evil of the united spirit of Woman. *Woman,* German woman or
American woman, or every other sort of woman, in the last war,
was something frightening. As every *man* knows. . . .

If a woman doesn't believe in a man, she believes, essentially,
in nothing. She becomes, willy-nilly, a devil.

A devil she is, and a devil she will be, and most men will succumb to her devilishness.

Let us make the distinction which Lawrence does not
now care to make. There is belief in a man, as he explained
in *Kangaroo,* which is personal. This belief Lawrence had
from his mother and his wife; and he has it from me. This
belief may be called acceptance. One accepts *him;* he is
what he is, a beautiful, suffering, divided, tormented being,
driven by destiny to deny his own most wonderful faculties.
This acceptance is love. It drove Lawrence to frenzy. The
belief that he wanted was impersonal belief; that is, belief
in the things he prophesied: a total belief in his message as
an infallible prophet. Belief of this kind he could not get,
and never will get, either from woman or man, for the simple
reason that his message is a compound of truth and falsehood, and the truth and the falsehood are so subtly inter-
twined that it needs more understanding and love than most
men possess to separate them out. So when he sought to
impose belief in his beliefs upon the woman, she refused it
instinctively. With perfect truth, she objected as Harriet
did to Somers, that he did not acknowledge his dependence
upon her. If he had acknowledged her, his message would
have been different, and she could have believed in it, as
well as accept him. But he could not acknowledge her. In

him the spiritual consciousness did verily hate the blood-consciousness. In a man so divided no true woman can believe. Lawrence could only be accepted by the woman; and her sentence stands. In the last resort, Lawrence can only be accepted and loved as a man; he cannot be believed in as a prophet.

Since the woman, instinctively, refused the belief in himself as true prophet, to which he had no right, she was inevitably the finger of an accusing conscience: a devil. She " destroyed him inch by inch "; " her very love was a subtle poison." Absolutely and terribly true — but true of Lawrence alone. Not her love only, but all love, was poison to him. And love was all he could get; all he had the right to receive: acceptance of the man, refusal of his message. A fearful fate: to be believed in as prophet only by those whose belief is not worth having, and by those whose belief is worth having only to be loved. A fearful fate in life, but not in death. In death, surely, a wonderful destiny, which few mortal men have attained: and those among the greatest. Centuries hence, Lawrence will be loved, and because he will be loved, his truth — his great truth — will be understood. Without love, there is no understanding of living truth. Love alone can distinguish the true from the false in Lawrence; distinguish them absolutely, and understand them both.

ᔓ

The great personal theme of woman the destroyer returns in the essay on Fenimore Cooper. Here it takes the positive form with which we are now familiar. The new society will be based on the relation between man and man. This, Lawrence assures us, was Cooper's deep desire in creating Natty Bumpo and Chingachook; the imaginative embodiment of this necessity is his great contribution to the myth of the new

America, which is the Utopia of Lawrence's dream. In this paradise there is no woman. The women of the story — *The Last of the Mohicans* — Lawrence brushes aside, packs them off, as it were, to the well-guarded security of the harem.

Beyond all this heart-beating stand the figures of Natty and Chingachook: the two childless, womanless men, of opposite races. They are the abiding thing. Each of them is alone, and final in his race. And they stand side by side, stark, abstract, beyond emotion, yet eternally together. All the other loves seem frivolous. This is the new great thing, the clue, the inception of a new humanity.

It had seemed, in *Kangaroo*, as though Lawrence had abandoned the dream of a man-to-man relation. But, in truth, he had abandoned it there only as an actual possibility in his own life. He was also on the brink of admitting that he was himself incapable of it; but this self-recognition would have been too vital, pierced too near the life-quick of the man. It had to be avoided; avoidance is natural and easy. It is not that he (so runs the new legend) is incapable of a man-to-man relation; it is that the men are not yet born who are fit to enter into such a relation with him. He utters the new conviction through the lips of Jack Grant at the end of *The Boy in the Bush*.

" Men ready to fight for me and with me, no matter against what. A little world of my own. . . . A little world of my own! As if I could make it with the people that are on earth to-day. No, no, I can do nothing but stand alone. And then, when I die, I shall not drop like carrion on the earth's earth. I shall be a lord of death, and sway the destinies of the life to come."

The patriarch with the harem; the womanless, childless pair of men — these are, as we have said, really identical

conceptions in Lawrence. Which has the prominence only
depends on the degree of imaginative freedom, or imaginative licence, he at the moment possesses. In *Kangaroo*,
where Lawrence himself is a character for the last time, it
is the friendship of childless, and, ideally, womanless men
which is the dream. For it is manifestly impossible that
Lawrence could imagine himself — " little Richard " — as
patriarch and polygamist. But when, as in *The Boy in the
Bush* or the essay on Hawthorne, his imagination is free
from the restrictions imposed by his own presence, the
patriarch and polygamist, who is, after all, the only adequate
embodiment of " the hardy indomitable male," emerges. The
motive of both dreams is the same — to escape from and
subject the woman.

In the essay on Fenimore Cooper it is the relation between
womanless and childless men which is " the inception of a
new humanity." The patriarchal, polygamical dream is
more convincing, because it does allow provision for the self-
perpetuation of new humanity. But that does not greatly
concern Lawrence: he himself is childless. *Après moi le
néant,* is never very far from his thoughts. And of all Fenimore Cooper's incarnations of the isolate man, the one that
most deeply attracts Lawrence is Deerslayer, whom he sees
as Natty Bumpo having sloughed off age.

Deerslayer seems to have been born under a hemlock-tree out
of a pine-cone: a young man of the woods. He is silent, simple,
philosophic, moralistic, and an unerring shot. His simplicity is the
simplicity of age rather than youth. He is race-old. . . . Almost
he is sexless, so race-old. . . .

Judith, the sensual woman, at once wants the quiet, reserved
unmarried Deerslayer. She wants to master him. And Deerslayer
is half tempted, but never more than half. He is not going to be
mastered. A philosophic old soul, he does not give much for the
temptations of sex. Probably he dies virgin.

And he is in the right of it. Rather than be dragged into a false heat of deliberate sensuality, he will remain alone. His soul is alone, for ever alone. So he will preserve his integrity, and remain alone in the flesh.

Here speaks the secret desire of Lawrence's soul — " to have preserved his integrity, and remained alone in the flesh," to have rejected " the crucifixion into sex." Deerslayer is the triumphant counterpart of the defeated Dimmesdale: the ideal that seemed possible to Lawrence, or which he dreamed to have been possible, whereas Jack Grant, the patriarch and polygamist, was impossible to him. To be virgin once more. How strange it will seem to some that this should have been Lawrence's most secret desire! Yet to those who can read through the letter to the spirit it is not strange at all. It is luminously self-evident.

Immediately after he has thus shyly revealed to us Deerslayer as the ideal, he bursts into a great generalisation of his own division. " The white man's mind and soul are divided between these two things: innocence and lust, the Spirit and Sensuality. Sensuality always carries a stigma, and is therefore more deeply desired, or lusted after." Again, it is not true; it simply is not true of the man and woman who have known love: but again it is true of Lawrence. And he turns Melville's *Moby Dick* into an allegory of the " crucifixion into sex." He is not concerned with Melville in and for himself, in his own quiddity. Melville exists only as a paradigm of Lawrence. But the projection of himself that Lawrence makes by means of Melville is amazing. It needs to be fully considered; but for the moment it is enough to remark the symbolism which Lawrence finds in *Moby Dick*.

What then is Moby Dick? He is the deepest blood-being of the white race; he is our deepest blood-nature.

And he is hunted, hunted, hunted by the maniacal fanaticism of our white mental consciousness. We want to hunt him down. To subject him to our will. And in this maniacal conscious hunt of ourselves we get dark races and pale to help us, red, and yellow, and black, east and west, Quaker and fire-worshipper, we get them all to help us in this ghastly maniacal hunt which is our doom and our suicide.

The last phallic being of the white man. Hunted into the death of upper consciousness and the ideal will. Our blood-self subjected to our will. Our blood-consciousness sapped by a parasitic mental or ideal consciousness.

In Melville's great story, the White Whale sinks the *Pequod*. That must mean, in Lawrence's symbolism, that the blood-consciousness overwhelms the ideal consciousness. And that, to him, is a fearful disaster. " We are doomed, doomed," he cries. " It is the doom of our white day." It does not matter in the least whether this is a true interpretation of *Moby Dick;* its importance lies in the self-revelation of Lawrence. The sinking of the ideal consciousness by the blood-consciousness is, for him, the supreme disaster. Even though by now we have become accustomed to paradox and contradiction in him, this comes to us with a shock of surprise. Even though we have been prepared, by the accumulation of many clues, for some such discovery, his naked assertion of it strikes us almost dumb.

For what does it mean? It means, first, in regard to Lawrence himself, that sex is the supreme disaster. It means that, in his secret soul, he identifies himself absolutely with that mental and spiritual consciousness " which *hates* the dark-blood potency." And, impersonally, it means that all the insistence on sex and the blood-consciousness, which is the constant obsession of all his books and by which he is generally known to fame or notoriety, was in his own secret judgment, a self-violation, a sin against the light. By it, he is tearing himself to pieces, killing the thing he loves, doing to death his own very soul.

And now he knows it. Than such a knowledge in such a man I can conceive nothing more terrible, more appalling. To me, the wonder is that he did not go mad, or kill himself, in the moment of full realisation. Kill himself in the spirit and by imagination, he did. He dies now finally out of his own books. Lawrence is no more; he is a spirit brooding over its own self-destruction. Whether the white world is doomed or not, he *is* doomed.

ॐ

By this convulsion of Lawrence's inward being the whole of his essay on Melville is convulsed. It is the strangest of all the strange documents which are the history of this strange man. The sense of doom, once we touch the quick of it with our souls, is unbearable. It is Lawrence's death agony; the cry of his final crucifixion. No wonder that it ends: " To use the words of Jesus, IT IS FINISHED. *Consummatum est."*

From the first Lawrence completely identifies himself with Melville. Melville was blue-eyed, a Northerner, sea-born. Lawrence is all these things. They cannot accept humanity, they cannot belong to humanity. " Let life come asunder, they say."

So they go down to the sea, these sea-born people. The Vikings are wandering again. Homes are broken up. Cross the seas, cross the seas, urges the heart. Leave love and home. Leave love and home. Love and home are a deadly illusion. Woman, what have I to do with thee? It is finished. *Consummatum est.* The crucifixion into humanity is over. Let us go back to the fierce, uncanny elements: the corrosive vast sea. Or Fire.

One has only to put the sentences together. This Melville *is* Lawrence.

Back, back, away from life. Never man instinctively hated life, our human life, as we have it, more than Melville did. And never was a man so passionately filled with the sense of vastness and mystery of life which is non-human. He was mad to look over our horizons. Anywhere, anywhere, out of *our* world. To get away. To get away, out! To get away, out of our life. To cross a horizon into another life. No matter what life, so long as it is another life. . . . The human heart gets into a frenzy at last, in its desire to dehumanize itself. . . . Melville hated the world: was born hating it. But he was looking for heaven. That is, choosingly. Choosingly, he was looking for paradise. Unchoosingly, he was mad with hatred of the world.

And Melville finds his earthly paradise — the South Seas; and he cannot bear it. He must escape. "The truth of the matter is, one cannot go back. Some men can: renegade. But Melville couldn't go back . . . and I know now that I could never go back. Back towards the past savage life. One cannot go back. It is one's destiny inside one." Yet, though Lawrence knows it, he cannot resist his blasphemy: the summons of his Holy Ghost is that he must blaspheme. Against Christ, against humanity, in one breath. (They are always the same breath.) Melville was repelled by the South Sea cannibalism. Not I, says Lawrence, "who cannot go back." " ' This is my body, take and eat.' . . . And if the savages liked to partake of their sacrament without raising the transubstantiation quibble, and if they liked to say, directly: ' This is thy body, which I take from thee, and eat. This is thy blood, which I sip in annihilation of thee,' why surely their sacred ceremony was as awe-inspiring as the one Jesus substituted. . . . The savage sacrament seems to me more valid than the Christian: less side-tracking about it." That is, in itself, hideous, and an abomination. Lawrence, who cannot go back, goes back: it is the sign of the inward convulsion. Part tears him forward, part tears him back. Now forward again.

It seems to me that in living so far, through all our bitter centuries of civilisation, we have still been living onwards, forwards. God knows it looks like a *cul de sac* now. But turn to the first negro and listen to your own soul. And your own soul will tell you that however foul and false our forms and systems are now, still, through the many centuries since Egypt, we have been living and struggling forwards along some road that is no road, and yet is a great life-development. We have struggled on, and on we still must go. We may have to smash things. Then let us smash. And our road may have to take a great swerve, that seems a retrogression. But we can't go back.

But what does it mean, for Lawrence, this not going back? Is this " swerve, that seems a retrogression " now anything more than empty metaphor? To this vital question there is no simple answer, as we shall try to explain. Again, we must content ourselves for the moment with noting that this is a moment of profound revulsion in Lawrence from all that he has been trying to believe. He has been round the world in search of the earthly paradise, looking for the humanity to which he could belong. He has not found it, he knows he will never find it. There is no going back. And he cannot go on drifting like flotsam. Always through Melville he utters these realisations. Melville couldn't " let his ship drift rudderless."

For a time, yes. For a time, he was rudderless and reckless. Good as an experience. But a man who will not abandon himself to despair or indifference cannot keep it up. Melville would never abandon himself either to despair or indifference. He always cared. . . . When he saw a white man really " gone savage "

. . . then Herman's whole being revolted. He couldn't bear it.
He could not bear a renegade. . . . As a matter of fact, a long
thin chain was round Melville's ankle all the while, binding him
to America, to civilisation, to democracy, to the ideal world.

So Melville returned; and Lawrence, in spirit, returns
with him. At this moment he acknowledges the truth that
" you can't fight it out by running away. When you have
run a long way from Home and Mother, then you realise
that the earth is round, and if you keep on running you'll
be back on the same old doorstep — like a fatality." The
realisation is good. But what does it mean? Lawrence sees,
but he cannot act: the power to act is not in him any more.
The Holy Ghost tells him that he must not run away; and
the Holy Ghost tells him that he must run away.

And so, when Melville does return, Lawrence rejects him.
The man who cannot choose, rejects the man who has
chosen. " Melville stuck to his ideal. . . . In his soul he was
proud and savage. But in his mind and will he wanted the
perfect fulfilment of love." Instantly, Lawrence reverts to
his own fantasy of himself as " the hardy indomitable male,"
and lectures Melville from that false eminence.

A proud savage-souled man doesn't really want any perfect
lovey-dovey fulfilment in love: no such nonsense. A mountain lion
doesn't mate with a Persian cat; and when a grizzly bear roars
after a mate, it is a she-grizzly he roars after — not after a
silky sheep.

Alas, this sort of thing in Lawrence has now become to
us an empty posturing, a sign of his own inward incoherence.
He cannot go back, and he must go back. We are tired of
this dream-reversion, this incessant form of revulsion from
himself, this " writing on the ideal pin," which he sees in
Melville. It is Lawrence himself who is writhing. And he
makes haste to show it.

It's our own fault. It was *we* who set up the ideals. And if we are such fools, that we aren't able to kick over the ideals in time, the worse for us. Look at Melville's eighty long years of writhing. And to the end he writhed on the ideal pin. From the " perfect woman lover " he passed on to the " perfect friend." Couldn't find him. Marriage was a ghastly disillusion to him, because he looked for perfect marriage. Friendship never even made a real start in him.

Yet to the end he pined for this: a perfect relationship; perfect mating; perfect mutual understanding. A perfect friend.

Right to the end he could never accept the fact that perfect relationships cannot be.. Each soul is alone, and the aloneness of each soul is a double barrier to perfect relationship between two beings.

Each soul *should* be alone. And in the end the desire for a perfect relationship is just a vicious, unmanly craving. *Tous nos malheurs viennent de ne pouvoir être seuls.*

This is not Melville, but it is Lawrence. *Tout son malheur vient de ne pouvoir être seul,* is not true of Melville, but it is true, in the height and in the depth, of Lawrence. He has used the quotation before, in the essay on Poe; and there he declared that there is no escape. " As long as man lives he will be subject to the yearning of love, or the burning of hate, which is only inverted love." The " vicious, unmanly craving " is in himself.

At the end comes a final identification with Melville, and a final revulsion from him.

Melville was, at the core, a mystic and an idealist.
Perhaps, so am I.
And he stuck to his ideal guns.
I abandon mine.

The incoherence is agonising, and was an agony. " There is no going back, but I am going back." As the next essay, on *Moby Dick,* rushes forward, Lawrence becomes more

and more penetrated with the horror of his doom. " That
great horror of ours! It is our civilisation rushing from all
havens astern." And the horror utters itself in a frenzied
shriek. " The spirit is doomed. . . . Oh God, oh God, what
next? " Lawrence tries to jeer at his own agony: he blasphemes again.

> *Boom!* as Vachel Lindsay would say.
> To use the words of Jesus, IT IS FINISHED
> *Consummatum est.*

The ultimate incoherence, the ultimate agony. We feel that
we have no right to be watching. But watch we must, and
listen we must. This is the agony of a great man.

৯

At this moment Lawrence knows that the spirit is doomed,
in him. He cannot go back, and he must go back. He cannot
betray the ideal, and he must betray it. The crucifixion into
humanity is over, for him; he puts the cup away from him.
He is a Jesus who has not had to find a Judas, his Judas is
in himself. He will, he can, maintain the struggle no longer
between the ideal and the animal. He abandons the ideal,
surrenders to the animal.

His final projection of himself is in the essay on Whitman.
This is his last identification. Let us try to be clear. Men
are not used to the kind of interpretation that is necessary
when a great human soul is to be understood. The art and
science of the human soul is in its infancy. " They are very
shallow people who take everything literally," said Keats.
" A man's life of any worth is a continual allegory, and very
few eyes can see the mystery of his life — a life like the
scriptures, figurative — which such people can no more
make out than they can the Hebrew bible. Shakespeare led

a life of allegory: his works are the comments on it." Lawrence led such a life, and his works are the comments on it.

The sinking of the *Pequod* by the White Whale was for Lawrence the symbol of the destruction of the ideal consciousness, of the spiritual by the animal, of the human by the non-human. This destruction was accomplished in himself: he abandoned the ideal. And this was death: death to the spirit in him, the spirit which he loved and was. *Moby Dick*, the book, was therefore a prophecy uttered in time, a vision of the doom which Lawrence must believe awaiting the white soul, because it had actually come to pass in Lawrence himself. There are two things: Melville's prophecy, as an event in time, which happened in the year 1851, and the event in Lawrence's soul. But Lawrence's method in *Classical American Literature* is a successive identification of the great American books with events in his own soul. Whitman comes after Melville; therefore Whitman represents the event or phase in Lawrence's soul which follows his surrender of the ideal, the death-blow consciously dealt to the spirit in himself. The question is: Is Whitman " a post-mortem effect "? The essay begins:

> Post-mortem effects?
> But what of Walt Whitman?
> " The good grey poet."
> Was he a ghost, with all his physicality?

If Whitman had been the perfect symbol of Lawrence's post-mortem phase, he would have been " a ghost, with all his physicality." That is what Lawrence had become. But no man can ever be the perfect symbol of a phase in another man: a man is always a man, a complete organism, obedient to its own individual destiny.

So that Whitman makes an inadequate symbol of the post-mortem effects: necessarily, because Lawrence himself did not know what the post-mortem effects in himself really were. The rest of his books alone could reveal them. But in Whitman, Lawrence traces himself again. First, he castigates him " for aching with amorous love, for gravitating to all he meets and knows." This is, of course, precisely what Lawrence did; this is that constant, undiscriminating urge towards intimacy, with which Harriet upbraided Somers. Lawrence castigates it, therefore, only the more vehemently. The disguise is so familiar by now that we need not dwell on it. Far more important is the reason which Lawrence gives for this yearning after universal love in Whitman.

You must have broken your mainspring. Your Moby Dick must be really dead. That lonely phallic monster of the individual you. Dead mentalized. You have killed your isolate Moby Dick. You have mentalized your deep sensual body, and that's the end of it.

It is Lawrence's demon speaking. Consciously, it is the last thing he would confess. " The curious thing about art-speech," says Lawrence in the preface of this very book, " is that it prevaricates so terribly, I mean it tells such lies. I suppose because we always all the time tell ourselves lies. Truly art is a sort of subterfuge. But thank God for it, we can see the subterfuge, if we choose." In Lawrence's art the subterfuge is the very man. It would have appalled him utterly to say, even to himself, that he ached with amorous love, and that the reason of the ache was that he had mentalized and killed his deep sensual body. But without a qualm he can say it of Whitman, though his identification of himself with Whitman is palpable, though " this maniacal hunt of the last phallic being of the white man " is precisely that urge of the individual consciousness with which he has completely identified himself at the end of the essay on *Moby Dick*.

Lawrence belongs to the *Pequod* of his symbolism, he is its last and strangest captain, carrying the hunt of the phallic being by the mental consciousness to lengths undreamed of, ultimately to lengths which even now he did not dream of. In speech, the sole prophet of the phallic being, in truth its last and most implacable enemy. Put sex into the place of sea, and his word concerning Dana is the absolute truth of himself. " Dana took another great step in knowing: knowing the sea. But it was a step also in his own undoing. It was a new phase in the dissolution of his own being. He would be a knower; but more near to mechanism than before. That is our cross, our doom." Lawrence knew, only too well, why Whitman ached with amorous love towards the universe. And, though he strives to repudiate Whitman, his identification becomes only the more complete. He traces in him the now familiar stages:

The great merge into the womb. Woman.
And after that the merge of comrades: man-for-man love.
And almost immediately after this, death, the final merge of death.
There you have the progression of merging. For the great mergers, woman at last becomes inadequate. For those who love to extremes. Woman is inadequate for the last merging. So the next step is the merging of man-for-man love. And this is on the brink of death. It slides over into death.

There we are given the exact sequence of the phases in Lawrence, from *The Rainbow* and *Women in Love,* through *Aaron's Rod,* to *Kangaroo* and *The Boy in the Bush,* with its final paean to the Halls of Death. For Lawrence was one of the great mergers, who love to extremes; and in Whitman he finds a comrade and a forerunner.

Whitman is a great poet, of the end of life. A very great post-mortem poet, of the transitions of the soul as it loses its integrity.

The poet of the soul's last shout and shriek, on the confines of death. *Après moi le déluge.*

Not wholly true of Whitman, but wholly true of Lawrence. " The poet of the soul's last shout and shriek, on the confines of death " — it is the perfect description of him. With a sudden and most touching simplicity Lawrence confesses his love for Whitman. "Whitman, the great poet, has meant so much to me." One of the simplest, most ordinary, and most lovely things ever said by Lawrence, who cast about so frenziedly to deny his loves. But now, for an instant moment, nothing but love and the admiration and understanding of love.

Whitman, the one man breaking a way ahead. Whitman, the one pioneer. And only Whitman. No English pioneers, no French. No European pioneer-poets. In Europe the would-be-pioneers are mere innovators. The same in America. Ahead of Whitman, nothing. Ahead of all poets, pioneering into the wilderness of un-opened life, Whitman. Beyond him, none. His wide, strange camp at the end of the great high-road. And lots of new little poets camping on Whitman's camping ground now. But none going really beyond. Because Whitman's camp is at the end of the road, and on the edge of a great precipice. Over the precipice, blue distances, and the blue hollow of the future. But there is no way down. It is a dead end. . . . Fearfully mistaken. And yet the great leader.

Then Lawrence becomes incoherent. The divided soul reveals itself again. Why was Whitman the great leader? Because he was the great poet of the transitions of the soul as it loses its integrity: that is, as it seeks successively to merge in woman, in man-for-man love, and finally in death: the poet of love that can find no fulfilment in woman, or in man, but only in death, or the dream of death: death that ends the crucifixion into humanity, which is the crucifixion into love. This is, for Lawrence, the necessary path of the soul: the soul's destiny of disintegration. Its pristine integrity is broken by desire and the knowledge of sin in desiring; it can never be recovered save in death. This is man's destiny, says Lawrence. " We have all got to die, and disintegrate. We have got to die in life, too, and disintegrate while we live."

〜

Death, then, actual and physical death, is not the great consummation. No, says Lawrence, we have to die in life. This is a great teaching, the greatest and deepest doctrine of the human soul. But what does Lawrence mean when he uses the words of this great teaching? Something utterly different from what the great teachers meant by it. He has told us in the essay on Melville. " Abandon the ideals," which means " Abandon love." This is the final disintegration, the final abdication: the acceptance of the doom of the spirit, the giving up of the Ghost.

And what will be the outcome of this surrender, this death? " Something else will come," he says. But for the moment he does not tell us what. " We've got to die first anyhow. And disintegrate while we still live. Only we know this much: Death is not the *goal*." It sounds right, too right, somehow, for Lawrence. Let us remember where we are, for it is easy, in this confusion, to forget; and the confusion is there, because Lawrence wants to forget. The human soul has passed through the love of woman, the love of man, the desire of death, wherein alone integrity can be restored. It refuses death, it clings to life, and pays the price: it abandons love. The soul commits suicide, *felo de se,* a felony in itself. " Then something else will come."

But what? Granted the possibility of this final suicide of spirit (which is impossible), *what* will come? After a pause,

Lawrence tells us: it is " the journey down the open road."
But what is that? Whitman will tell us. But how can Whitman tell us, when " he brought us to the edge of a precipice,
where there is no way down "? This was a mistake of Lawrence's, apparently; there is a way down, not a path merely,
but an open road.

The Open Road. The great home of the Soul is the open road.
Not heaven, not paradise. Not " above." Not even " within." The
soul is neither " above " nor " within." It is a wayfarer down the
open road.

Not by meditating. Not by fasting. Not by exploring heaven
after heaven, inwardly, in the manner of the mystics. Not by ex-
altation. Not by ecstasy. Not by any of these ways does the soul
come into her own.

Only by taking the open road.

Not through charity. Not through sacrifice. Not even through
love. Not through good works. Not through these does the soul
accomplish herself.

Only through the journey down the open road.

It is not clear, this doctrine; but that's no matter. What
we are hungry to know is how it comes that there is a soul
at all to make the inscrutable journey. Is not the soul dead,
is it not disintegrating still? Without love for woman, or for
man, without even desire for death? Yet here it is, journeying along the open road, meeting all the other wayfarers
along the road.

And how? How meet them, and how pass? With sympathy,
says Whitman. Sympathy. He does not say love. He says sympathy. Feeling with. Feel with them as they feel themselves.
Catching the vibration of their soul and flesh as we pass.

It sounds good. But how if they have not abandoned the
ideal, how if they still feel love for woman, or love for man,

or desire for death? How can the soul which has put away these things feel with the soul that feels them still? Whitman's own meaning we understand. Whether he said love or not, he meant it. That was his fearful mistake, says Lawrence. " He still confounded it with Jesus' LOVE and Paul's CHARITY." And this mistake was truly terrible. " He forced his soul to the edge of the cliff, and he looked down into death. And there he camped powerless. He had carried out his Sympathy as an extension of Love and Charity. And it had brought him almost to madness, and to soul-death." We are whirled in chaos. Have we not been told that this soul-death is necessary? And that Whitman is a great poet precisely because he brought himself, and led us thither? Because he taught us that we have to die and to disintegrate? Because he showed us the way?

Now it is all a fearful mistake. Because he believed in love, whereas he should have believed in " sympathy." Love brings madness and soul-death; "sympathy" brings life. Not to feel for — that is the poison; but to feel with — that is salvation. No, not salvation, the word is taboo. To feel with, anyhow. To feel with, as Dana felt with seaman Sam, and was sick, and Lawrence cursed him for it? To feel with, as Jack Calcott felt for the socialists with an iron bar, and Lawrence blessed him for it? The mystery of " sympathy " — who shall explain it?

Lawrence will, though he had better not have tried.

My soul takes the open road. She meets the souls that are passing, she goes along with the souls that are going her way. [There are none, but what matter?] And for one and all, she has sympathy. The sympathy of love [when love is *the* poison?], the sympathy of hate [wonderful phrase!], the sympathy of simple proximity; all the subtle sympathisings of the incalculable soul, from the bitterest hate to passionate love.

That is the great secret. We feared it. Lawrence will be
Lawrence still. He will react to everything; he will love, and
hate himself for loving, he will hate and love himself for
hating. He will go on the same open road, " backward from
all havens astern "; he will obey the impulse, hate the world,
run away, follow the god of the moment. Nothing shall be
changed, but the name: and the name for all this is
" sympathy."

Another handful of dust in our eyes, and in his own. It is
the same old Holy Ghost, who has led him to the brink of
death, from which he flinched, now ready to lead him back
again, under the name of Sympathy. Was Lawrence deceived? It seems incredible that he should have been. But
for the moment he was deceived. The divided soul must
connive for ever at its own deception. But " the sympathy
of hate "; it needed Lawrence to discover that with which
to cheat himself. But cheat himself he must. It is not easy
to kill the spirit in a spiritual man; it is not so easy for the
born idealist to abandon all ideals. All that he has rejected,
all that he has denied, returns upon him with a rush, on the
last page of this strange book.

The love for man and woman: a recognition of souls and a communion of worship. The love of comrades: a recognition of souls
and a communion of worship. Democracy: a recognition of souls,
all down the open road, and a great soul seen in its greatness, as
it travels on foot among the rest, down the common way of the
living. A glad recognition of souls, and a gladder worship of great
and greater souls, because they are the only riches.

It is the extremity of incoherence; a clean denial of all
that his book contains. The destroying woman, the womanless man, the flogging sea-captain, the hardy indomitable
polygamist, the sympathy of hate — everything is forgotten,
in the vision of the New Jerusalem. A recognition of souls,

a glad recognition of souls, and a communion of worship. Not far away from the Kingdom of Heaven, after all: not very far from the communion of saints.

" Right to the end," he wrote of Melville, " he could never accept the fact that perfect relationships cannot be." And he castigates Melville for his stupidity, his refusal to learn, his refusal to surrender. " Melville," he said, " was at the core a mystic and an idealist. So perhaps am I. And he stuck to his ideal guns. *I abandon mine.*" He will do his best; but it is not easy to kill one's soul. And the end is not yet, evidently not yet.

II

DEATH

THE most obviously significant thing in *The Plumed Serpent* is negative; it is that Lawrence does not appear in it. The Man disappears, the Woman remains. Anna Lensky, Ursula Brangwen, Tanny Lilly, Harriet Somers, and now Kate Leslie alone — these are unmistakable embodiments of the one woman. But now her husband is dead. Rupert Birkin, Rawdon Lilly, Richard Somers, is dead. His name, in this book, was Joachim. He had been an Irish patriot, with a consuming spiritual passion to regenerate his country. Now he is dead. Since Lawrence is not dead, this Joachim is not wholly Lawrence; one cannot even say that he is the *whole* of the spiritual and ideal Lawrence. But, so far as it is imaginatively possible, by killing Joachim, Lawrence has achieved that death, of which the throes convulsed *Studies in Classical American Literature.*

At the end of the book, a judgment is passed on the Woman. She is arraigned by another woman, who shows " contempt for her way of wifehood," and throws the blame for Joachim's death upon Kate. Says Kate: " He wanted to die."

" Ah, yes! " said Teresa, " he wanted to die."
" I did my level best to prevent him wearing himself out."
" Ah, yes, to prevent him."
" What else could I have done? " flashed Kate in anger.

" If you could have given him your life, he would not even have wanted to die."

" I *did* give him my life. I loved him — oh, you will never know. But he didn't want my soul. He believed I should keep a soul of my own."

Which may have been true of Joachim; but it was not true of Lawrence in *Studies in Classical American Literature*. There he demanded " newly submissive women — women who *choose* to experience again the great submission." And the woman, Teresa, who thus condemns Kate is one of these women. It is not surprising, therefore, that she is curiously unreal, lacking all solidity. Considering how vitally important the figure of Teresa is to the resolution of the underlying issue — for she is nothing less than " the new woman " — it is strange how little capable Lawrence is of presenting her. Strange, that is, theoretically; practically, the cause is clear. Lawrence cannot *realise* the new woman in his imagination. It is the counterpart and corollary of his being unable to realise the new man in himself.

Not the new woman, but the Woman, is therefore the chief character of *The Plumed Serpent*. Anna, Ursula, Tanny, Harriet — the Woman in these lives in the new book precisely as she lived before; but the Man is dead. The new man cannot be presented any more than the new woman. Lawrence is dead; and he experiences a kind of resurrection. He rises again as Ramon Carrasco, the saviour of Mexico: in his new life he has for mate " the newly submissive woman," Teresa. He has also the Jonathan to his David that he has so long desired, in Cipriano, the Mexican general. And Cipriano turns out to be the perfect mate for the Woman. Kate who would not submit to Joachim, submits to Cipriano — or seems to submit. Admittedly, this submis-

sion of Kate to Cipriano is precarious in the extreme: it is
as though Lawrence (like Aaron) could not really convince
himself that this submission of the Woman could ever be.
Kate is to the end reluctant and rebellious, accepting Cipriano rather as an experience than as a fundamental. And,
seeing that in the *Studies* Lawrence with horror repudiated
the notion of such an alliance between the races, it is surprising that his imagination should go so far. Cipriano is pure
Indian: the pureness of his Indian blood is insisted on again
and again. He is not Spanish-Indian, but pure Zapotec; and
Kate is, of course, pure Northern European. We remember
the *Studies*.

We can't go back. Whatever else the South Sea Islander is, he
is centuries and centuries behind us in the life-struggle, the consciousness struggle, the struggle of the soul into fulness. There is
his woman, with her knotted hair and her dark, inchoate, slightly
sardonic eyes. I like her, she is nice. But I would never want to
touch her. I could not go back on myself so far. Back to their
uncreate condition.

She has soft warm flesh, like warm mud. Nearer the reptile, the
Saurian age. *Noli me tangere.* . . . We can only do it, when we
are renegade.

Best then put down the abandonment of this apparent
conviction, in the perfect mating between Kate and Cipriano,
to the complete incoherence of the Holy Ghost in Lawrence
now: for if his convictions are coherent, then he is engaged
(even though unconsciously) in taking revenge on the
Woman by degrading her. That is possible, for the *Studies*
revealed clearly the depth of his hatred of her — the tempter,
the poisoner, the destroyer of his integrity.

༄

In Lawrence most things are possible. But perhaps the
tone and temper of *The Plumed Serpent* does not admit

of the idea of a wholly deliberate degradation of the Woman. Not merely is Cipriano a hero in the book; but, more deeply, Lawrence is, in regard to the Woman, now a dead man. In regard to her he is as it were disembodied: some of the bitterness of the personal struggle is past. He has lost the battle, and knows his defeat. She has not submitted to him, and never will. Nevertheless, he seems to say, he is right, although in life he has failed to make good his claim to her submission; and so he makes her submit to Cipriano, Cipriano with " the face at once of a god and devil, the undying Pan face." This from the beginning, from the time of *The White Peacock*, has been one of Lawrence's most cherished avatars: the desire thus to incarnate himself persists from Annable to Mellors, and is most curiously revealed in his own, quite unfaithful, drawing of his own face. Cipriano, like Count Dionys in *The Ladybird*, is one of these longed-for reincarnations of Lawrence as " the old masterless Pan-male, that cannot even conceive of service." To him the Woman submits.

" She could conceive now her marriage with Cipriano . . . the supreme passivity . . . the sheer solid mystery of passivity . . . where the soul of woman was dumb, to be for ever unspoken." This is the destiny which the Woman now accepts. She makes her submission, abandons the claims to individual being which Lawrence could never induce or compel her to resign in life. More than this, she surrenders her claim to sexual fulfilment. Lawrence is completely outspoken on this matter.

She realised, almost with wonder, the death in her of the Aphrodite of the foam: the seething, frictional, ecstatic Aphrodite. By a swift dark instinct, Cipriano drew away from this in her. When, in their love, it came back on her, the seething electric female ecstasy, which knows such spasms of delirium, he recoiled from her. It was what she used to call her " satisfaction."

But Cipriano would not. . . . And she, as she lay, would realise the worthlessness of this foam-effervescence, its strange externality to her. It seemed to come on her from without, not from within. And succeeding the first moment of disappointment, when this sort of " satisfaction " was denied her, came the knowledge that she did not really want it, that it was nauseous to her.

Oddly, or not at all oddly, this surrender is completely one-sided. It is in the case of the Woman quite explicit; but there is no indication, or faint hint, that the man forwent his physical " satisfaction." But the Woman is content with this ordering of the matter.

We need not dwell on this; but it would be criminal to slur it over. The sexual situation behind this imaginary consummation is fundamental in Lawrence; it is the physical cause of the extremity of his exasperation, and of his obsession with sexuality itself. Always, on the biological level, he felt himself inferior to the woman: he was radically conscious that as a male he was a failure. And he could not accept the fact. He persisted that it was not he, but the woman, who was wrong. She claimed from him as male what she had no right to claim; her idea of sexual fulfilment was not the true idea of sexual fulfilment. Through Cipriano he makes her accept this perversion of the truth, just as years before through Rupert Birkin he had made Ursula Brangwen accept it. But there is a difference now, and a great one. Rupert Birkin *was* Lawrence, Cipriano is not. Behind the crucial change is hidden the acknowledgment that in life the Woman will never accept his perversion of the truth; and, in reality, that acknowledgment is an acknowledgment of its falsity. For this is not a matter of mental conviction. You cannot by taking thought convince a woman that she is sexually fulfilled. She *knows*. The fact that she is not convinced is the proof that there is nothing to convince her of. But Cipriano might do what Lawrence himself cannot do: convince her physically that there is a sexual fulfilment beyond what ordinary men and women know as sexual fulfilment, that in sexual communion there is a " mystery beyond the phallic." Perhaps; but we fear it is a dream, a wishfulfilment. The truth is, that as Cipriano is an imaginary person, so the fulfilment he gives to Kate is an imaginary fulfilment, belonging to another order of existence than any we humans know. Once more Lawrence is evading the last reality of himself; and, as ever, the last reality of himself is the most intimate acknowledgment of the Woman's claim.

But now he has come very far. In *The Plumed Serpent* the Woman occupies the stage; she is the protagonist. On the realistic level everything depends upon whether she is convinced, not in this matter of sexuality simply, but in the great religious issues which the book propounds. Inevitably, these religious issues are not distinct from the personal and sexual issue. Kate's surrender to Cipriano in the flesh is only a particular manifestation of her surrender to the religion of Ramon and Cipriano; and the one surrender is as dubious as the other. It must be so, because the religion of Ramon and Cipriano is Lawrence's religion, a religion into which his own doubt of himself in regard to the Woman has entered. This religion is the perfected expression of his own " male creativity ": of that element in himself of which the Woman is justly suspicious. Her profound suspicion of it is just, because of the element of " compensation " with which it is vitiated. Inextricably mingled with the products of this " male creativity " in Lawrence is an imaginative surrogate for the independence he has never been able to achieve, or to maintain. Its creations are always too male, always characterised by the assertion in the world of imagination of a supremacy which cannot be asserted in the world of reality.

They have a febrile masculinity; they have the central weakness which comes of imaginative duplicity.

༄

This duplicity is evident, on more levels than one, in the religion of *The Plumed Serpent*. On the simplest level we are confronted with the obvious question: Why is Kate implicated in it at all? The new religion of Quexalcoatl and Huitzilopochtli is wholly a Mexican religion. This is not only admitted, but positively and repeatedly asserted by Ramon Carrasco. The dual divinity of Quexalcoatl and Huitzilopochtli is the Mexican manifestation of the one unnameable God; the Mexican contribution to the truly Catholic Church, says Ramon to the old Bishop. The thought is sound, but it is not new. It is characteristic of Indian religious thought; it was plainly enounced even by the boy John Keats. " The angel of the zopilotes must always be a zopilote," says Cipriano. But Kate is not a Mexican, and the Mexican saviour cannot be her saviour. She has her own saviour, the god-manifestation of her white race, if she is in need of god-manifestations at all. What she might do is to discern with the eye of the spirit that Quexalcoatl and Huitzilopochtli are necessary and right God-manifestations for the Mexican, more appropriate and more perfect manifestations than the Jesus and Mary of a degraded Indian Christianity; what she cannot do, except in violation of the Spirit that is within her, and at peril of becoming a renegade to her race, is to accept Quexalcoatl and Huitzilopochtli as manifestations of God to her. Yet this is precisely what Lawrence makes her do. Seeming to glorify her, he degrades her, by the same necessity which compels him to degrade her with Cipriano, under the guise of true fulfilment.

Here, on the visible circumference, is the palpable evidence of the divided soul within. As we advance towards the centre, it becomes still more manifest. Why, we must ask, is the divinity dual? This is not the great male and female duality, but a purely masculine duality. Nor is it a poly-theism, but a strict duality. Whatever those gods, Quexal-coatl and Huitzilopochtli, may represent in the old Mexican religion — and, after all, we know that Huitzilopochtli at least was an abomination of cruelty and blood and death — there is no doubt what they meant to Lawrence. They are the manifestations of love and hate. Ramon is a more deeply realised Kangaroo, and Cipriano complements him with the embodiment of those impulses to hate and murder and mind-less sensuality which were necessary, in the eyes of Richard Somers, to a complete manifestation of the "dark God." Cipriano celebrates his own apotheosis as Huitzilopochtli with the killing of four men and a woman. It happens that the slaying is just, Huitzilopochtli is, to this extent, regener-ated by his new incarnation. But, we feel, as Kate feels, that the justice is accidental, and the bloodshed is not. Blood-sacrifice, and the sacrifice of human blood, is the essential in the worship of Huitzilopochtli.

Huitzilopochtli in the new manifestation is subordinate to Quexalcoatl. Ramon is the master, Cipriano the servant; and the soul of Ramon, we are told at the beginning, is " es-sentially European." That is surely true, for the soul of Ramon is essentially the soul of Lawrence — a sensitive, generous, and loving soul; but the body of Ramon is not the body of Lawrence. And since souls and bodies are not distinct nor distinguishable, we are left to wonder whether Ramon is not a hybrid of the imagination, and, still more perturbing speculation, whether Cipriano would have been so obedient to him, if his soul had worn its wonted garment. Ramon might perfectly well have been a statesman and a soldier as well as a prophet and a poet. From his point of view there is no reason at all why he should need a complementary *divinity*. Cipriano could have remained his servant, instead of sitting on his right hand as a co-equal god. But the apotheosis of Cipriano satisfies discrepant desires in Lawrence: his desire for a blood-brother to save him from his own weakness, and his desire for an outlet to his hate.

∽

None the less, Cipriano is irrelevant to the inmost religious idea of *The Plumed Serpent*. The well-head of the new gospel is the essentially European soul of Ramon Carrasco. Cipriano is, confessedly, only an instrument for the realisation of Ramon's vision and purposes. On the impersonal level this religion of Ramon's is the spiritual quick of the book. On this level the conditions of its manifestation, Mexico, Cipriano, Kate herself, are accidental: they are, so to speak, the inevitable personal impurities, the eddies and stagnant back-flows caused in the stream of imagination by the obstacles of a personal destiny. Ramon-Quexalcoatl (if he is what he purports to be) does not need Cipriano-Huitzilopochtli, nor does he need Kate. Perhaps he does not even need Teresa, save in the capacity of a ministering Magdalen. And as we have said, the relation between Teresa and Ramon is not *realised* at all. To Kate it seems just like the relation between Joachim and herself, or between Somers and Harriet.

She thought of Teresa soothing him, soothing him, and saying nothing. And him like a great helpless wounded thing. It was rather horrible, really. Herself, she would have to expostulate, she would have to try to prevent him. Why should men damage themselves with this useless struggling and fighting, and then come home to their women to be restored!

Yet he would do it. Even as Joachim had done. And Teresa, with her silence and infinitely soft administering, she would heal him far better than Kate, with her expostulation and opposition.

Really, we know no more than this about the relation between Ramon and Teresa. She gives him that which Kate did not give to Joachim, nor Harriet to Somers. She surrenders herself absolutely to his service. " I kept my own life for a long time," she says to Kate. " And I tried to give it to God. But I couldn't quite." As a nun gives herself to God, so does Teresa give herself to Ramon. But the connection is not so virginal as it sounds. It is a sexual connection, the sexual self-immolation of a virgin in the service of her god — a sort of sacred prostitution. In it there is no thought of sexual fulfilment for herself — neither the " satisfaction " of the unregenerate Kate, nor the ultra-phallic mystery to which Kate submits in Cipriano — her sole object is to give Ramon from her body rest, and renewal, and sleep. And Kate is represented as acknowledging that Teresa is, in this, her superior.

Kate was accustomed to looking on other women as inferiors. But the tables were suddenly turned. Even as, in her soul, she knew Ramon to be a greater man than Cipriano, suddenly she had to question herself whether Teresa was not a greater woman than she.

Teresa! A greater woman than Kate? What a blow! Surely it was impossible.

Yet there it was.

Kate is the protagonist: she lives and fills the book. Teresa does not live, and enters only at the end. But she is intended to be the victor. She is the greater woman, and Kate must acknowledge it. She must be made to admit defeat. And her humiliation is pretty thorough. She is made to submit; and she is conquered, not by Ramon, but by Cipriano, whom in her soul she knows to be Ramon's inferior. Ramon does not choose her. She is second-best, and the bride of the second-best god; and even for that position she has to surrender all her belief, all her pride, all that she is. With his left hand Lawrence takes from the Woman all that his right hand has been enforced to give.

It is not simply an imaginative revenge. It is that, and we must see it. But it is also the dream of a weary man. Ramon is Lawrence himself, born again. " In the resurrection of the dead there is neither marriage nor giving in marriage "; but Lawrence cannot accept it. There must be, in some more perfect life, a marriage that is peace, for such a man as he. So he dreams it. He can dream his reborn self, but he cannot dream Teresa. She is shadowy — a nun, a priestess, a virgin who gives herself and is still virgin, one of " the spirits summoned west." And in Cipriano and Kate, he tries to slough off from himself that which, in actual life, has cankered him — his hatred, " the yearning of love and the burning of hate " which, he told us in *Studies,* must gnaw at a man all the days of his life. The love which is hate, and the hate which is love, are unknown to Ramon and Teresa. They know only a love which contains no hate within it, which Lawrence cannot imagine, but only assert; they are Lawrence and his bride in an earthly paradise. Alone they cannot make a complete divinity. Cipriano's hate and Cipriano's woman are necessary. But Cipriano and his woman bow down to them, and are governed by them: hate yields to love, and blood-sacrifice is governed by justice.

∽

A dream; but in its way a beautiful and significant dream, an attempt to imagine that harmony of which life denies him the attainment. A dream, moreover, purchased at the price of an imaginative death. It cost Lawrence, we are sure, no small pain to pass the knife thus through the great inward division in himself. And a sense of death, of doom and dissolution, hangs heavy over the book: death hangs in that Mexican air. Outwardly Ramon succeeds, the movement of regeneration seems victorious, but inwardly, he has no hope. Bitterly he says to Kate, towards the end, that this people will deify her one day, and murder and violate her the next. It is the old, terrible mistrust which comes over Lawrence when he lives among the unspiritual, pre-mental people, after whom he hankers — the same fearful mistrust that uttered itself in *Sea and Sardinia,* and in Pancrazio's grim warning to Alvina in *The Lost Girl.* " These people are bad." In *The Plumed Serpent,* Lawrence cannot conceal his terror and his mistrust. It is Huitzilopochtli who will master Quexalcoatl, not Quexalcoatl him. Ramon, who seems to triumph, has no confidence in victory. Kate, who cannot resist her destiny to be the nemesis of doubting man, asks him what he is sure of.

" I am sure — sure — ." His voice trailed off into vagueness, his face seemed to grow grey and peaked, as a dead man's, only his eyes watched her blackly, like a ghost's. Again she was confronted with the suffering ghost of the man. And she was a woman, powerless before this suffering which was still in the flesh.

" You don't think you are wrong, do you? " she asked, in cold distress.

" No! I am not wrong. Only maybe I can't hold out," he said.

" And then what? " she said coldly.

" I shall go my way, alone." There seemed to be nothing left of him but the black ghostly eyes that gazed at her. He began to speak Spanish.

" It hurts me in my soul, as if I were dying," he said.

" But why? " she cried. " You are not ill? "

" I feel as if my soul were coming undone."

" Then don't let it," she cried, in fear and repulsion.

But he only gazed with those fixed blank eyes. A sudden deep stillness came over her; a sense of power in herself.

" You should forget for a time," she said gently, compassionately laying her hand on his. What was the good of trying to understand him or wrestle with him? She was a woman. He was a man, and — and — and therefore not quite real. Not true to life.

There is, in this haunting passage, far more Lawrence than Ramon; far more of the living and dying Lawrence than of the reborn man of his dream: therefore at this terrible moment not Teresa, but Kate, is the comforter. This is that old suffering, that agony of inward torment, which wrung the heart of the Woman when she was Anna Lensky, and was flooded with pity for the suffering of Will. Her heart is wrung with pity, and the love that is born of pity: and she can do nothing, nothing at all. Neither by pity, nor by understanding, if that were possible, could she make him whole.

∽

But for the most part in *The Plumed Serpent,* Lawrence's imaginative detachment from himself is complete. What Ramon fears may happen to him, has actually happened to Lawrence: his soul has " come undone," split as it were into Ramon and Cipriano.

And, on the surface it appears that the religion of Ramon is simply this: that such a splitting of the man must not be. The ritual attitude of " the man of Quexalcoatl," standing erect and tense, with one arm taut towards the sky, the other downward to the loins and the earth beneath, is the symbol of the central mystery.

> Lower your fingers to the caress of the snake of the earth;
> Lift your wrist for a perch to the far-flying bird.

But it is, for all its beautiful elaboration in many poems and ritual songs, the old doctrine of *The Crown:* and it has all the old deceptiveness. It has, as of old, the appearance of truth. Spirit and flesh must dwell together and be one in man, it seems to say. It seems to proclaim the necessary unity of man. But, if it really meant this, and if Ramon-Quexalcoatl is indeed the symbol and embodiment of this unity, why is Cipriano-Huitzilopochtli enthroned beside him? And the answer is the same old answer. This seeming unity is not a unity at all; it is that mere " unity " of the body which unites, while bodily life endures, impulses that are implacably hostile to one another, the " unity " of unregenerate man. If it were a true unity of regeneration, Ramon-Quexalcoatl would need no Cipriano-Huitzilopochtli beside him. The religion of the Morning Star is the apotheosis of the divided man, of Good *and* Evil, of Love *and* Hatred.

The cause is the same old cause. Lawrence could not achieve the living unity for which he hungered and thirsted. Not by the undoing of his soul, not by the splitting of himself into Ramon and Cipriano, can he achieve it even in the world of imagination. Nemesis follows him into the secret places of his imagination. Now, when he has taken from himself the sediment of his hatred of the world, of the Woman, of all mankind, and made clay of it and moulded Cipriano to be the vehicle of his own revulsion against humanity, still he cannot keep Ramon pure of the contagion. The destiny marked out long ago in " Winter Dawn " cannot be escaped.

> I am washed quite clean,
> Quite clean of it all.
> But e'en
>
> So cold, so cold and clean
> Now the hate is gone!
> It is all no good,
> I am chilled to the bone

Now the hate is gone;
There is nothing left;
I am pure like bone,
Of all feeling bereft.

So likewise, when the hate is gone into Cipriano, there is
nothing left. What remains is nothing, and from nothing
nothing can be created. If Lawrence is to feel Ramon, then
Ramon must feel hatred. For hatred is the breath of life to
Lawrence. It must be so; for his hatred is his love, inverted,
denied, outraged. The passion of love that burned in him
is become a passion of hate.

He cannot conceive Ramon without plunging him into the
gulf of hatred. Ramon must fall headlong into the pit.

" My manhood is like a demon howling inside me," said Ramon
to himself, in Cipriano's word.

And he admitted the justice of his howling, his manhood being
pent up, humiliated, goaded with insult inside him. And rage came
over him, against Carlotta, against Cipriano, against his own people, against all mankind, till he was filled with rage like the devil.

His people would betray him, he knew that. Cipriano would betray him. Given one little vulnerable chink, they would pierce
him. They would leap at the place out of nowhere, like a taran-
tula, and bite in the poison.

There is no escape. The soul is utterly divided, even in
Lawrence's imaginative embodiment of the undivided soul.
When he has separated himself from his hatred, exorcised
it like a devil and bid it depart into another man, still it remains. The house is swept and garnished, but the spirit
cannot enter in, only seven devils worse, because more " an-
gelic," than the first.

Yet *The Plumed Serpent* is absorbing both as a document
and as an imaginative achievement. It is Lawrence's last

effort at complete expression of himself in his fulness. He can do it no longer by the familiar means, of presenting himself, with his thoughts, his feelings, his desires, his revulsions, as a single living person. The quick of himself is in dissolution, there is no point of vital coherence any more. The " I," the fundamental self, has fallen apart. He is become a pure succession of contradictory states. In *The Plumed Serpent* he seeks to express all these states, to give them, by imagination, the coherence that they cannot have in the living man. In the actual experience of the individual microcosm, one state destroys and annihilates the other: the self is delivered up totally to the condition of the moment. In the macrocosm of the imagination, these mutually destructive states can co-exist, and be given a specious unity. In other words, Lawrence, who discarded " art " for prophecy, has reached a point where he must discard prophecy for " art." And this is acknowledged, consciously or unconsciously, in *The Plumed Serpent*. It is Lawrence's greatest work of " art."

But the triumph of the " artist " is the defeat of the prophet. And, far more important, it is a triumph that cannot be maintained. Not merely because the energy necessary to maintain it must inevitably fail in a man who gives up the attempt to resolve his inward discords into unity; for this is the manifestation in consciousness of the vital urge of life towards more life, and it can fail only when life itself is failing. But also because for the man who is essentially a prophet, the return to " art " is manifestly the beginning of his decline. It is in itself the sign of the spent and ebbing wave, the indication that he has clutched more within his grasp than he can hold. Nothing remains but to relax the fingers, and let the precious stuff fall to the ground. From such a triumph of " art " as *The Plumed Serpent*, no growth of finer " art " can possibly ensue, nor any of equal " art ": for in this order, to cease to go forward is infallibly to begin to go backward. Lawrence knew it, more clearly than we. " A man's blood can't beat in the abstract," says Ramon. " And man is a creature who wins his own creation inch by inch from the nest of the cosmic dragons. Or else he loses it little by little and goes to pieces." It may not be true of all men; but of a Lawrence it is true, and it is the central truth of such a man. From the beginning he has been engaged, body and mind and soul, in the effort at self-creation. In obedience to that all-dominating impulse, he has abandoned " art " long ago, and made his books intimate and personal documents of his progress towards self-creation. This is now impossible, because the self *cannot* be created. He returns to art, knowing that it is a *pis-aller*, *because* it is a *pis-aller*. The death of Joachim, the sole survival of the Woman of the pair, and the renascence of Lawrence as " artist," are manifestations of the same inward dissolution. It is the beginning of the end, the brilliant and deceptive hectic flush of death.

The dissolution is everywhere. Finally, Ramon dissolves in our hands. As, physically, he seems to dwindle and to lapse from a strong and self-sufficient man into a careworn ghost with a voice whispering " I am sure — sure . . ." and trailing off into vagueness, so, spiritually, he falls together on himself like a house of cards. His faith fails him; the specious unity of his creed disintegrates. The Morning Star falls out of heaven. Bravely, at first, the Morning Star is the apparent symbol of a final human integrity, the twinatured unity of the individual man, the quick of life itself that seeks now the perfection of consciousness, now the warm oblivion of sleep and sexual love.

There is only one thing that a man really wants to do, all his life; and that is, to find his way to his God, his Morning Star, and be alone there. Then, afterwards, in the Morning Star, salute his fellow men, and enjoy the woman who has come the long way with him.

The old courage, and the old weakness. To be alone, and not to be alone. The old, impossible demand; the old self-deception. For if the Morning Star is verily what it seems to be, the sign and point of the surrender of the personal being to the unnameable and unknowable God, companionship in that place is unthinkable and impossible. No man or woman communes there save with the unknowable God himself. Ramon, no more than the actual Lawrence can accept his loneliness. He sees the path but cannot take it.

This was how Ramon felt at the moment; — I am attempting the impossible. I had better either go and take my pleasure of life while it lasts, hopeless of the pleasure that is beyond all pleasures. Or else I had better go into the desert and take my way all alone, to the Star where at last I have my wholeness, holiness. The way of the anchorites and the men who went into the wilderness to pray. For surely my soul is craving for her consummation, and I am weary of the thing men call life. Living, I want to depart to where *I am.*

Then why not go into the wilderness? Why not go as the great men of the spirit have gone before? They did not stay there; they returned. But only after they had been there, and endured the last agony of loneliness, alone, did they return with their message — always with the same message. The moment comes when the heroic human soul striving after self-creation *must* be alone. Friendship, marriage — these things vanish in the twinkling of an eye. There is no " I " to be bound by them; and they dissolve away. Then a man must choose. The choice is as Ramon puts it: to abandon the quest for self-creation, or to face the terror of an ultimate isolation. And Ramon, no more than Lawrence, has the power to choose; like Lawrence, he shrinks away from both, and cries for the impossible.

Yet, he said to himself, the woman that was with me in the Morning Star, how glad I should be of her! And the man who was with me there, what a delight his presence would be. Surely the Morning Star is a meeting-ground for us, for the joy.

There is no meeting *in* the true Morning Star; *in* the true Morning Star there remains to a man nothing with which he can meet a man, or meet a woman. A man who has been to the Morning Star, can return, and he can meet man and woman in the strength of his own integrity which is not his own: he is a re-born man. And it may chance that he may meet other men and women who have been to the Morning Star; and he may not meet them. He will not care. His *I am* has been annihilated in the great *I am*.

That annihilation neither Ramon, nor Lawrence, will meet. Let someone go with me, they cry. Nobody goes, nobody can go. And they will not go alone. They pause irresolute, and in that sickening pause decay begins. So Ramon, like Lawrence, ends by denying the Morning Star. The final declaration is that "the Morning Star rises between the two, and between the many, but never from one alone." That declaration is false and renegade; it is a lie. It is, moreover, a total denial of all that Lawrence first declared to be the truth of the Morning Star. The Morning Star rises always from one alone, never between two, never between many. The truth of the Morning Star is that when loneliness is ultimate, the individual being is not alone: he is, and knows himself to be, a living shoot of the great tree, a part of the whole, a "son of God."

Here, as ever, Lawrence must deceive himself. Because he has not achieved the Morning Star, it does not exist. It exists only in the relation between two: between man and man, and man and woman. A noble faith, it may appear. The appearance deceives. This noble faith is self-excuse. If the attainment of the Morning Star does not depend on one alone, if it is impossible that it should rise from one alone, why then, Lawrence is absolved. It is the fault of the others that he has failed to reach the Morning Star — the fault of the Woman, the fault of the Man, the fault of all men, who failed him in his need. He has been betrayed. Comfortable belief! More dust in his eyes, and in ours. As though, in this order, any man could ever be betrayed save to his own triumph. Jesus was betrayed by Judas, to his victory. Lawrence is betrayed, by Man, by Woman, by the Many, to his own defeat. There is the difference.

For to be failed by Man or Woman, is only to be left alone by them. It is a bitter thing, no doubt, but only part of the great process of suffering by which alone we learn, by which alone we can come to *be*. If Man and Woman and the Many did not fail us, in ways beyond their knowing, how should we ever pass into that isolation in which we are born again? The re-born soul knows well that those who failed him brought him, all unknowing, a great gift: they drove him into the loneliness that is fearful to be borne, into the agony whose travail ends in peace.

Lawrence is not re-born, nor ever will be. At the thought of the Man, the Woman, the Many, who have betrayed him, he is black and bitter hatred, blind to the simple truth (which he himself has uttered) that no man ever is betrayed except he betrays himself. That Lawrence has done irrevocably. Therefore he must believe that he has been betrayed by others. Therefore he must have revenge. In *The Plumed Serpent* he takes it — revenge on his race, revenge on the

Woman, revenge on both at once. He submits her to Cipriano in the flesh, to Huitzilopochtli in the spirit. " The power of the world was dying in the blond men, their bravery and their supremacy was leaving them, going into the eyes of the dark men, who were rousing at last." So great is his longing for revenge that the brave Morning Star, concerning which he has been so eloquent, sinks to its home in the mindless sexual consummation of a bloody minded pure-bred Indian, and a white woman murmuring to herself: " It leaves me insouciant like a young girl. What do I care if he kills people? His flame is young and clean."

So Lawrence, revenging himself, betrays himself again. It is not Man and Woman who have failed him, but he who has failed them. Instead of bread, he gives a stone; instead of fish, a serpent.

Thus ends the attempt to make " the great swerve in our onward-going life-course, and to gather up again the savage mysteries " — the attempt which Lawrence told us was necessary in *Studies*. Then he assured us: " This does not mean going back on ourselves." *The Plumed Serpent* shows that it means this and nothing else.

The Woman stays in old Mexico; but Lawrence himself, in the flesh, could not. A little of it was more than enough for him. Mexico as a world of the imagination, in which he could be resurrected, undergo apotheosis, and take a capable and wide revenge, was one thing; Mexico as actuality was another. He felt its malevolence, and fled to that safer Mexico — New Mexico — which is in the United States.

III

POST–MORTEM EFFECTS

LAWRENCE went to America in the fall of 1922; at the end of 1923, he made an abortive effort to return to England, in which I personally was concerned. The story of this episode can be briefly told.

I had been estranged from Lawrence from the middle of 1916 onwards. His quest of "mindlessness" during the Cornish period had put a gulf between us. We parted; and Katherine Mansfield and I went over to the other side of Cornwall. Lawrence came to see us there, and we had a few happy days, in which we nearly drowned ourselves in a small boat; but we shook hands "as it were, across a vast." After that there was a brief renewal of friendship between Katherine and Lawrence in the winter of 1918–1919, in which I barely participated. I saw him but once at that time. In the spring of 1919 I went to stay with him in his cottage at Hermitage in Berkshire. But the constraint between us was painful. And by that time the renewed relation between him and Katherine was frayed away.

He felt that we had failed him; we felt that he had failed us. We felt that he had denied the good thing that was between us. He felt we had refused to go along with him, and left him to his isolation. There was bitterness on both sides. When, eventually, *Women in Love* was published, I attacked it openly over my own name, in an article in *The Nation*.

Strangely enough there is scarcely a word in that article
which I should withdraw to-day: that in Lawrence which I
then instinctively refused, I refuse deliberately to-day.
What I did not know was that the book had been written six
years before, and that, when it was published in 1921, it
did not faithfully represent Lawrence's attitude. So that,
when *Aaron's Rod* appeared shortly afterwards, I was perplexed and disconcerted — most joyfully perplexed and
gladly disconcerted. The death-miasma that seemed to me
then, and seems to me now, to hang over *Women in Love*
was dissipated; and I welcomed the change with enthusiasm.
Again, I would not now withdraw a word of what I wrote
then. " *Aaron's Rod,*" I said in *The Nation,* " is the most
important thing that has happened to English literature
since the war. Mr. Lawrence's new book ripples with the
consciousness of victory; he is gay, he is careless, he is persuasive. To read *Aaron's Rod* is to drink of a fountain of
life."

As far as I then understood — and I understood but little
— the victory might have been final. It was temporary.
There was no victory possible for Lawrence on this side of
the grave. But *Aaron's Rod* and the *Fantasia* mark the pinnacle of Lawrence's achievement: the halcyon moment of
apparent harmony before the signs of disintegration begin
to show. The *Fantasia* at this moment — some time in 1922
— was unknown to me. If it had actually been published, it
had been published only in America. Meanwhile, beyond
the public salutation of *Aaron's Rod,* I had no contact
with Lawrence. Katherine Mansfield and I were in the
Swiss mountains, struggling with our own destiny. All we
knew about Lawrence was his book, a line of hearsay
telling us that he had gone to Australia, and a sudden
and unexpected postcard of friendship from Wellington,
New Zealand, Katherine Mansfield's home, where his

ship had touched on his journey from Sydney to San Francisco.

That was in the late summer of 1922. At the end of the year, when Katherine Mansfield was at Fontainebleau, I wrote him a letter — the first for several years — suggesting, I suppose, that our relation should be renewed. By the time his reply came (" Heaven knows what we all are, and how we should feel if we met, now that we are changed: we'll have to meet and see.") Katherine had died.

Yes, it's something gone out of our lives, [he wrote]. I always knew a bond in my heart. Feel a fear where the bond is broken now. Feel as if old moorings were breaking all. What is going to happen to us all? Perhaps it is good for Katherine not to have to see the next phase. We will unite up again when I come to England. It has been a savage enough pilgrimage these last four years. Perhaps K. has taken the only way for her. We keep faith. I always feel death only strengthens that — the faith between those who have it.

Still it makes me afraid. As if worse were coming. I feel like the Sicilians. They always cry for help from their dead. We shall have to cry to ours: we do cry.

I asked Seltzer to send you *Fantasia of the Unconscious.* I wanted Katherine to read it. She'll know though. The dead don't die. They look on and help.

But in America one feels as if *everything* would die, and that is terrible.

I wish it needn't all have been as it has been: I do wish it.

I read the *Fantasia* when it arrived; and I remembered exactly the time and place where I read it — late into the night in a solitary cottage in Ashdown Forest. It was to me then, as it is to me now, a wonderful book. I had just emerged from an experience which changed me radically. Lawrence's declaration of faith in the *Fantasia* was completely convincing to me in my new, half-convalescent, half-confident

condition. Here was something in which I did veritably believe with all my heart, and all my mind, and all my soul.
What I had glimpsed in *Aaron's Rod*, I had now a full sight
of. If this was what Lawrence believed and stood for, then
I was his man: he should lead and I would follow.

It clinched my half-formed determination to found *The
Adelphi*. He was willing to " unite up again "; he was in the
throes of a revulsion from America. Then let him come back,
and we would begin. In the meantime, I would prepare the
place for him. I would make a new magazine, and begin by
publishing the essential chapters of the *Fantasia*. We cabled
to him in New Mexico; he agreed to the publication. And
The Adelphi began.

I neither desired, nor intended, to remain editor of it. I
was in my own eyes simply *locum tenens*, literally lieutenant,
for Lawrence; and I waited eagerly for his coming. I was a
little dashed when his letters began to arrive. He couldn't
come to England, now, he said. Something inside him
wouldn't let him.

I mistrust my country too much to identify myself with it any
more. And it still gives me a certain disgust. But this may pass. I
feel something must *happen* before I can come back.

Hard upon this came a letter to say he had been in Mexico
City for five days, and found it unbearable. " I don't like
the spirit of this continent. It seems to me sub-cruel, a bit
ghastly." He had been to New York, he said, but he couldn't
stay there. He would look round Old Mexico a little longer,
and be in England by July. I was to look for a quiet cottage
for him.

I began to be perplexed, and my perplexity increased.
First, he was coming, then he wasn't; first, he didn't like
The Adelphi, then he did. First, it was too "apologetic";
then, " I like what you say about faith: one must have faith

to break an old faith "; then, " I begin to see *The Adelphi* building up like a little fortress." And, all at the same time, he hated the American continent: it was a place of death and despair. The Aztec cruelty made Old Mexico terrible to him; the emptiness of the United States wore him down. But, no, he couldn't come to England. " I feel such a ' sadness ' about England and Europe, as if I'd swallowed a lump of lead. . . . Ask the Lord to take away this heavy feeling in my belly, that I have when I think of England, and home and my people: or even when I think of Fontana Vecchia. . . . And America means nothing to me — yet I'm going right West again."

I was now bewildered. Did he mean, I asked him, did he really *mean* what he had written in *Aaron's Rod* and *Fantasia?* Had he really meant it when he asked for some man to join with him in trying to create a new world? Or was I just being a fool in having taken him at his word? Perhaps I had read those books all wrong, after all. (And, of course, I had.)

" I think you understand *Fantasia* and *Aaron* all right," he answered. " It's I — because the sense of doom deepens inside me, at the thought of the old world which I loved — and the new world means nothing to me. . . . I suppose I'm the saddest, at *not* coming."

In May he wrote that he had taken a house on Lake Chapala (the main scene of *The Plumed Serpent*). " You'll think I do nothing but change my plans. I can't help it. I go out to buy my ticket to New York and Europe, then don't buy it. . . . Wonder what ails me."

I did not know then what ailed him; I was simply bewildered by his strange irresolution. It did not occur to me that *Aaron's Rod* and *Fantasia* had been written nearly three years before, and that in those three years, Lawrence must have changed. The book that had meant so much to me had become for him the expression of an aspiration, no longer of a conviction. The sense of doom had begun to triumph over the resolution to act. All the process which this book strives to demonstrate, a process so plain to me now, was concealed from me then. I did not understand that the revulsion he felt from the malevolence and cruelty of Mexico was also the fascination that held him there, as it held him in Cornwall during the war. He wanted to feed his sense of doom and death and corruption; to fulfil his own injunction that "we must disintegrate while we live." In the last issue, he could not make the effort towards a new and fuller life. Part of him wanted this, desired it as ardently as any man has ever desired it — the part of him that wanted to love and to forgive; but deeper still was his longing for hatred and revenge. The world, his own life, had deceived him; and he was not going to take it lying down. Mingled with all his passionate but partial professions of desire to make all things new was a thirst for destruction, a nostalgia for chaos.

All that was apparent to me at this time was a strange instability in Lawrence. He wanted, and he did not want; he was coming, and he was not coming. He must have changed his intentions fully half a dozen times in as many months, before he wrote from Guadalajara on October 25, 1923: "Yes, I think I shall come back now. I think I shall be back by the beginning of December. Work awhile with you on *The Adelphi*. Then perhaps we'll set off to India. Quien sabe?" I was glad he was coming; I dearly wanted to set eyes on him again: but my nascent confidence in him as a leader had begun to wither. More than this, I half suspected that the real reason why he had at last decided to return had not very much to do with his declared purpose of trying to make a path into the uncreated future; it might be because his wife had already come to England, and he could not remain apart from her for long.

D. H. LAWRENCE

from a photograph taken in the Spring of 1930

However, in his letter announcing his decision, there was naturally nothing of this. The English, he said, had to pick up a lost trail, and the end of the lost trail was there, where he was, in Mexico. We had to learn to " modify ourselves to a distant end," to balance with something that was not ourselves. That was well enough in theory; it was the doctrine of the *Fantasia,* in which I believed. But in practice it seemed to come down to something more questionable, in which I could not believe. In practice it seemed to mean pretending a harmony between impulses which were varily contradictory; to mean denying the spiritual consciousness and asserting it, to mean loving the world and hating it at the same moment, to mean nailing the flag of the civilized consciousness to the mast and hauling it down in a single operation.

It was not long before I learned that the latter was the more important part of the process to Lawrence, when he had come to England. He looked positively ill, when I met him at the station: his face had a greenish pallor. Almost the first words he spoke were: " I can't bear it." He looked, and I suppose he felt, as though the nightmare were upon him again. All he had to suggest was that *The Adelphi* should attack everything, everything; and explode in one blaze of denunciation. I was feeling disappointed enough to be momentarily tempted by the plan. But the moment was brief. I did not need a Lawrence to show me the way to nihilism. I had been there, and emerged again; it was not possible for me to return. I turned the notion aside, as though it had been a joke. Then he changed his ground. Would I not give it all up and go back with him to New Mexico, and there begin the nucleus of a new society? This was a far more serious temptation. After all, since the real purpose of *The*

Adelphi had been to make a place for Lawrence, and Lawrence now refused it, why not give up? Lawrence said he needed me badly. Why not do what he wanted?

At first I agreed, then I hesitated; for I found in myself an obstinate instinct against yielding. It was only another running away. Lawrence by this time had no belief at all in America. The little ranch in New Mexico was a pleasant place to live in, the best place that Lawrence had found; but that was all. It was a very good reason why he should return there, but no reason why I should return with him. If I did return with him, I should do it purely out of personal affection for him; and I told him so. No! there must be nothing personal about it, he insisted; the motive must be impersonal. But, unfortunately, there would be no impersonal motive at all in my going to New Mexico. I could not really believe that this was the way to create the nucleus of a new society. If the birth of the nucleus of a new society depended upon people having money enough to go to New Mexico, and a profession which would comfortably maintain them there, then it was hardly worth thinking about. On the other hand, if I went with him there simply out of personal affection, it was a preposterous situation if he continued to repudiate, in all his open professions, the worth of that personal affection which alone would take me with him. Further, if the plan was that we should simply go there and live to ourselves, rejecting the world, washing our hands of it altogether, that seemed to me renegade to the doctrine of the *Fantasia;* and certainly I knew it would be a retrogression in myself.

It was a painful time, and painful things happened in it. I am conscious that this retrospective account makes the issues much clearer than they were to me at the time. Lawrence's personal appeal was pretty desperate; so were my struggles to avoid being involved in a situation which I felt instinctively would be disastrous. He talked to me much about Death, in a way I could not understand, trying in particular to convince me that Life was a form or manifestation of Death, not Death of Life, as I believed and believe. What we had to do, he said, was to shift from the Life-mode into the Death-mode, and to do this Mexico was necessary. I listened, and tried in vain to understand; it seemed to me completely alien to the *Fantasia*, and still more alien to my own small fragment of personal conviction. It was hardly possible for me to believe in it, and I told him so. I insisted that if I went with him, it would be from personal affection, and that he must accept this. If there was any tacit understanding that I had accepted this new and unintelligible, but faintly alien creed, then I must withdraw, because it was bound to end in disaster.

The upshot of it all was that Lawrence returned to New Mexico, and I stayed in England. As so often before, each felt that he had been let down by the other, although on this final occasion the full realisation of the feeling came gradually. It was not till three years later, at the beginning of 1926, when Lawrence had finally left America and settled in Italy, that he definitely broke with me; and by that time I was prepared for it as inevitable.

I remember vividly more than one moment during this last sustained contact of mine with Lawrence. One is memorable. We were at a dinner-party together, and Lawrence was talking with all his quick gaiety and sensitive response. Suddenly the feeling came upon me: *Why* is there a gulf between this Lawrence and the writer? I sat watching him, and became more and more bewildered and depressed by the strange discrepancy. I felt rather sore about it; it seemed to me that this was the cause of all the failure. After dinner, he took me aside into a corner, and said: " You're angry with me about something. What is it? " I said that I wasn't sure

that I *was* angry with him. " Yes, you are," he persisted.
" What is it? "

" Well," I said, " if you really want to know, I *am* angry,
and I'll tell you why. You always deny what you actually
are. You refuse to acknowledge the Lawrence who really
exists. And as far as I can see, you'll go on doing it to the
end."

For a moment, he was quite silent; he was obviously
moved and distressed. Then he said, simply: " I'm sorry
. . . I'm sorry."

There it was; and there it is. The criticism I made of
him then is substantially the criticism I make of him now.
In the last issue he would not accept himself; he would be
something that he was not. In the books of this period the
inward discrepancy becomes more and more glaring. The
more closely we study them, the more deeply we are distressed by their essential incoherence, until at last the distress passes into a kind of terror. We are witnessing a lapse
from humanity.

It was all very well for Lawrence to propound it as a
universal truth that " we must disintegrate while we live."
It was a manifest destiny that Lawrence himself should disintegrate while he lived. But to turn this into a universal
truth was a self-deception, a deliberate denial of the self-
knowledge momentarily achieved in the *Fantasia*. There he
had seen and admitted that his was a peculiar destiny, a destiny which coming generations must avoid. To make disintegration a universal necessity was, in reality, to deny
that his disintegration was disintegration, by making himself a forerunner on a path which mankind must follow.
This Lawrence was not; he was the very opposite of this.
And he could not admit it. Lawrence could not surrender him-

self. His pride is become a madness. He cannot admit that he is wrong, that he has failed, that he is beaten, even though his mind is distraught in a chaos of contradictions.

In the essays in the volume *Reflections on the Death of a Porcupine,* published in 1925, the old, old themes are hunted to death. Love must give way to " Power." " Why limit man to a Christian brotherhood? " he cries against Tolstoy.

> I myself, I could belong to the sweetest Christian-brotherhood one day, and ride after Attila with a raw beefsteak for my saddle-cloth, to see the red cock crow in flame over all Christendom, next day. And that is man!

To anyone who knew Lawrence the bravado is preposterous. If that *is* man, Lawrence was not man, nor anything remotely resembling man. But we need no private knowledge to unmask this rhodomontade. In the essay on the death of the porcupine, Lawrence tells us that never in his life before had he shot at any living thing; he could not bring himself to do it. It was repugnant to him even to try to shoot at a target. Guns were sinister and mean. But the porcupine had horribly maimed a dog; so Lawrence overcame his repugnance and shot him.

> And in the moonlight, I looked down on the first creature I had ever shot.
> " Does it seem mean? " I asked aloud, doubtful.
> Again Madame hesitated. Then: " No! " she said resentfully. And I felt she was right.

Is it not the height of self-deception for such a man to imagine that he could ride after Attila? He is, after all, a grown man, not a day-dreaming child. And now, because he has suddenly summoned up the resolution to shoot a porcupine, he turns and says that " the Buddhist who re-

fuses to take life is really ridiculous." Is he one whit more
"ridiculous" than Lawrence with his forty years of constant repugnance to shoot at a living thing? Does Lawrence
admit that he was "ridiculous" up to the moment he resolved to shoot the porcupine? He never dreams of it; indeed, the question never occurs to him.

This is only a simple and flagrant instance of the old
internecine conflict in Lawrence. He wants to deny the love
that is in him; he wants to posture to himself as a bloody,
and brutal savage, a born hunter, a perfect male, a man of
"power." He has two whole essays to tell us what "power"
is, and we reach the end stupefied. "Power" is that which
brings a new thing into the world: George Stephenson invented the steam-engine, and that was a manifestation of
"power"; Napoleon had "power." But it turns out, dis-
appointingly, that this is quite the wrong kind of "power."
Ultimately the only right kind of "power" is derived from
the sun. "He who has the sun in his face, in his body, he
is the pure aristocrat. . . . Or he who, like Dostoevsky, gets
nearest the moon of our not-being." All one can say to this
is that it is the utterance of a weary man whose mind is become a chaos. All Lawrence knew at the moment of writing
his essay on "power," is that he wanted something different
from what is, and to be something different from what he
was. But to stiffen up the sinews of his imagination, to
realise what he did want, and decide whether what he wanted
was compatible with other things that he also wanted —
this was an effort which he must shrink from making: it
would bring him too close to his own inward chaos.

⌇

What can only be described as a vicious and inverted sen-
timentality begins to manifest itself. The long and feeble

story *St. Mawr* depends upon this same unrealised imagination of "power"; and since the central conception is incoherent, the story itself is futile. St. Mawr, the stallion, is the symbol of "power" to two discontented and unconvincing women. "Why can't men get their life straight like St. Mawr, and then think?" asks Lou. It seems a sound question, and is a foolish one; as though thinking were not life, and in equal need of straightening. It assumes that adult men could put off their mental consciousness, and could begin by being animal. Actually, men do thus begin. A small child does have its life straight like a foal; and then it passes inevitably into the mental consciousness, and the divided being. The problem for man is to pass beyond this condition: precisely the problem from which Lawrence shrank to the end; precisely the problem from which the spiritual teachers before him did not shrink. Lawrence always instinctively refused their solution — isolation, death and rebirth. Hence his feverish desire to escape backwards to the pre-mental, which weakens and vitiates the whole of this story of St. Mawr.

In it are all the new conventional figures, Phoenix the mindless Mexican, and Lewis, the detached and isolated male, the direct descendant of Annable and ancestor of Mellors. Why doesn't St. Mawr get foals? "Doesn't want to, I should think — same as me," says Lewis. The idiosyncrasy, by which the males are so male that they do not beget children, is now familiar. St. Mawr is savage, and gets no foals; yet he is not to be cut, even after he has nearly killed his rider and put his hoof in another man's mouth. No the animal is right, and the men he maims are wrong. St. Mawr merely feels "a great woe: the woe of human unworthiness." His sentimental mistress Lou, who prefers him to her husband, has the stallion tenderly taken to New Mexico. There she discovers a ranch, which is obviously

Lawrence's own ranch. Her solution of the problems of life
is to live there on an independent income, and become virginal once more. She is sick of sex. Not, of course, that she
is becoming " conventy."

" I don't hate men *because* they're men, as nuns do. I dislike
them because they're not men enough: babies, and playboys. . . .
I only wish, with all my soul, that some men *were* bigger and
stronger and *deeper* than I am."

What Lou needs is the human equivalent of St. Mawr; a
sterile stallion. But these are as scarce in the human world
as in the animal. In other words, she is, like Teresa, one of
the new women whom Lawrence imagines for himself, and
since she talks more, she is more tiresome and less real even
than Teresa.

The whole story — it is really a short novel — is a tissue
of dishonesties: from the beginning to the end it is one long
and unworthy evasion. Febrile and sentimental in temper,
unstable and incoherent in substance, it is a monument of
Lawrence's disintegration. It is Lawrence's most substantial piece of fiction between *The Plumed Serpent* and *Lady
Chatterley's Lover*.

ری

Its companion story, " The Princess," is not much better; but it deals with a new theme which is now recurrent.
Once more the story plays in New Mexico. The " Princess,"
this time, really is a virgin; aloof, remote. Lawrence imagines her sexual surrender to a Mexican guide. It is, in fact
though not technically, a violation, which ends in the girl's
madness and the guide's death. The theme of " None of
That," the concluding story of *The Woman Who Rode Away*,
is a technical and sickeningly brutal violation, this time of an
unpleasant American high-brow millionairess, at the instiga-
tion of a Mexican *torero*. The impressive title story, " The

Woman Who Rode Away," tells how a white woman is cap-
tured and offered up as a human sacrifice by a tribe of primitive Indians in the wild Mexican interior. We remember —
how should we forget? — how in Cornwall Richard Somers
felt the ecstasy of human blood-sacrifice, and how Lawrence glorified it in Cipriano; now, once more, Lawrence
seeks the sensual, or imaginative thrill of it. He identifies
himself with the sacrificers. In the last lines of the story he
thus describes the priest.

In absolute motionlessness he watched till the red sun should
send his ray through the column of ice. Then the old man would
strike, and strike home, and accomplish the sacrifice, and achieve
the power.

The mastery that men must hold, and that passes from race to
race.

This imaginative self-persuasion that human sacrifice is
lawful in a man who is so tender that only by an immense
effort he can bring himself to shoot the vermin on his ranch,
is a sickening perversity. We do not blame Lawrence for his
tenderness — God forbid! — we condemn him for allowing
his imagination to violate it. This is horrible. This seeming
courage is a supreme cowardice; it proceeds from a refusal
to accept one's own nature, and to take the consequences.
This licence to the imagination to commit the extremity of
horror is given only by a soul that is sick unto death, and
seeks release by self-laceration.

If this imaginative participation in violation and human
sacrifice is the " great swerve in our own onward-going "
that we must make in order to take up again the savage mysteries, it must be replied peremptorily that we cannot make
it. To attempt to make it is to paralyse the life that is within
us. So doing we force back the flow upon itself and turn it
into a stagnant eddy of corruption. We inevitably begin to

decompose. We are not, and we cannot be all-inclusive. We have to accept our destiny as a particular species of the genus homo, distinct from others, with its own peculiar limitations. Whether these limitations, these organic reluctances which manifest themselves in our finest conscience, are universal or not is totally irrelevant. Our organic reluctances are our own, they are we.

Doubtless, it is true that we assume reluctances that are not really our own. The very process of education is to come to possess reluctances by assuming them. And these reluctances may be inimical to life, because they are too alien to our animal nature. The duty of every living responsible man, who takes his share of the burden of life upon his shoulders, is to make his conscience and himself agree. This is the delicate work upon which all advance towards fuller life depends; this is that exploration of life to which the conscious soul is always committed. It is the discovery of the ultimate self; that inmost core in a man which *must* not be violated save on pain of self-destruction. The point to be discovered is the point where the spiritual does not violate the animal, nor the animal the spiritual. At that point — which is the secret quick of the individual man — there is no longer either spiritual or animal. Both are inevitably one. When it has been discovered, then a man can be described indifferently as having no conscience, or being all conscience; as being completely unspiritual or wholly spiritual. It is the point of integrity.

This point in himself Lawrence gave up even the attempt to discover. We admit, abundantly admit, that it was infinitely harder for him than another man. He was far more spiritual, far more capable of love, than other men; he had far more reluctances to reconcile with his animal self than most men have. He was doomed from the first to a lonely struggle, having for the crown of achievement an exceeding great reward. If he had been able to attain his own point of integrity, then he would have been the forerunner of a new kind of man; he would have been himself the first of a new race of men. But the burden of that destiny he could not bear. He shrank from it; his strength failed him. He became not the forerunner of the integration of a new man, but the perfect paradigm of the disintegration of an old one. In him was manifest the last extremity of the conflict between animal and spiritual in man; the final abandonment of all hope of unity.

Hence comes the horror which preys upon a sensitive reader as he submits himself to the works of this period. He is watching the decomposition of a greatly gifted human soul. Only the old Christian metaphors are really adequate to describe what is happening, Lawrence is now possessed by devils. There is *no* Lawrence. For who can say now which is Lawrence — the man who loves, or the man who blasphemes against love? The man who seeks life, or the man who imaginatively exults in violation and murder and death? Lawrence himself could not say. He had no longer the strength to be either. He was both, and he was nothing. The doom had overtaken him.

IV

THE DREAM OF RESURRECTION

THE theme of murder and violation and blood-sacrifice, in which Lawrence's hatred of woman and of mankind finds expression, had already been plainly indicated in *The Plumed Serpent;* so had the second striking theme of the minor works of this period — the imagination of a consummation of his relation with woman *after death*. It may be that the definite emergence of this theme coincided with Lawrence's own definite knowledge that he had not much longer to live.

In *The Plumed Serpent*, the theme was indicated rather horribly in the complete submission of the Woman to the pure Indian Cipriano and his rejection of all her Aphrodisiac demands, while Lawrence-Carrasco finds comfort in the virginal, but physical and sexual tenderness of the vaguely imagined Teresa. The consummation of Lawrence's own unfulfilled relation is accompanied by an act of imaginative revenge upon the Woman.

But in two remarkable stories — " The Border Line " and " Glad Ghosts " — there is a manifest revulsion from this imaginative horror. In " The Border Line," the Woman unmistakably appears as Katherine Farquhar. Her husband, Alan, a Highland officer, has been killed in the war, and she has married again. Her second marriage is a relation of the kind which she is represented, here and elsewhere, as having desired: her new husband, Philip, a journalist, is completely dependent upon her, and completely submissive; he makes her "feel like a queen." Whereas her first husband, Alan, had stood his ground against her overweening demands, asserted his claim to be her lord and master, and, when she refused it, withdrawn himself completely from her and spent his days watching the heavens through a telescope.

Married now to Philip, after a brief period of voluptuous content, a sense of degradation steals over Katherine Farquhar. "She realised the difference between being married to a soldier, a ceaseless born fighter, a sword not to be sheathed, and this other man, this cunning civilian, this subtle equivocator, this adjuster of the scales of truth." So, she leaves England, and even on the Channel boat begins to feel that Philip has never existed and only Alan has ever been her husband. At Strassburg, the ghost of Alan appears to her — more than a ghost, the physically resurrected man. He puts his hand upon her arm, and they walk together.

And as she walked by his side through the conquered city, she realised that it was the one enduring thing a woman can have, the intangible soft flood of contentment that carries along at the side of the man she is married to. It is her perfection and her highest attainment.

Now, in the afterwards, she knew it. Now, the strife was gone. And dimly she wondered why, why, why, she had ever fought against it. No matter what the man does, or is, as a person, if a woman can walk at his side in this dim full flood of contentment, she has the highest of him, and her scratching efforts at getting more than this, are her ignominious efforts at self-nullity.

Now she knew it and submitted.

The story ends in a ghostly, ghastly fashion. Philip follows Katherine abroad, and falls ill. Engrossed by her renewed marriage to the resurrected Alan, she nurses Philip

grudgingly, and his illness grows to a crisis. He calls to her at
midnight to hold him.

Curiously reluctant, she began to push her hands under his
shoulders, to raise him. As she did so, the door opened and Alan
came in, bareheaded, and a frown on his face. Philip lifted feeble
hands, and put them round Katherine's neck, moaning faintly.
Silent, bareheaded, Alan came over to the bed and loosened the
sick man's hands from his wife's neck, and put them down on the
sick man's own breast.

Philip unfurled his lips and showed his big teeth in a ghastly
grin of death. Katherine felt his body convulse in strange throbs
under her hands, then go inert. He was dead. And on his face was a
sickly grin of a thief caught in the very act.

But Alan drew her away, drew her to the other bed, in the silent
passion of a husband come back from a very long journey.

*

" The Border Line " is really a sort of " sequel " to " The
Captain's Doll," which was written some two or three years
before. In both the woman is the Woman, and in both the
man is the same man — not recognisably Lawrence, but a
recognisable avatar, something half-way between a Cipriano
and the reality: a soldier, silent, slim, taciturn, determined
and masculine, who turns away from the Woman who will
not submit herself to him, and finds contentment, like Somers at the end of *Kangaroo,* in impersonal contemplation of
the heavens. The difference between the two stories is that
in " The Captain's Doll " the Woman submits in the man's
life, in " The Border Line " only after his death. In " The
Captain's Doll," Hannele, who has turned her man, in her
soul, into a manikin (for that is the import of the doll in
that odd and unsatisfying story), promises to do so no
longer. She accepts Martin's ultimatum:

" If a woman honours me — absolutely from the bottom of her nature honours me — and obeys me because of that, I take it my desire for her goes deeper than if I was in love with her, and adored her."

Hannele is, for the moment, recalcitrant. She pits her creed of love against his demand to be honoured and obeyed. " It's the same thing," she says. " If you love, all the rest is there — all the lot: your honour and obedience, and everything. And if love isn't there, nothing is there."

But only for the moment does she resist. Martin stands his ground and she yields; she burns even the portrait of the doll she has made. " The Border Line " is the acknowledgment that she has not yielded, and is not likely to yield, in the man's life, but somehow she will submit to his demand after his death. It differs from *The Plumed Serpent* in that there is no element of revenge upon the Woman in its ghostly consummation. Lawrence's hatred is diverted to the unfortunate Philip who has dared to supplant him.

Something of the same curious relation holds between the earlier *Ladybird* and the later " Glad Ghosts." In these stories the woman is not the Woman. Daphne in the earlier, and Carlotta in the later, story are embodiments of the same type. They represent the virginal woman, which the Woman so emphatically and convincingly is not. The type is persistent in Lawrence's work; in its most significant manifestations (Teresa of *The Plumed Serpent* and the priestess of Isis in " The Escaped Cock ") it is shadowy. Daphne and Carlotta are more distinct, and based, one would imagine, upon some known woman. In *The Ladybird* she is released into fulfilment by the familiar figure of the dark Pan-male.

Count Dionys Psanek comes from the aboriginal dark inhabitants of Europe; his " ladybird " emblem is really the Egyptian scarabaeus beetle, which, according to the hieratic tradition (or Lawrence's version of it), created the cosmos out of corruption by rolling the débris of dead worlds into a ball. Count Dionys is therefore very dark, and very old, cosmically speaking. An aboriginal, aristocratic Pan, he belongs to the mindless world, is a priest of the dark God, and a perfect incarnation of " power." Daphne responds to the " power " in him, and so finds her sensual fulfilment. The beneficent change wrought in her is such that her kindly, intellectual and ineffectual young husband, who, of course, believes in " love " and not in " power," gladly surrenders all claim to Daphne. He recognises that she belongs to Dionys, though she will never be Dionys' wife, for Dionys happens to be married. But she is fulfilled, for Dionys possesses the masculine authority, also possessed by Alan Farquhar and Jack Grant and Cipriano, which comes from being " a Lord of Death."

It is impossible to form any distinct conception of what Lawrence meant by this phrase, which is recurrent in his writing of this period. Alan Farquhar is a Lord of Death, perhaps because he has died and is resurrected. Jack Grant is a Lord of Death perhaps because he nearly dies when lost in the West Australian bush. Both of these may be understood as having gained their lordship at a price. But Dionys and Cipriano are born to this dim purple. The phrase carries a multitude of meanings, ranging from having been dead and being alive again, to being an addict of blood-sacrifice. It is, indeed, just as vague and various as the Dark God, to whom it corresponds. The Lords of Death are the initiates into the mysteries of the Dark God, the God of " the faceless flame," and " power " is their attribute. The conception is, in reality, purely negative: at the impersonal level it is sim-

ply the antithesis of the " spiritual," and since no one has
ever conceived the " spiritual " more variously or more in-
consistently than Lawrence, its opposite must needs be
equally various and equally inconsistent; at the personal
level, the Lord of Death is simply all that Lawrence is not
and dreams of being — the final form of the dream of the
hardy indomitable male.

෴

In *The Ladybird* Daphne finds her fulfilment through the
dark " power " of Count Dionys. In " Glad Ghosts " (which is
a much more impressive story) the solution for her counterpart, Carlotta is, apparently, quite different. Yet the problem
is precisely the same problem, the conditions the same conditions. Carlotta's husband, Luke, is Daphne's Basil; and
Luke has separated himself from Carlotta, exactly as Basil
separated himself from Daphne. But whereas the agent of
Daphne's fulfilment is the dark, aboriginal Pan-male, a Lord
of Death, the agent of Carlotta's fulfilment is a man indis-
tinguishable from Lawrence himself. There is a consummation between them; but the strange and significant thing
about this consummation is that it takes place in a shadowy
after-world: whether of dream, or of some other realm of
experience, we are not, and cannot be, told. Colonel Hale
gives a kindred fulfilment to the unsatisfied ghost of his
dead wife Lucy; she returns to him from the dead, as Alan
returned to Katherine in " The Border Line." But instead
of revenge being taken by the first Mrs. Hale on the second,
as Alan took revenge upon Philip, the second Mrs. Hale
finds her fulfilment in Carlotta's husband, Luke. In this
case, it is true, Lawrence's masculine pride is not involved,
and he can afford to be kinder. But we feel that for the moment all desire of hatred and revenge has disappeared from

Lawrence's soul. All the ghosts, whether of the dead or the living, are satisfied.

But this imaginary peace is achieved only through the miracle of a bodily resurrection. What the " ghosts " all long for is physical tenderness. It is their failure in life to give or to receive this physical tenderness which has made them "ghosts." "Was your body good to poor Lucy's body? " Luke asks Colonel Hale; and the question comes to the Colonel like an illumination; he acknowledges his failure, and with a touching humility bares his bosom before them all that the unquiet ghost of the dead Lucy may have rest. The physical fulfilment of Lucy and the Colonel is be-tween the ghost of a dead woman and a living man; Car-lotta's is in a twilight realm of dream or mystical experience — " Was it the innermost of the cosmos that he touched," or " a very woman "? Lawrence asks and does not answer; Mrs. Hale's appears to be between a living woman and a living man. But, in fact, Luke also is physically resurrected. He is changed in the body. In the story, Lawrence looks at the metamorphosed Luke and asks himself: " Could one so change as to become another creature entirely? " And a little while after, he answers: " I always believed that people could be born again, if they would only let themselves."

Did Lawrence really believe it? Probably, he did not know; what he knew was only that he desired to believe it. For it was all that was left to him. To this necessity Law-rence has been inexorably driven: and to him a bodily resur-rection is necessary for one reason alone, in order that he may experience the physical tenderness, the ultimate " bodily compassion," which he has never been able to give, or to receive. Says Luke, who is " inspired ":

" Worship with the body. . . . We all want it. And before we die we know it. I say before we die. It may be after. . . . It's awfully important to be flesh and blood. Think how ghastly for Jesus, when he was risen and wasn't touchable. Oh, God, I'm glad I've realised in time."

In time? Death, for Lawrence, was drawing very near. And what is it that he has realised? That his craving is for physical tenderness: that for him the veritable heaven is that physical tenderness between a man and a woman that is the prerogative of love — of love which he has rejected and denied.

His cry is desperate, anguished, piercing the heart. He turns to the great language of the Bible for utterance. Says Luke:

" Don't cry, Carlotta. Really don't. We haven't killed one another. We're too decent, after all. We've almost become two spirits, side by side. We've almost become two ghosts to one another, wrestling. Oh, but I want you to get back your body, even if I can't give it you. I want my flesh and blood, Carlotta, and I want you to have yours. We've suffered so much the other way. And the children, it is as well they are dead. They were born of our will, and our disembodiment. Oh, I feel like the Bible. Clothe me with flesh again, and wrap my bones with sinew, and let the fountain of blood cover me. My spirit is like a naked nerve on the air."

The cry is terrible to hear — the wail of a disembodied man; and though in the story Luke who utters it is clothed with new flesh, and has his happiness, Lawrence from whom it is wrung is, even in his own imagination, a disembodied man. His consummation with Carlotta is ghostly and beyond the flesh. Yet after it a child is born.

৵

Behind it all is Lawrence's anguished desire for love and tenderness in the flesh, and the fearful knowledge that it

can only be had by a bodily resurrection. At this crucial
moment, Lawrence turns desperately upon the accusing
figure of Jesus. He will justify himself against Jesus, prove
that the Son of Man and not the Son of Woman has betrayed
mankind.

Carlotta had ceased to weep. She sat with her head dropped,
as if asleep. The rise and fall of her small slack breasts was still
heavy, but they were lifting on a heaving sea of rest. It was as
if a slow, restful dawn were rising in her body while she slept.
So slack, so broken she sat, it occurred to me that in this crucifixion business the crucified does not put himself alone on the
cross. The woman is nailed even more inexorably up, and crucified in the body even more cruelly.

It is a monstrous thought. But the deed is even more monstrous. Oh, Jesus, didn't you know that you couldn't be crucified
alone? — that the two thieves crucified along with you were the
two women, your wife and your mother? You called them two
thieves. But what would they call you, who had their women's
bodies on the cross? The abominable trinity on Calvary!

For a moment it strikes us as a strange aberration, a veritable madness, an irrelevant blasphemy. Suddenly we realise that Lawrence has identified himself with Jesus; that
Jesus is become for him Lawrence, only with the mighty and
agonising difference, that he is Lawrence who chose another
way — the Lawrence who might have been. And this Jesus
— the Lawrence who might have been — is wrong, and the
Lawrence who is, is right.

For Jesus had the courage to deny his mother —
" Woman what have I to do with thee? " and he had the
courage to withhold himself from woman at the summons
of the spirit. In order that he might love mankind in the
spirit he tore himself away from his love of the body. In
order that his spirit should not be violated and crucified,
he suffered his flesh to be violated and crucified. He went his

way, courageous and alone, to the bitter end. And Lawrence
stares, transfixed with anguish, at the Cross; and seeks to
justify himself. The courage and the isolation of Jesus were
wrong; he, Lawrence, who was denied the strength to tear
himself from his mother or his woman, is right. The love
that Jesus gave to all mankind should have been given to
woman, as Lawrence gave it.

The judgment is fearful. On the Cross, the man who kept
his spirit whole, and let his flesh be crucified; standing beneath, the man who would keep whole his flesh, and let his
spirit be crucified. On the Cross, the man who severed his
bodily love from Woman, that he might give it to all women
and to all men for evermore; standing beneath, the man who
would not sever his bodily love from Woman, so that it
turned into hate for all women and for all men. On the
Cross, the man who himself took and preached the eternal
way of resurrection in the spirit; beneath it, the man who
refused it, or could not take it, crying in anguish for the
resurrection of the body. " O abominable trinity on
Calvary! "

Inevitably, the two men stand over against each other.
Lawrence is henceforward a Jesus-haunted man. For there
are only two ways open to man who pushes his exploration
of life so far as Lawrence has done. Either he must make
his peace with the nature of things, or he must change the
nature of things; and to make his peace with the nature of
things, he must change himself. That is to say he must either
achieve a spiritual resurrection or cry for a bodily one.
Lawrence, the unsatisfied and isolated, must either be reconciled to his hunger and his isolation, or demand a second
physical life wherein he will be satisfied and not isolated any
more. He must choose: to seek the possible, or cry for the

impossible — to be reborn in the spirit, or reborn in the body. Here we touch a veritable ultimate: the absolute difference between true religion and false.

Lawrence is a prophet of the false religion: which denies or will not understand the reality of Spirit, and cries for miracle instead. For only by virtue of the Spirit can man accept the nature of things, and make his peace with the world of existence, wherein human desire goes for ever unfulfilled, and human love is doomed inexorably to death. False religion denies the fact of death. True religion accepts it, and in that act of acceptance, the soul of man dies and is reborn into the Spirit. The love of the Spirit is the love which seeketh not its own; the love which contemplates the drama of existence in all the beauty of its own necessity, the drama in which all the personal being of man, even to the most sacred and secret aspirations of his soul, is wholly involved. One thing, and one thing only, is absolved from this flux of existence, of unsatisfied desire and inevitable death — the pure spirit which discerns it. The wisdom is old, and ever new. Lawrence could not acquire it; because he could not pay the price of it. He could not surrender desire. " My desire must, and shall be satisfied," he has said. Now he stands at the brink of death and cries for a miracle.

ॐ

It is his destiny. He has denied the spirit, which is love; he must pay for the denial. Spirit is real. There are moments in this period when he seems to tremble on the verge of acknowledging its reality, but a strange compulsion turns him aside. Thus he writes in *The Death of a Porcupine:*

Any creature that attains to its own fulness of being, its own *living* self, becomes unique, a nonpareil. It has its place in the fourth dimension, the heaven of existence [he means, " of being," as the sequel shows], and there it is perfect, beyond comparison.

At the same time, every creature exists in time and space. And in time and space it exists relatively to all other existence and can never be absolved. Its existence impinges on other existences and is itself impinged upon. And in the struggle for existence, if an effort on the part of any one type or species or order of life, can finally destroy the other species, then the destroyer is of a more vital cycle of existence than the one destroyed.

It seems impossible that a man could come nearer to acknowledging the distinction between the realm of spirit, and the realm of matter; between the world of being, and the world of existence. Yet, if Lawrence had really believed even the second article of this creed alone, how could he have spent his energies in exalting the mindless Indian? Why was he so constantly renegade to his once declared intention of being faithful to " the civilised consciousness "? The only answer is that he did not believe it, because he did not want to believe it; it would have meant a sacrifice of his appetite for hatred and revenge.

But still more important, he does not really believe in the first article of his creed. He asserts quite truly, that " even an individual dandelion has *being*," as distinct from existence; and it follows, inexorably, that an individual man has being. Every individual man or woman, whether loved or hated by Lawrence, is a nonpareil. But this Lawrence would not accept. To safeguard himself from having to accept it, he introduces the perfectly alien conception of " fulness of being," which means " fulness of life." Every individual dandelion has " fulness of being," according to Lawrence, but not every individual man. And, of course, it is perfectly true that very few men or women have " fulness of being " in the sense (if such a sense there really was) in which

Lawrence required it. Assuredly, Lawrence himself did not possess it; or he would not now be longing for the miracle of a physical resurrection for himself. Nor, in all his writings, as far as I remember, is there any acknowledgment that any actual human being has possessed it. Jesus, Kant, Napoleon — " they were all failures." That is the burden of his song. But who, we finally ask, was a success? And, when Lawrence is put to it, he has only two answers — both false. Either he will point us to the " mindless " savage, the indomitable and aboriginal male; or, as now, when he cannot suppress the cry of his own experience that the consciousness of the savage and the civilised consciousness are implacably opposed, he points us to the miracle of a physical resurrection. When man is totally changed in the body, then he will have " fulness of being." So Lawrence, without knowing what is happening to him, falls finally into the creed of the superstitious " Christian," with " his happy land, far far away," or the superstitious Mohammedan, with his vista of houris in Paradise.

Beneath it all is the old equivocation, the old refusal. The vision that declares every dandelion to be a nonpareil, and to have its place in the heaven of being, is the spiritual vision. To that same vision, every man is a nonpareil, and has his place in the heaven of being. But to turn his spiritual vision upon his fellow-men, to acknowledge their uniqueness, to love them for what they are — that was asking too much of Lawrence. That would have made him altogether too much like Jesus. Perish the thought! The Apache is a nonpareil, but not his own white brother.

The Apache warrior in his war-paint, shrieking the war-cry, and cutting the throats of women (of women, of course), is still part of the mystery of creation. He is godly as the growing corn.

That is true, absolutely true; but only on one condition, without which it is false, damnably false. And the condition is that you acknowledge that the business-man in his swivel-chair, or Mr. Lloyd George, or any of the white men whom Lawrence held in such contempt, are also part of the mystery of creation, and godly as the growing corn. Without that universal acknowledgment, the vindication of the Apache warrior is no more than a desire for murder — or, more truly, a desire to see murder done by others upon others — a vicious and horrible perversity.

You cannot dictate terms to the spirit, which is love; you cannot bid it look on this with love, and on that with hatred. It is not a slave; it is the only free thing that humanity has ever known. You may love and hate to your heart's content in the world of existence, but you cannot make the spirit participate in your passions. Spirit is utterly indifferent to them, it will not, and it cannot be implicated. And that is Lawrence's continual effort, to implicate the spirit in his passions, to assign *Being* at his own personal will, and petulant caprice. He wants to grant absolution from the world of existence, which is the world of good and evil, at his own particular discretion. Therefore he confuses Being, in which the whole universe, created or imagined, must necessarily share, with " fulness of life," which is a personal conception. It is within Lawrence's right to say: This man has " fulness of being," and this man not, which is only a way of saying: I assert that this man is better than that. It is not within his right, and it is not a manifest presumption, to say: This man has Being, and that man not; this man is a nonpareil, that man a nonentity.

Lawrence knows full well the issue that is at stake. He may not be a metaphysician, but his language does not fail him. " So," he says, " we still find ourselves in the tangle of existence and being, a tangle which man has never been able to get out of, except by sacrificing one to the other." He knows where he is. He is confused, only because he cannot pay the price of not being confused. On this issue, he does not want to think straight, or to tell himself the truth. Man is perfectly well able to escape from the tangle of existence and being, and many men have escaped from it; but there is only one way of escape: to acknowledge the sovereign independence of the spirit, to admit the reality of that which some great men have called the divine love — the vision of the eye which sees all things and all men *sub specie aeternitatis,* in the perfection of their indefeasible uniqueness.

This does not mean that one is sacrificed to the other. Existence is not sacrificed to Being, nor Being to Existence. When Spirit is pure, Spirit does not prey upon Life, nor Life upon Spirit, for the pure Spirit is far beyond what men ordinarily call the spiritual. Our so-called spiritual impulses belong entirely to the flux of existence, where they must maintain themselves or perish. We have to distinguish absolutely between the Spirit and the Ideal. The Ideal may prey upon life, and often does, because the Ideal in man is often in necessary and beneficent conflict with sheer animal impulse. But for Spirit an ideal impulse is an impulse like another, and the battle between impulses belongs wholly to the realm of existence. This totality of existence, to which the total personal being of man — ideal and animal — belongs, is the object which the pure Spirit contemplates. Spirit is therefore impersonal; it cannot judge, it can only watch, and love, with a love that is not human, but transcendent and divine.

This detachment of the pure Spirit Lawrence could never attain. In *The Death of a Porcupine* he came as near to it as he ever came; because at that moment he came as near as he ever came to admitting the truth of his own nature. But his nearest was far away. " Sacrifice is useless," he maintained. Sacrifice is the very condition of existence. For the human being, existence means that one is, irrevocably, this man and not that. No greater sacrifice can be imagined, or only one greater — namely, the sacrifice by which man may consign all that he is to the flux of existence, in order that the spark of the pure spirit may be kindled within him. Only by sacrificing his all, man gains the realm where nothing is sacrificed. He dies in his personality, to be raised again in impersonality.

In the last work of this period, the dramatic poem *David*, all the old and sickening irresolutions are manifest. Lawrence still stands facing both ways, incapable of decision, while the quick of life decays. Is God with David, or with Saul — with Saul, the servant of the Dark God, or David the servant of the White? Lawrence veers about between them, indentified now with one, now with the other; and the anguish of his own division is heard in the cry of Jesse:

" The heart of man cannot wander among the years like a wild ass in the wilderness. The heart at last stands still, crying: *Whither? Whither?* Like a lost foal whimpering for his dam, the heart cries and nickers for God, and will not be comforted."

In *David* the heart of Lawrence cries in vain. He is distraught by utter confusion. Samuel anoints David, knowing that the Lord has chosen him, and anoints him unwillingly; yet at the end he turns backward on himself in complete denial. " Saul yearneth for the flame," Samuel says to David at last, " thou for thy to-morrow's glory. The God of Saul hath no face. But thou wilt bargain with thy God." So Samuel turns upon and denies the Lord, of whom he is the prophet.

SAMUEL: Yea, I will bless thee! Yea, I will bless thee, my son. Yes, for now thy way is the way of might, yea, and even for a long space of time it shall be so. But after many days, men shall come again to the faceless flame of my Strength and of Saul's! Thou art brave, and alone, and by cunning must thou live, and by cunning shall thy house live for ever. But hath not the Lord created the fox, and the weasel that boundeth and skippeth like a snake!

DAVID: O Samuel, I have but tried to be wise! What should I do, and how should I walk in the sight of men? Tell me, my father, and I will do it.

SAMUEL: Thou wilt not. Thou walkest wisely, and thy Lord is with thee. Yea, each man's Lord is his own, though God be but one. I know not thy Lord. Yet walk thou with him.

It is in vain that we ask questions any more. If each man's Lord is his own, how is the Lord of Saul and Samuel the same? Whose Lord was it that Samuel obeyed when he took the power from Saul and anointed David?

As with Samuel, so with Jonathan. At the last he too turns back upon himself, and denies the love that he has compelled David to give him. He joins with Saul and Samuel, in looking for the end of the dispensation of David's power:

" Thou goest, David! And the hope of Israel with thee! I remain, with my father, and the star-stone falling to despair. Yet what is it to me! I would not see thy new day, David. For thy wisdom is the wisdom of the subtle, and behind thy passion lies prudence. And naked thou wilt not go into the fire. Yea, go thou forth, and let me die. For thy virtue is in thy wit and in thy shrewdness. But in Saul I have known the magnanimity of a man. Yea, thou art a smiter down of giants, with a smart stone. Great men and magnanimous, men of the faceless flame, shall fall from Strength, fall before thee, thou David, shrewd whelp of the lion of Judah! Yet my heart yearns hot over thee, as over a tender, quick child. And the heart of my father yearns, even amid its dark wrath. But thou goest forth and knowest no depth of yearning, thou son of Jesse. Yet go! For my twilight is more to me than thy day, and my death is nearer to me than thy life. Take it! Take thou the kingdom, and the days to come. In the flames of death, where Strength is, I will wait and watch till the day of David at last shall be finished, and wisdom no more be fox-faced, and the blood gets back its flame. Yea, the flame dies not, though the sun's red dies! And I must get me into the city."

Thus ends the play: one more monument of the indecision and nostalgia of the divided man. For what is " the faceless flame " of Saul, and Samuel, and Jonathan, but the familiar dark God, that composite of Lawrence's unlawful and unsatisfied desires? If it is the unknowable source of all existence, then David springs from it no less than they, the fox-faced wisdom no less than the wisdom that is not fox-faced. But it is not the source of all existence, only of some: the source of magnanimity, and depth of yearning, and the flame in the blood. The imagination becomes childish. Magnanimity and depth of yearning and the flame in the blood did not perish from the earth since a rod came out of Jesse. Those brave old days of the dark God and the faceless flame, when all the good things were, are a sentimental imagination; a recrudescence of the old desire for mindlessness.

There Lawrence stands, at this moment. Two dreams haunt his imagination. The old dream of mindlessness, of the dark God, of "power," of the savage mysteries; and the new dream of a physical regeneration and a consummation of perfect felicity with a woman. They are complementary: one is to escape the crucifixion into sex by returning backward to a point where it has not begun, the other is to escape it into a heaven where there is no unsatisfied desire. Both escapes are imaginary, and impossible: denied by the nature of things.

They are the extreme and contradictory assertions of the ideal, which Lawrence declared that he abandoned. Mindlessness is an ideal, resurrection in the body is an ideal. They are the more ideal in that they are impossible. Neither is spiritual, for the spiritual is not impossible. It is a simple reality; it happens, when a man finally gives up, as childish, the desire to escape, and refuses to delude himself with the hope of a miracle, when he acknowledges, once for all, that he is irrevocably caught in the *engrenage terrible de la responsibilité et de la souffrance humaine.* Lawrence has circled the round globe in the effort to escape the realisation; and now he has returned. He has not found the earthly paradise, which is only a name for happiness. He comes back to Europe, back to the old conclusion, that to be happy he must be changed, he must be changed by a miracle. The miracle has not happened, and will not happen. He is a weary, and a beaten man: a prophet without a message, save of a mindlessness he cannot enter, and a resurrection of the body in which he cannot believe.

v

THE MAN WHO HAD DIED

IN *Lady Chatterley's Lover,* Lawrence goes further towards imagining his physical resurrection. The figure of
Annable, with which his novels began, returns in the figure
of Mellors to end them. But there are great differences between Annable and Mellors. In *The White Peacock,* Annable
had his counterpart and opposite in Cyril. Cyril the spiritual,
Annable the animal man who has killed the spiritual —
these belonged together. They were bound by a bond, and
the nature of the bond was manifest; it was the bond of
Lawrence's own nature which included them both. Lawrence
the spiritual, and Lawrence who desired to renounce the
spiritual and revert to the animal: and including and brooding over both, the prophetic Lawrence who foresaw, who
knew within himself, the disaster of misery that would over-
take him if he renounced his spiritual being. In *Lady Chatterley's Lover,* there is no Cyril, nor any analogue to him.
Lawrence the spiritual has disappeared; he has been swallowed up. He is dead, and wanders in limbo, an uneasy
ghost. Lawrence is completely identified now with Annable;
and the name of the new Annable is Mellors. " I thought I'd
grown a solid middle-aged man," Annable had said to Cyril,
" and here I feel as sore as I did at twenty-six, and talk as
I used to." The prophecy of eighteen years ago was not quite
true. Mellors is more bitter, more wholly surrendered to

his humiliation and his hatred than Annable was, more naked in confession. Not an imaginary Lady Crystabel is the figure of woman now — " all vanity, screech and defilement " — but the very women whom Lawrence knew. The sexual youth of Mellors is Lawrence's own youth: there is barely an effort at disguise.

" The first girl I had, I began with when I was sixteen. She was a schoolmaster's daughter over at Ollerton, pretty, beautiful really. I was supposed to be a clever sort of young fellow from Sheffield Grammar School, with a bit of French and German, very much up aloft. She was the romantic sort that hated commonness. She egged me on to poetry and reading: in a way, she made a man of me. I read and I thought like a house on fire, for her. And I was a clerk in Butterley offices, a thin, white-faced fellow fuming with the things I read. And about *everything* I talked to her: but everything. We talked ourselves into Persepolis and Timbuctoo. We were the most literary-cultured people in ten counties. I held forth with rapture to her, positively with rapture. I simply went up in smoke. And she adored me. The serpent in the grass was sex. She somehow didn't have any; at least, not where it is supposed to be. I got thinner and crazier. Then I said we'd got to be lovers. I talked her into it, as usual. So she let me. I was excited, and she never wanted it. She just didn't want it. She adored me, she loved me to talk to her and kiss her: in that way she had a passion for me. But the other she just didn't want. And there are lots of women like her. And it was just the other that I did want. So there we split. I was cruel and left her. Then I took on with another girl, a teacher, who had made a scandal by carrying on with a married man and driving him nearly out of his mind. She was a soft, white-skinned, soft sort of a woman, older than me, and played the fiddle. And she was a demon. She loved everything about love, except the sex. Clinging, caressing, creeping into you in every way: but if you forced her to the sex itself, she just ground her teeth and sent out hate. I forced her to it, and she could simply numb me with hate because of it. So I was balked again. I loathed all that. I wanted a woman who wanted me, and wanted *it*."

That is the most veracious account of Lawrence's early sex life that he has given. The two women are Miriam and Helen; and the true origin of *The Trespasser* is plain to see. Lawrence is now nearing the end of his mortal career, and he comes nearer to acknowledging the truth about his relation with Miriam than ever before. We had guessed it long ago; it is no revelation now. His entry into sexual life was self-imposed, willed, mental: everything that Lawrence condemned. It was a violation of himself, and of Miriam. " I got thinner and crazier. Then I said we had got to be lovers." It was a willed and personal purpose they had to fulfil; Lawrence had to make himself a man, to crucify himself into sex, and *use* her as his means. It was disastrous, and Miriam reacted away. Her reaction was instinctive, inevitable, and right. It was Lawrence who was, judged by any standards and above all by his own, wrong.

The second phase in Mellors' sexual life is his marriage to Bertha Coutts. The description of that is not, under present conditions, to be quoted. It is full of physical horror and loathing, the manifest product of a mind which has brooded incessantly over the naked facts of the situation that underlay Ursula Brangwen's " annihilation of the core of intrinsic male " in Anton Skrebensky. Bertha Coutts is the woman who would not, or could not make herself the man's physical slave; who would not, or could not, make herself his instrument; who sought her own Aphrodisiac satisfaction, who " tore at him down there, as if it was a beak tearing at him." She is the woman who " wanted *it*."

And, alas! she is *the* Woman. There is no mistake possible. The description of Bertha Coutts is the final and most fearful act of imaginative revenge upon her.

Now, in Oliver Mellors the gamekeeper, Lawrence is physically reborn, and he imagines a woman for himself. He is thirty-nine years old in his reincarnation; Connie Chatterley is twenty-six. The whole book really consists of detailed descriptions of their sexual fulfilment. They are not offensive, sometimes beautiful, but strangely wearisome. The sexual atmosphere is suffocating. Beyond this sexual atmosphere there is nothing, nothing. The world beyond Mellors and Connie is unspeakably grey, dreary and hopeless; more hopeless by the flashes of the wild tender beauty of nature which make the grey surrounding murk more grey.

It is an utterly hopeless book, hopeless on the surface, with its simple and monotonous insistence that physical fulfilment between man and woman is the be-all and end-all of human existence; more hopeless beneath, when we know that the one thing needful is, for Lawrence himself, absolutely and for ever unattainable; more hopeless still, and filled with a grinding misery, when we realize that Lawrence cannot accept his destiny, and that he is declaring that he has been cheated of a happiness which might have been his. If it had only been another woman, he might have known in his own body this physical fulfilment which he seeks to enjoy imaginatively between Mellors and Connie Chatterley: physical fulfilment *and* manly independence. It is not his fault, but only the woman's and he cannot forgive.

With Connie Chatterley he imagines fulfilled all those demands he made in vain upon the actual Woman. He is, in their sexual relation, the leader, she the led; she is dependent, he independent; even, most paradoxically, she submits completely to the demand for the dark sensuality of

" mystic otherness " which she resisted in *Women in Love*. She suffers her innocence to be shattered; " she had to be a passive consenting thing, like a slave, a physical slave " ; she discovers that " what one supremely wanted was this piercing, consuming, rather awful sensuality." And this is necessary, because Lawrence, though he speaks of " physical tenderness " and " bodily compassion " as the one thing needful, cannot change himself. Reincarnated, he is still dual and divided, and divided as before between love and hate. In Mellors' reactions to the great world of men and women this is painfully and childishly manifest. But even towards the woman of his dream, it is still the same. Inevitably; because Mellors is the man who receives all that Lawrence desired but did not get from the Woman in life. And he desired physical tenderness, which is bodily love; and he desired sensuality, which is bodily hate. And the reason why he desired bodily hate was that he was incapable of bodily love. We need not enter into the old arguments again. He distinguishes in *Lady Chatterley's Lover* as he needs must do, between " real tenderness " and " real sensuality," and he tries to make it appear that both alike are innocent. But it is notable that, though his descriptions of sexuality are outspoken to an extreme degree, he is completely reticent about the sensuality. The reason is obvious. He cannot achieve any sort of innocence about it; it is simply impossible for him. It is evil, because he believes it to be evil.

Neither, on the other hand, could he leave it out. His demon demanded that it should be there. Mellors is Lawrence, only Lawrence satisfied. The satisfactions of a divided man must needs be still divided. Lawrence cannot imagine himself really whole; all that he can imagine is that he is physically strong and capable, and in this physically capable reincarnation of himself, he can only imagine his own

divided soul. In order that *Lady Chatterley's Lover* should
be indeed what it has the specious appearance of being,
namely a truly innocent book, Lawrence would need to have
achieved precisely the condition of inward integrity which
would have made the writing of the book unnecessary and
impossible. It is, in fact, the product of the last stage of
inward disintegration: a final and despairing effort at self-
annihilation by the spiritual man, the deliberate sinking
of the *Pequod* by the White Whale.

ري

There is in the novel much talk of tenderness, and no
doubt a deep yearning for it, for tenderness of different
kinds. It claims to be a gospel of tenderness, physical and
spiritual. It makes the noblest professions.

After all, one may hear the most private affairs of other people, but only in a spirit of respect for the struggling, battered thing
which any human soul is, and in a spirit of fine discriminative
sympathy.

It is admirable, the very doctrine of charity; but it has
surely fallen into the wrong book. Lawrence is so pitiless
and inhuman to Clifford Chatterley that he makes him a
fantastic and quite incredible figure; his hatred of Bertha
Coutts reaches a pitch of vindictiveness that is scarcely
sane. But Lawrence, we discover, is cheating himself with
words. He continues:

For even satire is a form of sympathy. It is the way our sympathy flows and recoils that really determines our lives. And here
lies the vast importance of the novel properly handled. It can
inform and lead into new places the flow of our sympathetic consciousness, and it can lead our sympathy away in recoil from

things gone dead. Therefore, the novel, properly handled, can reveal the most secret places of life: for it is in the *passional* secret places of life, above all, that the tide of sensitive awareness needs to ebb and flow, cleansing and refreshing.

It sounds plausible, until we realise that Lawrence is using the word "sympathy" in the old deceptive fashion of his essay on Whitman: it includes the "sympathy of love" and the "sympathy of hate." It is merely a thread-bare covering for the old demand that he should love *and* hate. And if we examine the relation of Mellors and Connie carefully, we find that the physical "tenderness" is of precisely the same order. The whole episode of the "sensuality" begins in anger and hatred, and in spite of the fact that Connie is supposed to discover that "what one supremely wanted was this piercing, consuming, rather awful sensuality," in the morning after she whispers anxiously: "But you'll keep the tenderness for me, won't you? I loved last night. But you'll keep the tenderness for me, won't you?" We understand, only too well, her pathetic anxiety; but not her wistful confidence. She has been abused and made a victim, and though Lawrence dare not confess it, her sexual innocence has been outraged.

The serpent of conscious evil lurks behind it all. The "tenderness" is only a veneer; and it must be so. For in Mellors, Lawrence is attempting a final justification of himself, or trying to imagine a final triumph of his own defeated masculinity. He represents himself as bringing sexual salvation to a young and naive woman; in fact, he is indulging himself with the idea of a final sexual submission of a woman to his divided man. It is his perfect triumph; all that he demanded and did not receive of woman in life is yielded to him. It is the supreme gratification of his male pride.

That superficially and consciously, but underneath, and unconsciously, his final surrender to Woman. In *Lady Chatterley's Lover* sex blots out the universe. The great religious and creative purpose which, according to the *Fantasia,* a man must have and to which he must be obedient even to the gates of hell, in order that there should be a true relation between man and woman — this great purpose has wholly disappeared. There is only one purpose in life, and it is the sexual act. The sexual act is all in all, and the great creative purpose has dwindled, in Lawrence, to the writing of the most detailed celebration of the sexual act the English language has known, or is likely to know again. That " acknowledgment" which the Woman always claimed and justly claimed, and which Lawrence always refused and wrongly refused, is now lavished — but not upon her. She is loathed and vituperated as a symbol; she is made a thing of horror. But the goddess which she serves is the only deity. The broken man recants all his old professions and prostrates himself before the Magna Mater. Her mysteries are the only mysteries.

The defeat of the creative purpose of man is, indeed, the second theme of the book; and it is more or less deliberately propounded. Sexuality is the be-all and end-all, because there is nothing for a man to do in the modern world of industrialism. "I believe in the little flame between us," says Mellors in the letter to Connie with which the book closes. "For me now it's the only thing in the world." We cannot but remember Harriet's demand in *Kangaroo* that she and Richard Somers should settle down together in a little place, and be happy, and leave the world to look after itself. Somers had then insisted that he had work to do with the world of men. It has come to nothing; it consists now in proclaiming the truth of Harriet's simple gospel. The only difference is that the woman is not Harriet. That would be impossible: for it would mean his final submission to her. Over her he must triumph. And he does. His male pride takes revenge. As a person he annihilates her in Bertha Coutts; in Lady Connie he resurrects her, with all the re-calcitrant elements in her left out, in order that he can make her completely submissive; and then, when his own personal victory is secure, he is free to accept her gospel that nothing matters except " love " between a man and a woman. " But of course what I live for now," says Mellors at the end, " is for you and me to live together."

ᔓ

There is, indeed, little more to be said about *Lady Chatterley's Lover*. Regarded objectively, it is a wearisome and oppressive book: obviously the work of a weary and hope-less man. It is remarkable, indeed notorious, for its de-liberate use of unprintable words. But in a very little while the mind becomes simply accustomed to them; they become simple glyphs which do nothing to diminish or to enhance the value of the book. With each successive reading that value seems to dwindle. The book leaves no permanent im-pression, as though it had been from the beginning devoid of all vital energy of soul. And this curious effect, as of a neuter thing, with no real power of vital disturbance, appears on reflection to be inevitable, The great " thought-adventure," of which Lawrence made us once the partakers, is over. It has been abandoned, or rather it has collapsed. We are at the beginning of life again. Lawrence has accomplished the destiny he prophesied for himself in Annable. The struggle has been in vain.

As a purely personal document, the book throbs with a pathetic and poignant interest. Its inevitability is appalling; its internal contradictions pitiful. Complete surrender to woman masquerading as complete victory over the Woman; the conscious proclamation of tenderness unconsciously derided by the extremest indulgence of hatred; a physically regenerated Lawrence brooding over a personal past which would have been impossible if he had been the man he now dreams himself to be — the essential contradictions of the book are terrifying. So are Lawrence's various and repeated defences of it. It is a good book, a salutary book, a moral book, he insists. The great repudiator of the " ideal " must, even *in extremis* have his ideal sanction for the final repudiation of the " ideal." He cannot acknowledge the sheer compulsion that is upon him, and be silent. It is his doom to write *Lady Chatterley's Lover;* the avenging Furies require this of him. The man who refused to be humble must be made to touch the extreme of humiliation, by committing what is, or was, in his own eyes the unforgivable crime — " the mentalization of the phallic mystery." " To-day," he he writes in defence of his book, " the full conscious realization of sex is even more important than the act itself. . . . Only fresh mental realization will freshen up the experience." It fills us with pity and horror. The completeness of the recantation, the sordidness of the phrasing, comes to us like a grim and ghastly joke. We feel that there are Powers, whose majesty Lawrence has outraged, and that they have taken a fearful revenge.

Lady Chatterley's Lover is a book which lacerates the mind that is sensitive to its personal significance, to the point of agony. It is impossible not to be pierced by the undertone of anguished yearning which throbs beneath. It aches with the desire for tenderness, and with the knowledge that the desire can never be satisfied. The spirit of Lawrence is " like a naked nerve upon the air " seeking rest and peace and oblivion. We hear again the clairvoyant cry of Luke in " Glad Ghosts ": " It's awfully important to be flesh and blood."

Awfully important, and now for ever impossible. The dis-embodied ghost of Lawrence wanders up and down through the pages, seeking the warm oblivion of the body and seek-ing it in vain; a tired and tortured ghost conjuring up re-incarnation, dreaming of the simple fulfilment of love, yet unable even to dream of it, and tearing itself in sunder. And when we are responsive to the full implications of the book, and understand it as the culmination of a life-long struggle and the confession of complete defeat, the sheer human pathos of certain passages stabs the quick of the heart.

" Ma lass! " he murmured. " Ma little lass! Dunna' let's fight. Dunna' niver fight. I love thee and the touch on thee. Dunna' argue wi' me. Dunna'! Dunna'! Dunna'! Let's be together! "

" The Escaped Cock " is the necessary counterpart of *Lady Chatterley's Lover.* Lawrence is incapable even of imagining life lived together with a woman in simple tender-ness. Let him be a resurrected and regenerated man, let the woman be young and tender and submissive, let all the dreams be fulfilled, and still it cannot be. The man is still divided, be-tween love and hate, and between good and evil; and the de-sires of the divided man must be enforced upon the woman. The moment Lawrence seeks to make real to his imagination this dream of happiness, this life of man and woman together, it lapses back into a mere assertion of victory for his pride. He remains what he was, he sacrifices nothing, but he is victorious.

In " The Escaped Cock " he turns away from this act of realization. The new woman in this story is an unsubstantial ghost. Let him not think any more of what the life together of the reborn man and the woman of his desire would be, for the black tide of hatred comes flowing, when he thinks of it, irresistibly into his heart. Let him, instead, imagine what he would have been if he had not suffered this destiny of love turned into hatred.

What would he have been? He would have been like Jesus, nay, he would have been Jesus. This is no blasphemy. Lawrence must face this final reckoning. It is his destiny, and he cannot avoid it. For Jesus and Lawrence stand over against each other. If Jesus is right, Lawrence is wrong; if Lawrence is right, Jesus is wrong. At every point the opposition is now naked. They are true opposites, complementary and in a sense necessary to each other. And Lawrence knows it. The reckoning had to be settled. Either Lawrence must destroy Jesus, or Jesus will destroy him.

In " The Escaped Cock," Lawrence sets himself to destroy Jesus. "Destroy" is a harsh and clumsy word. Lawrence loves Jesus, as he needs must do; but Lawrence also hates him, as he needs must hate a man whose life and teaching deny his own. But it is not in hatred, rather in love, that he sets himself to destroy Jesus. He must destroy Jesus in order to save himself. If Jesus is right, he himself is wrong, and he is damned. He must persuade Jesus that he is wrong. He must make Jesus acknowledge that he is wrong; he must make Jesus acknowledge that he, Lawrence, is right.

With this intense and agonising purpose the story of " The Escaped Cock " quivers in every phrase. It is a wonderful story; one of the most wonderful stories in the world — the masterpiece of a great and dying genius on the brink of judgment. Nowhere in the story does Lawrence name the name of Jesus. He is always simply " The Man who had Died." The reticence is instinctive, and necessary. It made it easier for Lawrence to do what he needs must do — namely, identify himself completely with Jesus. For Lawrence is also " The Man who had Died." Lawrence had died in the spirit, where Jesus died in the body.

The story is that Jesus rose in the body from the dead. He came back painfully to life in the rock-tomb, and, hidden in the garden of a nearby peasant, slowly healed. While his body is healing, he thinks with pain about the life which ended in his crucifixion. He sees now that it was utterly mistaken. He goes back to the tomb and sees Mary Magdalen, and speaks to her, and says:

" My triumph is that I am not dead. I have outlived my mission and know no more of it. I have survived the day and the death of my interference, and am still a man. The teacher and the saviour are dead in me; now I can go about my own business, into my own single life. Now I can wait on life and say nothing, and have no one to betray me. . . . I wanted to be greater than the limits of my hands and feet, so I brought betrayal on myself. Now I can live without trying to sway others any more. For my reach ends in my finger-tips and my stride is no longer than the ends of my toes. Yet I would embrace multitudes, I who have never truly embraced even one."

And he comes to a further realisation:

Risen from the dead, he realised at last that the body, too, has its little life, and beyond that, the greater life. He was virgin in recoil from the little, greedy life of the body. But now he knew that virginity is a form of greed; and the body rises again to give and to take, to take and to give, ungreedily. Now he knew that he had risen for the woman, or women, who knew the greater life of the body, not greedy to give, not greedy to take, and with whom he could mingle his body.

The rest of the story tells how this " greater life of the body " comes to him. A virgin priest of Isis, by her ministrations, perfects his wholeness. Through an agony, he becomes an entire man again.

She looked up at him suddenly, her face like a lifted light, wistful, tender, her eyes like many wet flowers. And he drew her to his breast with a passion of tenderness and consuming desire, and a last thought; — My hour is upon me, I am taken unawares.

So he knew her, and was one with her. . . .

So the days came and the nights came, and days came again, and the contact was perfected and fulfilled.

The woman conceives, and is with child. But the man must leave her. They are hunting him as a malefactor. He escapes. " When I am gone," he says to her, " live in peace with the growing child. And I shall come again. All is good between us, near or apart."

That is the outline of the story; much of its substance, though only the faint shadow of its wonderful agonising beauty, is to be found in an essay, and in a poem, both entitled " The Risen Lord." Its implications are tremendous. The resurrected Jesus comes to two fundamental realisations, which are, in reality, one realisation — namely, that Lawrence is right, and he himself wrong.

Jesus recognises and admits that the love for all men with which he was consumed and by which his life was determined was simply the consequence of his being physically unable to love a woman in the flesh. Had he been sexually fulfilled in bodily love of a woman, he would never have felt this devouring love for mankind nor been led by it along a path which ended inevitably in his agony and bloody death.

Now this may conceivably be true in fact. I believe it false, though I cannot prove it false. But even if it were true in fact, it is none the less utterly irrelevant. In the order of total human life, wherein creation and newness are perpetual, the effect is everything, the " cause " nothing; or rather they are completely incommensurable. To say that Jesus was not physically an entire man, and that if he had been whole, his life would have been different, cannot invalidate his life. His life and teaching and death, whatever their physical "cause," are unique and eternal, events that happened once for all. The question is what value they have for the men who followed after.

Just so, in the case of Lawrence himself, the fact that he was not an entire man, does not invalidate his life and teaching. They likewise are events that happened once for all; and again the question is what value they will have for the men who follow after.

The difference between the teaching of Jesus and the teaching of Lawrence is tremendous. But it can be reduced simply to this: that for Lawrence, the accident of physical destiny is irreparable. It maims a man for ever; it condemns him, beyond hope of reprieve, to imperfection. He is, like Clifford Chatterley, by the accident of his body, irremediably damned. Jesus, on the contrary, held that the true perfection of a man was the perfection of his soul, and that bodily limitations were utterly irrelevant to the attainment of it; nay, that they might even be a positive help to progress along the path of this spiritual perfection. The difference, finally, is this: that in Lawrence's eyes, Jesus and himself are inevitably and irrevocably damned to imperfection, unless the miracle of a physical resurrection and a second bodily life is vouchsafed to them; while, in the eyes of Jesus, both Lawrence and himself are not only as capable of salvation as other men, but by their infirmity perhaps privileged to attain it more swiftly, and communicate it more directly, than their more bodily fellow-men.

To Jesus, a physical resurrection is not only not necessary; it is inconceivable that he should desire it. To Lawrence, a physical resurrection is the one necessity without which his own life is utterly barren; it is inconceivable that he should not desire it.

One thing at least is clear: that the teaching of Jesus, if it is true, is the only teaching that can save Lawrence from his own teaching, which demands a physical miracle, or ends, if the miracle be denied, in blank and irrecoverable despair.

But how can Lawrence accept the teaching of Jesus? How can he accept his own bodily limitations, whose whole life has been spent in rebellion and hatred of them? How can he, who has saved his life to lose it, turn back to one whose teaching is that he must lose his life to save it? It is not possible: the doom is irrevocable. He cannot accept the teaching of Jesus, it is no longer in his power to accept it. He knows that in men of the order to which he belongs, the stories of death-bed repentance are childish tales. He *cannot* change. It is Jesus who must change. Lawrence cannot accept the teaching of Jesus. Jesus must accept his teaching. Jesus must accept at his hands that physical resurrection in which he did not believe, and which he could not have desired, in order that he may disown his teaching and proclaim his belief in the teaching of Lawrence: namely that without the miracle of a physical resurrection, his own life was futile, mistaken and mad.

The inward drama with which " The Escaped Cock " is tense is almost beyond endurance. To understand that story is to have one's soul appalled by the thought that a man could suffer as Lawrence was suffering then. Jesus must renounce his mission in order that Lawrence may not be lonely at the last. Jesus must admit that his life was mistaken in order that Lawrence may believe that his own was not mistaken.

No doubt Jesus would have loved Lawrence as his own brother; if he could have made him happy at the last, he would have done so, and laid down his life to do it. But to deny his own truth: that he could not. It would be impossible for Jesus to do what Lawrence would have him do, namely to violate the spirit that was in him. Lawrence has done this, therefore Jesus must do likewise, that Lawrence may be happy at the last: and it is beyond Jesus' power to do.

But, says Lawrence, Jesus wanted to save the world; and that is an impossible dream. "From what, and to what, could this infinite whirl be saved?" the man who had died asks himself, and has no answer. Lawrence is deceiving himself, because now he *must* deceive himself. The value of his own life is at stake. Jesus did not want to save "the infinite whirl" itself; he wanted to save men from being engulfed in it, as Lawrence is now finally engulfed in it. His purpose was to save men from becoming what Lawrence has now become, a man dead to the spirit, swirled aimlessly in the flux on unsatisfied and unsatisfiable desire.

"Men cannot be saved," cries Lawrence; "it is impossible." He implores Jesus to admit it, he makes Jesus admit it. But his Jesus is not Jesus — only Lawrence himself. The man who died on the Cross cannot speak to Lawrence. Between Jesus and himself is a great gulf fixed, and when Lawrence cries across it, the only answer he receives is the echo of his own despairing voice.

Jesus must rise in the body from the dead, simply in order that he may comfort Lawrence. Unless he is risen in the body from the dead Jesus cannot repudiate his mission and his truth, for in his own life he obeyed it to the last. Neither can he desire what Lawrence desires, for in his own life he chose the way of isolation, and followed that road also to the last. Therefore he must rise in the body from the dead to recant, to tell Lawrence that it is a mistake to die in order to save one's soul alive or to save alive the soul of humanity (for these are the same salvation). He must rise in the body to tell Lawrence that the only thing that matters is to be alive: that the one thing needful is not love, or

courage, or self-sacrifice — but simply to be flesh and blood.
Jesus rises in the body and recants, at Lawrence's summons.
" My triumph is that I am not dead."

It is strange and terrible. Lawrence himself will not be
flesh and blood much longer. If the one thing needful is to
be flesh and blood, it will be taken from him, and for ever,
in a little while. Why should he call upon Jesus to recant
his truth and declare it as a new revelation that " a living
dog is better than a dead lion? " And the real answer
is that Lawrence himself cannot believe it. In his soul he
knows that Jesus is right and he is wrong, that Jesus
had the courage and that he had not, and that the one
thing needful is to love, and that to be alive is nothing
beside it.

But how can he admit it now, who has denied it all his
life? How can he thus annihilate himself, his message, and
his life? He, who had the greatest power of love of any
man in his generation, suffered it to turn into hatred, hatred
the more fierce and terrible in that it was love denied. How
can he at the last admit that the one thing needful is love?
He cannot; but neither can he go to the grave that yawns
for him proclaiming hatred still. He will find a way out.
Yes, love is needful, and it is needful to be alive. And you
must not love all men, because that leads to death. You
must only love one. Physical tenderness between man and
woman: that is the one thing needful.

But this is a childish dream. Physical tenderness between
man and woman is the beginning of life, not the end. Let a
man and woman love with simple tenderness, and all the
ills that flesh is heir to may come between. The woman dies.
What then? Shall she also be resurrected in the body that
she may love and be loved again? Men and women have
loved each other with simple tenderness all through the ages,
but the miseries of the loving heart are not diminished. The

bliss of perfected love is but the prelude to the agony of inevitable separation, by disease or death.

It is not physical tenderness to each other that men and women need to be taught as the one thing needful. What they need to learn is something to avail them when physical tenderness is torn away, and happy love is a faint and far-off dream; what they need to learn is how to endure suffering alone. And what has Lawrence to tell them? Nothing, nothing at all. But Jesus had something to tell them. True, it was not easy to learn; but there it was, and it was true, and he died rather than deny it. It was what he discovered when he was utterly alone; it was what other men, great and small, have discovered when they also have been utterly alone. The truth is simple. " He that loseth his life, the same shall save it."

The one truth that Lawrence never learned; the one truth out of which the life and death of Jesus inevitably grew. And this truth, and the perfect life and death which grew from it, Lawrence would have annihilated, and replaced by a simple fairy-tale. The one perfect tragedy of the entire world blotted out for " Once upon a time . . ." and " They lived happy ever after."

✍

The pathos of " The Escaped Cock " is unbearable: unbearable when we know that the man who died is Lawrence, still more unbearable when we realise that to the dying Lawrence this simple fairy-tale was more wonderful, more throbbing with the promise of beatitude than the life and death of Jesus. And truly it is unbearable to peer into that anguished heart and find in it that childish dream of happiness in love — Did he believe that once it lay within his grasp, had he been brave enough to stand free and take it, but that he was a coward and thrust it away? Or did he believe that a cruel destiny had denied him even the possibility of it? " I have sowed the seed of my life and my resurrection," says the reborn man at the last, and his heart is glad at the thought of his woman, and their child within her womb.

Was his desire at the last so simple and so impossible: love, tenderness, and a child? I think it was. All the brave speech in " The Escaped Cock " concerning " the greater life of the body," all the sordid speech in *Lady Chatterley's Lover* concerning " warm-hearted f . . . g," melts away, leaving behind only the ache of a simple and now for ever unattainable human desire. To Lawrence, now on the brink of the grave, it shines within the dark with the mysterious wonder of the impossible — this simple love between virgin man and virgin woman issuing in the birth of a child. For this, and this alone, man must be resurrected in the body: in this he is perfected and content. To this simple love the man yields himself, with all his heart, and all his soul, and all his mind. No enforced slavery is required of him; he yields in a willing and blissful surrender, as the woman also yields. There is no vestige, in this dream, of that loathing for the bondage of sex which cries, and shrieks aloud in the pages of *Lady Chatterley's Lover.* In that book, in spite of all the conscious homage done to it, sex is the supreme degradation: a doom to which man is dragged as a victim, and to which he surrenders blaspheming. For Mellors is Lawrence, with Lawrence's past; but the Man who died is another man.

The first and final love of which destiny had cheated him, the sex which is not a crucifixion and a violation for the man, not a crucifixion and a violation for the woman, but a tender unforced flowering into manhood for the man, into womanhood for the woman — this is Lawrence's last dream of happiness. For this he must be born again in the flesh, and for this alone is it worth while to be reborn. It is a personal dream, shaped by a personal destiny, and coloured by the haunting regret for that virginal love which his strange doom compelled him to violate in his lover and in himself.

It is a childish dream; but its fearful pathos lies in this very childishness — that at the end of his own life, and in the act of trying to contemplate the end of the life of Jesus himself, he should be borne back to the beginning, as though in the unconscious yearning that all his life and all his work between should be blotted out and forgotten. If only he could have been a different man! The dream is childish, so is the judgment of Jesus: the judgment as innocent as the dream. Lawrence has blasphemed many times, but " The Escaped Cock " is utterly devoid of blasphemy. It is the judgment of a perfect child upon a perfect man.

What then has been his life? If now, at the point of death, he is become a child, what have been the years and the works between? One long illusion, one long nightmare, one long and unavailing attempt to deny the thing he was: to deny the love that possessed him, and the spirit that visited him. A man cannot deny his inmost self, and *be*. " We must disintegrate while we live," he cried in anguish, when the knowledge of his destiny came full upon him. It was true of him. He did disintegrate while he lived. Back, back, he went. His life is the story of one long, tormented effort to be, to be a man, to be whole; of its utter failure; and of the slow inevitable return into the womb of woman. In *Lady Chatterley's Lover* he creeps back, shrieking, in " The Escaped Cock " he is born anew. His life, his true life, is now to be lived. And it is over.

We cannot regret it. If his impossible dream had been realised, his agony would only have begun again. Death would finally have loomed before him, as it looms before him now: death and the same final despair, the same anguished dream of a miracle. Somewhere, somehow, at some time, the same sacrifice would have been demanded of him, that " he should lose his life to save it." The man who will not, or cannot, die in life, must die in death: a death is required of him. There is no escape. Integration means a death, it cannot be had at a lesser price. " We must disintegrate while we live," which was Lawrence's message, means only we must avoid death while we live. We shall not avoid it at the last. " We must integrate while we live," is the eternally opposed doctrine; it means only that we must seek our death while we live. And that is best. We cease to be torn in sunder, we cease to desire miracles. They, and they alone, are immune from the longing for the resurrection of the body, who have endured the rebirth of the soul. " Men *are* their own flesh," says the risen Lord of Lawrence's poem. It is the fatal lie: the half-truth that is more deadly than a thousand lies, and leaves humanity without hope. For men are indeed their own flesh; but they are also the spirit which knows it, and is content.

Pansies is the voice of the final disintegration. In uttering himself in this form, Lawrence is as it were absolved from the semblance of coherence; and it is obvious that it came to him for that reason. He is conscious of the condition. He asks:

> Must we hold on?
> Or can we now let go?
> Or is it even possible we must do both?

To hold on, that is, to human integrity, to the necessity of a total unity. He universalises his own disintegration. " Is the time come for humans now to begin to disappear? "

That is the counterpart of his dream-resurrection. If nothing remains for him but the impossible miracle of being born again, and born different, then one of two things must be true. Either the race of human beings is at the end of its course, or Lawrence is no longer a man, in the sense that his destiny, or his composition, are quite peculiar, so that his necessities are not compulsive on his kind. If Lawrence's destiny is inevitable to the sensitive human being, then manifestly it is proved in him that the race of men is doomed.

That is the question. How far is Lawrence significant? In the precarious halcyon moment of the *Fantasia*, he saw the true answer clearly. He is tremendously significant, but negatively significant. In him is made manifest the way to disintegration, to a form of life which cannot live. The future of humanity depends on making impossible the conditions which produced him. And he is negatively significant in a deeper sense than this. Whether or not under the compulsion of his own conditioning, he has refused the spiritual way, the way of integration. In him is manifest the choice which lies before fully conscious man: either to achieve a rebirth in the spirit, or be left vainly clamouring for a rebirth in the flesh.

Whomever we personally may regard as the master of the spiritual way, there is no doubt whatever that for Lawrence it was Jesus. Whether he understood Jesus at all, Jesus was for him the incarnation of the spiritual way. Consciously and unconsciously, he pitted himself against Jesus. The way of the Spirit, the way of love — these were anathema to Lawrence: the more deeply abhorrent, precisely because he felt, far more deeply than other men, their compulsion. He would prove, in himself, that there was a better way; he would fight against it to the end. He did fight to the end.

And what is the end? In the essay, " The Risen Lord," he

once again asserts the necessity of a physical resurrection, the necessity of a new Christ.

The virgin birth, the baptism, the temptation, the teaching, Gethsemane, the betrayal, the crucifixion, the burial and the resurrection, these are all true according to our inward experience. They are what men and women go through in their different ways.

But the image of our inward state to-day is beyond this. It is the resurrection of the body.

Jesus was risen flesh-and-blood. He rose a man to live on earth. The greatest test was still before him: His life as a man on earth. Hitherto He had been a sacred child, a teacher, a messiah, but never a full man. Now, risen from the dead, He rises to be a man on earth, and live his life of the flesh, the great life, among other men. This is the image of our inward state to-day.

In so far as it was the image of Lawrence's desire, at the point of death, as we have seen, this is true. But what does it *mean*? It corresponds to nothing in Lawrence's experience. He is dying: and no such resurrection will come to him. As a dream-image it means the total repudiation of his own life; it means that for him his life on earth had not begun. As a symbol for other men, it is childish and pathetic. Men must have the wholeness and integrity of animal life. We can agree. But how is it to be attained? If men go the way of Lawrence, they will be at the end like him, dreaming of a new and quite different life, desiring an integrity which can never be theirs. The dream and the reality, as in him, will be divided by an impassable gulf. How is the dream to be made real?

And Lawrence has no answer, no answer at all. For him, and for other men (if he is typical), it is a simple miracle for which he calls. This new world into which he bids men enter does not exist. Not this earthly paradise, but the darkness of the grave, is actually before him. Still, he must dream, if only to dream death away. His dreams are all the old dreams of love and comradeship — dreams which in his life he has found impossible, and because he has found them impossible, has poured scorn and hatred upon them. And, now, at the end, they are as far from him as ever. In the published *Autobiographical Sketch* he writes: "Something is wrong with me, or with the world, or with both of us."

I don't feel that there is any cordial or fundamental contact between me and society, or me and other people. There is a breach. And my contact is with something that is non-human, non-vocal.

I used to think it had something to do with the oldness and the worn-outness of Europe. Having tried other places, I know that it is not so. Europe is, perhaps, the least worn-out of the continents, because it is the most lived in. A place that is lived in lives.

It is since coming back from America that I ask myself seriously: Why is there so little vital contact between me and the people whom I know? Why has the contact so little vital meaning?

By this time, we know more about Lawrence than Lawrence knew. He is a disintegrated man; he has fled from, and denied, the spirit which makes vital human contact possible for such a man as he — "the love that seeketh not its own." And now, as ever, it is not he that is at fault. The something that is wrong is wrong with the world, not him. It is class. He comes from the working-class, and cannot tolerate that denial of the "old blood-affinity with my fellow-men" which middle-class contacts demand; neither, of course, can he live with the working-people. They are, "narrow in outlook, in prejudice, and narrow in intelligence." Both are impossible.

If there were no class, then Lawrence would be able to make his vital contact. And class is money. If money-values were abolished, then the world of men would be possible for him. It is Mammon he now hates, it is Mammon which prevents him, and other men, from simple fulfilment. So far as there is any single sustained thought at this last moment, it is that Mammon is the evil. In *Pansies* a few thoughts are dominant: the thought of his own final nullity.

> When a man can love no more
> and feel no more
> and desire has failed
> and the heart is numb
> then all he can do
> is to say: It is so!

Then there is the ever-recurrent dream of the resurrection of the body into wholeness. And, third, the cry for the destruction of Mammon. The first two we understand; we have watched them come to birth. What is the meaning of the third? As it is uttered in *Pansies,* it comes to this. Let men not mistrust each other any more, let them be generous, let them give from the heart to their brother in his need, let each man feel that men are near to help, let there be no money any more, let all men be allowed that the tender springing life may flourish within them. We know this cry from of old. " Ho, every one that thirsteth come ye to the waters, and he that hath no money; come ye, buy and eat; yea come, buy wine and milk without money and without price."

It is the old, old cry for love and loving-kindness among men which Lawrence at the end can keep from his lips no longer. Unless there is more love, the world of men is doomed. Yet even now he cannot admit the word; but there is no mistaking the meaning.

The world is waiting for a new great movement of generosity or for a great wave of death.

So Lawrence died, proclaiming that the one thing needful was Love. Whether he knew what he was doing, who can say? But what his lips at the last must utter, his whole life reveals. He has denied Love, and he is shattered; he has fought against it, and he is broken; he has refused it, and he implores it. Two things, at the last, he asks for — another life for himself, where love may be his portion, and for his fellow-men " a new great wave " of love.

∽

So, Lawrence, you died. " Even the dead," you wrote of Maurice Magnus, " ask only for *justice.*" But what is Justice? " Anger," you wrote again, " is just, and pity is just; but judgment is never just." Shall we be angry with you then, or shall we pity you? Would even pity bring balm to your uneasy ghost?

Neither anger, nor pity, nor judgment is just. There is only one justice in the world worth having, and it is neither anger nor pity, nor judgment but the simple understanding which is love indeed: the understanding which accepts the things that are in all the beauty of their manifest necessity.

The evil that you did, is done; and it *is* evil. You muddied the spring of living water that flowed in you more richly than in any man of your time. In the world of good and evil, wherein men must struggle for ever while they live, you quenched the light more often than you kindled it. You bewildered men who might have learned from you, betrayed men who would have followed you. We needed a leader and a prophet, you were marked by destiny to be the man; and you failed us. It was your destiny to fail us, as it was your destiny to fail yourself. In the measure in which you failed yourself, you failed your fellow-men.

But there is a world beyond the world of good and evil: the eternal world of Being, whose reality you denied, known by the Spirit, which you would not suffer to lodge within yourself. In this world you are a perfect thing, which those who understood must love, and those who love must understand. In this world, love and understanding are one. Neither is possible there without the other.

This understanding, so far as I am capable of it, I have given you in this book. In life you asked something of me which was not in my power to give, nor in your power to take. I did not know what it was you asked of me, neither did you know. But I know now. I remember how, one night, when you had returned to England, after all the pain of separation and the torment of love that had turned to hatred, you became to me once more the wonderful Man: super-human by the anguish and excess of your humanity. Suddenly, you put your arm about my neck, for the first and the last time, and said " Do not betray me! " I did not understand, but I never forgot. The words, and the suffering in the words, have never ceased to echo in my soul.

In this book I have betrayed you? Was it this, that I have done, of which you were afraid? There was nothing to fear. This " betrayal " was the one thing you lacked, the one thing I had to give, that you might shine forth among men as the thing of wonder that you were.

For truly you were wonderful among the sons of men, and you gave the world a gift beyond price: not a gift of prophecy or wisdom, for truth and falsehood are mingled to utter confusion in your work — but the gift of yourself. Without someone to " betray " you, it could never have been given. No man in these latter days has given to men so marvellous or so terrible a picture of Man as you have given.

No such picture of Man existed in the world before you came. You were a man of destiny, driven to sacrifice yourself in order that men might know themselves and the eternal laws they must obey, the laws which, even in denying them, still they obey. Two eternal things you denied, two things of which the promise was richer in you than in any other man whom living men have known: Love and the Spirit, which cannot exist apart. You denied them to the end. Yet to those two things your appeal will be enduring. That which you sought to strangle, you are doomed to bring to birth, in men.

CPSIA information can be obtained
at www.ICGtesting.com
Printed in the USA
BVHW04s1442171018
530437BV00008B/79/P